RUNNING AWAY FROM STALIN

The Life & Times of Alfred Hecht, PhD, Dr. (h.c.)

MARK HECHT

*

Heidl Media Company

Published by

H

Heidl Media Company

Copyright © 2025 by Mark Hecht
All rights reserved, including the right to reproduce this book or portions thereof in any form whatsoever.

For purchasing multiple copies or for more information contact Heidl Media at: laurier1007@gmail.com.

Book cover design by Matthew Burmafalk of Syndicate Vision. Illustrations, graphs and photographs are sourced from Alfred Hecht and Mark Hecht and may not be reproduced for commercial purposes without written permission.

Print and bound in Canada.

ISBN: 978-0-9951770-4-8
Registered with Library and Archives Canada

Heidl Media Co.
British Columbia
Canada

Dedicated to those who died on the road to freedom.

Preface

As the author of *Running Away from Stalin*, I was deeply blessed and honoured by those who allowed me to tell their stories. Some stories have been told many times before while others were told to me for the first time. Some were told without emotion and some with tears.

Running Away from Stalin takes place over a span of time covering the last hundred years or so; a very long time. One realization for me while listening to the stories was how wildly different memories and interpretations of an original event can be and how those memories could also shift quite dramatically over time. Where versions of an event differed among those telling the oral history, when verifiable facts were not possible I used the version that seemed to make the most sense to me. It is quite likely my interpretations contain errors.

Any omissions, errors, mischaracterizations or misrepresentations of people, places and events are mine and mine alone.

Many people contributed to *Running Away from Stalin*. I will surely fail to list everyone and offer my general gratitude instead—*thank you*.

Some individuals were not mentioned in this book who may believe they should have been. The decision to tell some stories and not others is not synonymous with importance but is instead a matter of literary flow and the structural framework in which storytelling must occur. The decision to tell some stories and not others rests solely on my shoulders.

Lastly, I want to acknowledge that Alfred Hecht was an absolute pleasure to work with in the telling of his life story for which I am eternally grateful. I hope that in all respects I have given the appropriate care and attention his biography deserves.

- Mark Hecht

Table of Contents

1. The Professor — 1
2. The Storyteller — 3
3. Borderlands — 8
4. Middle Name — 12
5. Wrong Name — 17
6. The Great Trek — 22
7. Suza is Lost — 25
8. The Terrible Trade — 29
9. Niemandsland — 33
10. Redisposition — 39
11. Grönau — 43
12. Paraguay — 46
13. New Life in the Chaco — 50
14. Utopia — 56
15. Warkentin — 64
16. Canada — 70
17. The First House — 72
18. Linda — 75
19. Decisions — 86
20. Master's Degree — 88
21. Ambition — 92
22. Spring Memories — 97
23. PhD — 101
24. WLU — 103
25. Return to Stalin's Empire — 109
26. Marburg — 118
27. The Graduate Program — 122
28. Pletsch — 125
29. The Boilermaker — 128
30. Horse & Buggy Mennonites — 133
31. Berlin Wall, 1989 — 138
32. East Germany Cleanup — 141
33. Reconciliation with Mother Russia — 145
34. Laurier International — 149
35. Behind the Back of Bureaucracy — 153
36. Conscience — 156
37. Boots — 160
38. Wenn schon, denn schon — 164
39. Return to Paraguay — 170
40. Speaking of Ethnicities — 184
41. Return to Laurier — 188
42. Inside Laurier — 190
43. Sharpe — 205
44. Salloum — 213
45. Side Hustle — 217
46. Fishing Stories at Jack's — 222
47. Regrets — 225
48. Legacy — 227

References — 232
Appendix — 233

1. The PROFESSOR

"According to my Canadian passport I was born in the village of Steinfeld, Ukraine on February 26, 1942 during the Second World War but my aunt insists the village was Gruenfeld."

Dr. Alfred Hecht was born thirty-nine months before the Second World War ended. His young age saved him the worst of the trauma that his older siblings had to endure while they fled the Ukraine in October, 1943.

More than 20 million people in Europe were displaced from their homes during the Second World War. Nazi Germany could be blamed for instigating the displacement. The consequences, retributions and repercussions against Germans everywhere at the end of the war and afterwards were immense.

It is estimated that approximately 15 million German speakers either fled, evacuated or were forcibly expelled from central and eastern Europe in the single largest instance of ethnic cleansing in recorded history. The number of people who died during that mass migration is estimated to be anywhere between 500,000 and 3,000,000 people.

The Soviet Union in particular saw vast numbers of people from all ethnic groups flee the communist regime under Joseph Stalin during the upheavals of WWII. Approximately 325,000 were German-speaking peoples who fled southern Russia in the fall of 1943 and went to Poland and Germany. Around 37,000 of those were German-speaking Mennonites.

Two-thirds of those Mennonites were forcibly sent back to Russia at the end of the war. Six months after the war ended, only 11,000 Mennonites remained, trapped in Germany, their fate unsettled. They were homeless and near hopelessness. They needed to escape. They needed to find freedom.

Like an abusive husband, Russia wanted them all back.

Germany was not safe.

America rejected them.

Canada rejected those without a male provider.

Alfred's mother, without a husband, like so many other widows with children, had one last reasonable option. She could go back to Russia and face almost certain death or go to one of the most remote regions on the planet in the only country that would accept them unconditionally—Paraguay.

Alfred Hecht as a young boy was one of the incredibly few individuals who survived that tumultuous moment in history. His family and those around them, as Mennonites with German backgrounds but Russian citizens by birth, had to navigate the dilemmas and vagaries of war and national loyalties. They had been caught between the proverbial rock and a hard place and by basic probabilities alone should have perished on the northern plains of Europe somewhere between 1943 and 1945.

Not everyone in Alfred's family did survive, but somehow he made it through. After fleeing Europe as a refugee and being resettled with his family in Paraguay he would eventually immigrate with his mother and siblings to Canada in 1955 and start anew.

In spite of his early upbringing, or perhaps because of it, he rose to the top of his field in Canada as a university professor of economic geography and went on to shape the economic trajectory of his adopted country and mentor countless students who would go into the halls of business, politics, international affairs and academia to shape the world.

He would also return many times to his former childhood homes in Germany, Poland, Ukraine, Russia and Paraguay, to help those less fortunate than himself.

It all began for Alfred Hecht in the Ukraine but we began in Paraguay.

2. The STORYTELLER

I flew in from British Columbia to hear the stories of Alfred Hecht's life and to write his biography. I stayed for almost a month at the home of Alfred and his wife Linda, at their unassuming suburban home in Kitchener-Waterloo, Ontario. Being his nephew, I had heard many of the stories in one form or another throughout my own life but not all, and by no means the most shocking.

Alfred and Linda had decided the guest bathroom upstairs needed a few renovations before their guest arrived. The contractor's work resulted in a leaky faucet which in turn led to water dripping through joists and onto the kitchen floor below.

Wooden floor boards warped and buckled.

The insurance company was called in.

The restoration company appeared shortly afterwards with a half-dozen industrial-sized moisture vacuums. They set them up inside the house and then ran the fans for the next four days.

I arrived just in time to experience the mayhem of a noisy renovation fix.

"My insurance guy says I have $1,000 deductible," Alfred said while running his hand through silver hair in reflexive frustration as we moved into the family room, away from the awful din of an incessant hum.

Large windows looked onto a backyard where grapes hung from an overhead trellis built over a wooden deck. Inside, on the far wall, beside a brick fireplace hung a trophy perch. The fish looked small against tree-bark backing.

Noticing my intrigue, Alfred said with a quirky smile as though there were more to the story, "It fits into the Master Angler Award of Manitoba."

He sat down on one end of a comfortable brown leather couch. I sat in an adjoining chair that was turned toward a big-screen television.

Alfred's straight, full head of hair had turned colour but had not thinned a wisp in eighty-two years. Rimmed glasses and a casual repose gave the impression of an affable man. I knew it was mostly an accurate impression, although all impressions come with illusions.

Alfred returned to the insurance issue and said, "A thousand bucks is not what it used to be."

"Just like when you lived in Paraguay with high inflation?" I replied.

Well, not exactly.

When the Hecht family fled Germany after the Second World War, they went as refugees to Paraguay and had to live there for seven-and-a-half years. When they arrived in 1947, the right-of-centre Colorado Party was in power under Federico Chaves and inflation was debilitating.

One of Alfred's older brothers, Rudy, remembered working in the capital of Asunción and getting paid at the end of every week. With inflation ripping away purchasing power on a daily basis, the moment that workers received their paycheques they would spend the entire thing before the value of the money dropped again. If paid every two weeks, the paycheque had lost so much purchasing power as to be nearly worthless. The situation was untenable and everyone knew it.

In 1954, there was a military coup attempt. From the chaos of the coup, General Alfredo Stroessner (1912–2006) emerged and came to power as the President of Paraguay. He remained as a dictator for thirty-five years, which had its advantages.

Until 1954, "there was bad inflation," Alfred remembered. When Stroessner took over, "he pegged the Guarani to the American dollar. That was pretty good...until he was kicked out. Then inflation became a problem again."

Chronic convulsions of political unrest, coup d'états and civil war plagued nearly every Latin American country during this time period, except Paraguay. Other than the short civil war in 1947 and the quickly resolved coup attempt in 1954, Paraguay was relatively stable.

Of course, suggesting the country was free of political strife would be dishonest. Dissidents were often tortured or murdered during *El Stronato*—the reign of Alfredo Stroessner's dictatorship. Comparatively speaking, however, Paraguay was one of the most stable Latin American countries.

"When Stroessner was in power, people around the world wondered why there was no revolution against him," Alfred said and went on to explain that the dictator knew the importance of a stable currency. Not only did Stroessner need monetary stability so his own government could plan for the future, he also recognized that the peasants wanted to plan for the future, too. "They had to know that the Guarani today was going to be the same tomorrow," said Alfred.

The downside of Stroessner's economic policy was that Paraguayan products had trouble launching into the international export market at competitive prices. It also resulted in high interest rates. Yet, with the Guarani pegged to the US dollar, the perils of inflation were avoided.

While Stroessner was often brutal in the suppression of dissidents, there was no revolution against him. Alfred Hecht, as an economic geography professor, attributed the lack of revolution largely to Stroessner's monetary policy.

"The guy made sure the peasants knew they could plan. In Brazil, Argentina, Bolivia, if you got paid today you had to buy stuff today because (inflation was so high that) tomorrow it would only buy half the stuff."

Alfred explained. "When I taught courses on Latin America, we looked at different countries in terms of inflation and what it meant." And one of the intriguing and most visually apparent outcomes of inflation was the appearance of buildings perpetually under construction.

Since it's more important to hold hard assets rather than cash in an inflationary economy, people invest in tangible assets even if it means owning just a few bricks as soon as one can afford to buy them.

"Today you bought five bricks. Tomorrow maybe another five but the price would be higher tomorrow. It's called *in-situ development*, investing in hard stuff," Alfred said and shook his head a little.

In the Latin American countries with high inflation, *in-situ development* is still common even today. But in Paraguay, under Stroessner, it was rare to see buildings sitting unfinished.

As long as Paraguayans could count on a stable currency, while watching those in neighbouring countries suffer through inflationary uncertainty, it was probably enough to ward off revolution against Stroessner. Not that some people hadn't thought about it.

The Mennonites were not one of the latter. They liked to keep to themselves and never had much of a problem or distaste for the dictator. In fact, they often liked his strongarm tactics and held favourable impressions of the man. Also, they were not terribly affected much by the Guarani's stability or instability since they had their own internal economic barter system that was relatively independent of the country's currency. In some ways, Stroessner's monetary policies had little effect, positive or negative, on them. And Stroessner in many ways had a soft spot for the Mennonites, often supporting them directly and indirectly.

The Indigenous peoples of the Chaco on the other hand suffered quite heavily under Stroessner's dictatorship, less due to monetary policies and more to do with land rights. And ironically, the Indigenous peoples, regardless of the fact that Stroessner came from a Spanish family, often referred to the South American military dictator as "the Mennonite President."

It was an indication that the relationship between the Mennonites and the Indigenous peoples in the Chaco of Paraguay was not always a convivial one. Even Alfred, an ardent believer that the presence of Mennonite farmers in the Chaco was a benevolent good for the Indigenous peoples, could see parallels with the often tense relationship between Mennonites and Indigenous peoples in Paraguay, as there had also been between Mennonites and Russians in the Ukraine. It was a foreboding insight we would return to later.

For now, the industrial fans ran loud in the kitchen while the Canadian dollar in 2024 lost value as we spoke. Latin American-style inflation was creeping into Canada. It was returning to Alfred's life just when he thought it was something left behind in his past.

In fact, it was strange to consider how Alfred and his family ended up in one of the most isolated regions of the world—the Paraguayan Chaco—after fleeing one of the most catastrophic regions in history—the

Ukraine—only to end up in the safety of suburban Canada. And then, for him to go on to influence the trajectory of Canada's economic development into the 21st century, only to see much of the peril at the beginning of his life slowly returning at the end of his life.

That beginning started shortly after Adolf Hitler invaded Russia and drove his tanks through Alfred's village.

3. BORDERLANDS

Since Alfred's life began in one of the world's most nefarious borderlands, things were bound to go badly at some point. Fortunately, it happened early.

The regions of the world colloquially known in geopolitical parlance as the borderlands are places where one finds a chronic predilection for violence and turmoil. These are lands not easily defended. They usually exist on open ground, have valuable resources and disunited peoples. They are usually surrounded by rival powers that are willing to invade and disrupt whenever opportunity is given. The expansion and contraction of small and large empires alike across these lands results in a nearly predictable displacement of populations at regular intervals throughout history. Alfred Hecht was bound to be caught up in the machinations of conflict simply by the unfortunate circumstance of being born in a borderland. The Ukraine is in fact one of the world's most notorious borderlands. It is and always was, one of the most unstable places on Earth to make a living.

The year before Alfred was born, the German Army under Adolf Hitler had invaded Joseph Stalin's Russia. The German Army arrived in Alfred's village of Steinfeld[1]—east of Krivoy Rog in the Dnipropetrovsk Oblast, Ukraine—in the spring of 1941. Most of the ethnic Germans, including the Mennonites who'd lived in Russia for a long time, saw the arrival as a blessing, not because of a shared ideology but a shared lineage.

Southern Russia (Ukraine) is more than a thousand kilometres from Germany but an important connection between the two regions began in the late 1700s. Russia had been a small entity desiring greatness at the time. The Empress of Russia, Catherine the Great (1729–1796), began to successfully take over and control the open grasslands south of her but she encountered a serious problem with her expanding empire.

The newly acquired *steppe* composed of rolling grasslands had thus far been occupied by nomadic peoples that showed little willingness to be subjects of the expanding Russian empire. Being nomadic, they were difficult to control and offered little economic benefit.

The climate of the steppe was temperamental and unpredictable and had deterred attempts at agriculture. The grasslands of the steppe, controlled by nomadic peoples such as the Nogai and Cossacks, were much like the pre-1870s grasslands of North America, home to the Blackfoot and Lakota tribes prior to agricultural settlement.

If the Empress could bring farmers to settle the region, they could provide a larger monetary-based economy, bring in taxes, be willing subjects and create the foundations of a much more powerful Russian empire.

Catherine the Great would need exceptionally skilled farmers and she would need to entice them to live in this less than desirable place. It would help if the potential farmers were mild-mannered, had good reason to leave their homelands and had a culture of independence that would not rely on government support or subsidies.

The Empress looked to western Europe and focused on one group in particular—Mennonites. They were good farmers; they were being persecuted for their faith; they were mild-mannered pacifists that would not threaten the government with revolt; and they were willing to operate their own communities without asking for help from the government. She offered the Mennonites free land, military exemption and the right to operate their own schools, institutions and religious facilities. Some Mennonites accepted her offer.

There were other groups of people, mostly ethnic Germans of Lutheran faith, who were given similar offers. Each group, whether Mennonite, Lutheran Germans, Catholic Germans, Latvians, or others, went to Russia at slightly different times to set up their own communities.

In 1789, the original group of 228 Mennonite families—mostly from Danzig—went and built their first settlement on the west side of the Dnieper River. They named it Chortitza. It grew to encompass 405,000 acres plus large tracts of rented land and privately owned farming estates.

In 1803, another group of Mennonites arrived and established the Molotschna settlement on the east side of the Dnieper River. It would become the largest of the two settlements with 324,000 acres and an estimated population of 6,000 in 1835. Throughout the 1800s, the Mennonite population increased and many sister colonies were constructed throughout the larger region.

In spite of the steppe's climatic difficulties, the Mennonites proved to be fantastic farmers and businessmen. They became agriculturally and economically successful. They ran their own communities, continued to speak their Low German dialect—Plautdietsch—and remained relatively autonomous. Some Mennonites, especially the early landowners, rose up in the social hierarchy of the Russian empire and would become almost indistinguishable from the Russian gentry but the average Mennonite preferred to keep their traditions and insular way of life.

By the late 1800s, the Russian government was beginning to renege on its agreements with the Mennonites over issues of autonomy and loyalty. Population pressures and a shortage of land were also causing serious problems. Some of the Mennonites decided to leave Russia in 1870. They resettled in the United States and Canada.

As time passed the problems only increased. The Mennonite community suffered immensely, as did many others. They suffered raids on their villages from anarchist revolutionaries ("Makhnovchina") in the turmoil of the Russian Revolution of 1917. There were the killings of landowners ("kulaks") in the 1920s by the new communist government. A famine in 1922 was particularly devasting and the state-induced famine ("Holodomor") of 1932–33 was even worse. Increasing attempts by the state to assimilate also encouraged them to leave, except they weren't permitted to do so.

On top of it all, erratic visits by the secret police (NKVD) that resulted in extrajudicial murders and disappearances led to a general atmosphere of fear especially from 1935 onward.

The lives of the Mennonites had become immeasurably worse over the course of a century-and-a half since they had first arrived under invitation from Catherine the Great.

Although conditions had worsened and the population actually declined, the presence of Mennonites in Russia was still extant and remained relatively unchanged since 1789.

In the fall of 1943 it all came to an end.

4. MIDDLE NAME

"Why don't you have a middle name?" It's a question Alfred Hecht gets asked a lot.

"Maybe because my father Leonidas Hecht, as well as my mother Susanna Hecht, did not have second names."

His father would leave very little direct influence on Alfred, as he would die in the war when Alfred was only three years old. Yet, his father did leave a strong indirect and indelible impression on Alfred for the rest of his life. In a way, Alfred's father was more influential in death than in life.

The full extent of what Alfred knows about him comes partially from a letter written before Leonidas was sent to the frontlines of the German-Russian front in WWII. The letter, below, was an account of Alfred's father's life. His father left the letter with his wife Susanna before he went off to the army.

> I, Leonidas Hecht, born on December 9, 1909 in Alexandrovka, Rayon, Izyum, USSR, Region Charkow.
>
> My father's family sold the estate in 1911 and moved to Tambov Oblast, Rayon Koslow. Here they bought a new estate with 320 hectare land. When the war of 1914 started, our family was sent to Siberia, more precisely, the Ural mountain region.
>
> In March 1915, we returned to the Ukraine and settled in Eugenfeld, Rayon. Melitopol. Both mother and father died in 1921.
>
> I started my elementary education in Eugenfeld in 1917 and finished the 7th grade in 1921. In the same year I started in the Taedtechinicum and completed it in 1929. As a distance

education student I finished in 1939 at the teacher's education Institute in Kriwoj-Rayer.

I have been a teacher from 1929 till now. From 1929 till 1935 in Gruenfeld. In 1935 I was in prison for 3-months. From 1935 till 1938 I was teaching in Neuland, Rayon Tjatichalva and from 1938 till 1941 on the Artjomorva school, Rayon Kriwoj-Rog. From 1941 till now (Feb 28, 1943) I again was teaching in the elementary school in Gruenfeld.

My family consists of 7 people of which 5 are children, all under 10 years of age.

Gruenfeld February, 28, 1943

---

*Written by Leonidas Hecht in German. Translated by Alfred Hecht into English. See Appendix for full geographic references.

Alfred's mother's lineage is less well known but is in many ways more detailed and complicated. Unlike his father, Susanna Hecht had a direct and very powerful influence on Alfred's life from the moment he was born. Her own history was deeply connected to one of the bizarre Russian government social experiments of the 19th and 20th centuries.

When Catherine the Great welcomed new immigrants to the steppe, the population was sparse and scattered. By the mid-1800s, the situation had reversed. There was an over-population problem that left many people landless. Among Mennonites, landless individuals and families were considered the lowest of the social classes. The Mennonite leadership was open to almost any option the Russian government could offer. The Russian government came up with various plans to solve the problems.

One of those solutions was to build new settlements. One in particular, near the Ukrainian city of Krivoy Rog (Kryvyi Rih), saw the Russian government survey a 10 sq. km area that had fertile soils, upon which were six farming villages for Jews to occupy.

The place was approximately 150 km west of the main Mennonite settlement at Chortitza. The Mennonites referred to the Russian government's planned farming communities as "the Judenplan" (roughly translated as, "the Jewish settlement").

The Russian government expected the Jews to become independent subsistence farmers much like the Mennonites. Being more culturally oriented toward business and crafts, the Jews did not take well to subsistence farming.

The Russian government sought a novel solution for this problem, as they saw it. They offered Mennonites the possibility to live among the Jews as model farmers who could teach the Jews how to be good farmers.

The Mennonite leadership endorsed the idea, especially since it offered an opportunity for some of their landless people to own property. From the Russian government came tax breaks, rights to operate their own schools and an opportunity to own land. This enticed many landless Mennonites to move into the Judenplan.

"The Krause family moved to the Jewish village in 1852 from Kronsweide in the Chortitza colony. They must have been one of the first settlers to come from Prussia around 1785 since in the list of Mennonite migrants was listed a person by the name of Krause, classified as a servant. My mother's maiden name was Krause and she was born in the village of Novovitebsk, which was part of the Judenplan in the same village (where my) grandmother was born. Hence, both could speak excellent Yiddish," Alfred explained.

Between ten and twenty Mennonite families lived in each of the six villages and prior to WWII, as many as eight hundred Mennonites in total lived in the Judenplan.[2] The Jewish population was double that number.

The intermingling of Jews and Mennonites did not go as smoothly as the Russian government hoped. Cultural attitudes were quite different, in spite of the fact that each group spoke linguistically similar languages that were somewhat mutually intelligible.

"The Mennonites were never able to influence the Jewish people to become successful peasant farmers and the experience further convinced the Mennonites that multi-ethnic or multi-religious communities weren't a good idea."[2]

By the end of the 1800s, population pressures were again the cause of housing and land shortages. Near to the Judenplan, a number of Mennonites bought up land and estates from the Russian gentry that included ten thousand acres, which subsequently became known as Schlactin-Baratov. Four Mennonite villages were built here—Steinfeld, Gruenfeld, Neu Chortitza, Gnadenthal. Many Mennonites from the Judenplan moved into the nearby Schlactin-Baratov villages including the Krause family.

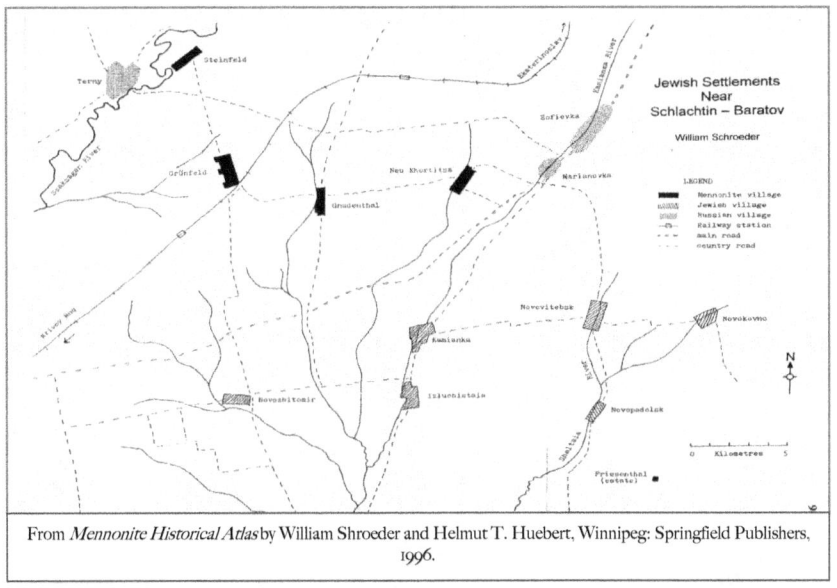

From *Mennonite Historical Atlas* by William Shroeder and Helmut T. Huebert, Winnipeg: Springfield Publishers, 1996.

After the Russian Revolution, turmoil and terror were common and constant in this region. "During the Stalin persecution era, both my grandfather and great-grandfather Krause died by forced drowning, by the communists," Alfred pointed out.

"My father, Leonidas Hecht, married my Aunt Helene (my mother's sister) in 1934 and they had two children, Rudolf and Elsa. Shortly after Elsa's birth her mother died. In the same time period my mother married Johan Friesen and they also had two children, Franz and Susanne (Suza). But Johan was taken by the communists and died in captivity."

"By 1939 both of my parents had two children and no spouses and so they married. This was the period of collectivization. Food was scarce and having a reliable partner was crucial. They then had children of their own. Alfred the first died at six months and Alfred 'the second' was born in 1942 (the subject of this book). Helene was the second, born in 1943 and Johanna the third, born in 1945. Now the family had seven children—the older four and the younger three."

While the question of a second name was never resolved, it was their last name that was the real problem. It almost sent the whole family off to a concentration camp.

5. WRONG NAME

Their lives were about to be uprooted in 1943 but when the German Army had invaded southern Russia two years earlier, many ethnic Germans who were living there, including the Mennonites, saw them as liberators who had come to save them from Soviet Russia's communist oppression.

The lives of most ethnic Germans did actually improve quite dramatically and immediately upon the arrival of the German Army, but it came at a price. It did not take long to realize they had become engaged in a dance with the Devil.

The *Final Solution* and removal of *Untermenschen* was implemented as soon as the German Army rolled in. All Jews in the villages where Alfred's mother and grandmother were born were taken away and shot. The same happened in all the villages across the region. Once a village was ethnically cleansed of their Jewish population, signs were proudly posted announcing it was *Judenfrei (Free of Jews)*. Anyone who was mentally ill, Romani, a collaborator, or a Bolshevik was also taken away and in most circumstances killed.

Ethnic Germans living in Russia had not been exposed to the same Nazi propaganda and indoctrination as those living in Germany itself. The Mennonites, a religiously passive people, quickly became acquainted with the ideological fervour displayed by some of the German soldiers and their officers. Upon seeing Jewish friends and acquaintances being taken away to be deported or killed, sometimes shot right in front of them, the Mennonites began to understand the complications of living under their new 'liberator.'

Some, of course, were more than willing participants in the extermination of the Jewish population but many were less than enthusiastic. The reticence and unwillingness to engage in the atrocities was noted in German Military Command reports. It found that the further east the German Army went, the more unlikely it was for local ethnic

German populations to willingly participate in the genocide. Those who refused were demoted to lesser social positions, sent to labour camps or executed. The Mennonites, whether fervent supporters of Nazi ideology or not, had little choice but to go along with it if they wished to survive.[3]

When a nefarious branch of the German Army—*Einsatzgruppen C*—went searching for Jews in the Ukraine, they found Alfred Hecht's family. Suddenly, the ethnicity and race of the Hecht family was in question and it all began with their surname.

Mennonites as a whole were usually considered to be ethnically German under Nazi ideology but Hecht was not a common Mennonite surname. While the other surnames in their family lineage such as Friesen, Janzen and Krause were considered Mennonite and thus Germanic, Hecht was not.

Hecht is a common Jewish name.

"When the Nazis overran southern Ukraine, my mother was married to my dad, Hecht. They were asked, 'Are you Jewish or Mennonite or German?'" Alfred recounted.

If the answer had been, "We are Jewish," they would have been given 'special treatment' (murdered).

Fortunately, the Hecht family had a recorded lineage going back to the early 1700s. As far as they understood, they weren't Jewish but they needed official confirmation to avoid being murdered, and the Gestapo were not the kind to give the benefit of the doubt. The Hechts had to prove it.

"The Burgermeister in Staffort, Bavaria, Germany from where the Hechts had come, had to write a letter to southern Ukraine saying, 'I can vouch for it. The Hecht family has been Lutheran since 1760. So there is no Jewish background in them,'" Alfred explained.

When Alfred revisited the records that saved his family back in 1941, he received a letter from Councillor Wilhelm Hauck of the Municipality of Stutensee-Blankenloch, Baden-Wurttemberg, Germany. Below is Mr. Hauck's abbreviated letter from 1984.

Alfred's father, Leonidas Hecht, had a father named Karl Hecht who was born in Altmuntal on 12.7.1853 and died in Eugenfeld in 5.5.1921. Karl Hecht's second wife was Loise Waechter and one of their children was Leonidas Hecht.

Leonidas' grandfather was also named Karl Hecht (24.6.1826–2.2.1900)

Leonidas' great-grandfather was Christian Freidrich Hecht (29.10.1781) married to Nina Han.

Christian and Nina migrated to Prischib, Ukraine in 1813 from Staffort, Stutensee, Germany.

Leonidas' great grandparents were Johanna Martin Hecht (8.5.1755—28.11.1820) and Barbara (Ernst), (10.11.1740–9.9.1812). They married January 12, 1779. She was 15 years older than him.

Leonidas' great-great-grandparents were Johan Martin Hecht (same name as father) (27.4.1730—27.5.1789) who married Eva Barbara (Waidmann) on 14.5.1750. She died on 2.1.1762.

*Source: Letter from the Amtsrad Wilhelm Hauch, aus Stutenensee-Blankenloch, Germany, dated 1984

They were registered Lutherans not Jews but Alfred clarified the point. "There are quite a few Hechts in Germany. So, it's a common German name too," not exclusively Jewish.

"So, you were saved from being sent to a concentration camp?" I asked rhetorically.

"Argh," Alfred said with a tinge of disbelief in his voice as though the event had happened yesterday.

They were by no means the only family caught up in the fanaticism of Nazi ideology and yet, like everyone else, it forced them to choose sides whether they wanted to or not. Neutrality was not an option and sometimes, every option led to death no matter the choice offered.

Historians often debate whether the German invasion of the Soviet Union in 1941 would have turned out differently if Chancellor of the Third Reich, Adolf Hitler had allied himself with the Ukrainian nationalists who were desiring independence from Russia.

Those who lived in Russia's southern state of Ukraine had experienced a devasting famine in 1932–1933 that many believed had been purposely created by Joseph Stalin to suppress nationalist stirrings among the Ukrainian population. Ukrainians, like ethnic Germans in southern Russia, initially saw the German Army as a potential liberator. Many Ukrainians were willing to fight with the Germans against the Russians. Many in fact, did so, initially.

Within the ranks of Hitler's generals, some were more practical than ideological. The Eastern Front general, Heinz Guderian, famously said, "We lost the war the day we failed to raise the Ukrainian flag over the cathedral in Kiev; that day is when the Ukrainians lost their hope and faith in the Third Reich as the liberators I intended."

The fiercely ideological Adolf Hitler had chosen racial purity instead of practical alliance.

"(The Nazis) thought themselves a superior race against any people living in the East, except those of German ancestry," Alfred said.

Being of German ancestry, albeit from a long time prior, the Mennonites were welcomed into the fold of the German occupiers. Clearing up the origins of the Hecht family origin spared them a one-way trip to a concentration camp or bullet to the head, but their alignment with Nazi Germany under Adolf Hitler simultaneously made them traitors to the Soviet Union under Joseph Stalin. In the eyes of the Russians, they would have to be punished.

The traitor designation would stalk the family for the next five years but it would haunt Alfred for the rest of his life. It would even force him later, as a Canadian citizen, to test the Soviet Union's long-term memory. But that was not yet. Alfred was still an infant in 1943 when the war went badly for the German Army and the family was forced to leave with them as they retreated.

The whole Mennonite community and all other peoples of Germanic origin living in Russia, who had become comfortable and loyal to the Nazi's apparatus of security and protection, had to decide in fact, if they were going to remain when the advancing Red Army retook the territory or leave with the retreating German Army.

The answer was obvious, yet there was still hope in the summer of 1943 that it wouldn't come to that.

6. The GREAT TREK

After losing in February 1943 at the bloodiest battle in history—The Battle of Stalingrad—the German Army would spend the next two years fighting a rearguard retreat.

The city of Stalingrad was nine hundred kilometres east of Alfred's village. For many, it seemed far away. By the summer, however, the Battle of Dnieper erupted and forced the evacuation of the original Mennonite colonies of Molotschna and Chortitza. Yet, that was still nearly two hundred kilometres east of Alfred's village. The Red Army continued its rapid advance westward through the summer and into early fall.

Alfred's mother and the rest of the Mennonites in the area knew they would be better off remaining under the protection of the German Army rather than being under the control of the Soviets, if forced to choose. They prepared to leave if necessary.

It happened faster than expected.

On the night of October 25, 1943 the Red Army advanced to within a few kilometres of their villages of Steinfeld, Gruenfeld, Gnadenthal and Neu Chortitza that comprised the Schlactin-Baratov Mennonite colony. Word spread that the Russians were already transporting residents in the overrun villages east of theirs to Siberia or other unknown places.

The next day was tense. Alfred's father and mother loaded up the wagon with the six children plus Alfred's grandmother and aunt.

Some ethnic Germans in other areas had been evacuated earlier by train but those further afield, including everyone in the Schlactin-Baratov colony, had to go by horse-drawn wagon, or on foot.

The Hecht's wagon joined the convoy of thousands who were heading west on dirt roads toward somewhere deeper inside the safety of Nazi Germany.

They travelled a number of months through the winter until they arrived near the Polish border at Reichshof (Rzeszow, Poland). Here, they abandoned their horses and wagon and were loaded onto a train that then took them to Freihaus (Zdunska Wola) in Poland.

Under the Third Reich's ideological premise of "Germanization" and "Lebensraum," Germany had expelled 630,000 Poles from the region and renamed it Warthegau.

The Hecht family was accommodated in a house that had previously belonged to Polish owners who were expelled under the previously mentioned policies and subsequent actions. The house was in the village of Shieratz (Sieradz). Here they would stay for ten months.

Alfred's father began teaching again and for a brief time it seemed as though life might return to some normalcy. His last teaching contract was issued May 4, 1944. He taught in the summer and then on September 6, 1944 in Freihaus, the German government conferred German citizenship on all members of the family and almost all other refugees of German ethnicity. This allowed the German government to promptly send all able-bodied men with German citizenship to war, including Alfred's father, Leonidas Hecht.

The ability to speak both German and Russian naturally led Alfred's father to be posted into a communications role. He was assigned to a position as a radio operator.

With the Soviet Army continuing its advance and the frontline shifting ever westward, the family had to flee again in November 1944. They said goodbye to their father and hoped he would survive in the German Army fighting against the Russians. Leonidas Hecht was posted to Poznan in early January 1945. "At the end of January 1945, we got the last letter from him."

The last letter was addressed to Rudy and dated January 13, 1945 but not received until later in the month. It was translated by Alfred.

"Verbal communication from fellow soldiers told us that a Russian bomber attack hit his fox hole. We never received formal information from the German or Russian Governments about his death. He died at the age of 36."

Dear Rudy:

I am glad that you wrote me a letter.

But that your shoes are already broken is not good. Study eagerly. Everything you have you can lose but what you have in your head no one can take away from you. Make sure you take care of mother and grandmother also. How many times in the week do you have school? Say Hi to Alfred as well as Lena. Greetings also to Susa and Franz. For Elsa I am including a separate little note.

I remain,

Your Papa

While Alfred lost his father, his mother was pregnant again and the family was on the road to an illusory freedom. Alfred's mother was going to give birth to a daughter soon but lose another.

7. SUZA IS LOST

On the road from Poland it took many weeks to get to Germany in the bitter cold of winter.

The last refugees fled Poland in January 1945 with the Soviet Red Army at their heels. While the Great Trek out of the Ukraine in 1943 had been somewhat organized by the German military, this time, the situation was chaotic, unplanned and desperate. The German authorities had lost control and were in complete disarray.

Some refugees had horses and wagons. Some dragged makeshift sleds but most had nothing other than the clothes on their backs and whatever they had grabbed as they ran from their houses, often in sight of Russian tanks rolling into their villages.

The winter of 1945 was bitterly cold and on that flight to freedom, they lost Suza.

"Everybody was feeling restless because the Russians were coming," Alfred explained. The convoy of refugees were desperately on the move, being unable to linger for long. War planes would strafe their wagons from the air. On the ground the sound of artillery, gunfire and the rumbling of tanks was rarely silent. On some days the battle was far in the distance but sometimes it was so close it seemed they would be overrun by the Red Army at any moment. In some instances, that's exactly what happened.

Those caught up in the advancing Russian frontline were taken and sent back to Russia. Others were able to carry on and quite literally outrun the Russian Army.

One day at a fork in the road, Alfred's older sister Suza and one of Suza's friends, a neighbour from Steinfeld, had walked on ahead of the convoy. They waited at a small village but when the convoy seemed to take too long, they went back only to find that everyone had disappeared.

Unbeknown to Suza and her friend, the convoy had taken a different road and suddenly they were all alone. They managed, just barely, to find help and with the kindness of strangers they eventually ended up at an orphanage where they stayed until the war ended.

Alfred's mother had no idea where Suza had gone or whether she was still alive.

"We lost her there on the road," remembered Alfred's oldest brother Franz.[4] Suza was lost but the family had to keep moving, hoping she wasn't dead, hoping to be reunited with her later somehow, somewhere. Now was not the time to stop.

A couple of days later, they entered Germany and came to rest at a farm in a village called Oberdorf, north of the Czechoslovakian border.

In Oberdorf, six months passed in which spring came and went, Alfred's mother gave birth to Johanna and there was still no word of Suza's whereabouts. However, good news did eventually arrive while they were trying to figure out what to do next. They learned that the Red Cross organization had picked up Suza and her friend and were taking care of them in an orphanage along with over 100 other children, inside Czechoslovakia.

"Mom said, 'We are not gonna go with our people,'" Franz recalled. They were going to rescue Suza instead.

It would not be easy. There were two inconceivably difficult problems. The orphanage was one hundred kilometres away. It was also inside Czechoslovakia, which was now controlled by the Russians. They would have to go back into the hands of the Russians; back into the hands of those they had been fleeing from for the past two years but it was a risk Susanna was willing to take to get her daughter back.

According to Alfred, his mother took a small wagon, her eldest son Franz, the baby carriage and baby Johanna, and rode off toward Czechoslovakia. Meanwhile, Alfred's grandmother and his Aunt Tina left with the rest of the Mennonites heading further west. The other four children—Rudy, Elsa, Helene, Alfred—were left behind with the farmer in Oberdorf.

Susanna and Franz went off to find Suza. As they came to the German-Czechoslovak border, on the horse-drawn wagon, she turned to Franz and said, "Let's not speak in Russian. We can only speak in German."

She didn't want the Russian soldiers to hear them speaking Russian because they would be recognized as Russian citizens and be immediately transported back to Russia, if not immediately shot.

They rode into Czechoslovakia in what was a loosely governed, semi-lawless, post-battle territory that the Russian Army had only recently captured.

Franz vividly recalled what he saw. "Tanks on the side of the road all bombed up, upside down. And the Russians could do whatever they want. They could shoot anybody."

Russian soldiers were standing at nearly every intersection directing people where to go. They were trying to send people back from where they came but Susanna and Franz needed to go deeper into Czechoslovakia. The soldiers kept telling them to turn around.

Franz said to the soldiers at each intersection, "Yes, we're going to turn around at the next corner," but they never did. When they came to the town where the Red Cross was working and where Suza was supposedly located, they stopped for a moment. Here, without Susanna's strong sense of intuition and gut instinct, they would have gone no further.

"My mom talked to a Russian soldier on the sidewalk," Franz remembered, and the Russian soldier directed Susanna to go to a certain location nearby where "'you get lodging and food and then you can go on.'"

Susanna knew the soldier was lying.

Franz remembered her saying, as they rode away from the soldier, "Let's get out of here as fast as we can because if we go (where the soldier instructed) we don't see my sister and...we would be back in Russia."

They kept going and soon found the orphanage, and Suza!

It was lucky Suza was still there at all. Food was scare and it was common to send children off to be billeted at farms where food was more plentiful and labour was needed. The nuns at the orphanage had actually planned to send the girls individually to different homes but a strong protest spearheaded by Suza and her friend convinced the nuns to let them stay. The children and nuns raised their own vegetable gardens on the grounds of the orphanage through the spring.[5]

By the time Susanna and Franz arrived at the orphanage there was fresh food, warm beds and companionship, and a looming terror. The Russian soldiers at night would rape the nuns and the older girls in the orphanage. The only reason Suza avoided it as a young teenage girl, she claimed, was because with so few beds in the orphanage she would sleep in a crib, deep under covers and out of sight of the Russian soldiers.

But that day, upon seeing her mother and brother at the entrance of the orphanage, Suza was ecstatic, after six months of wondering. She left with them immediately.

Susanna, Franz and Suza returned to Germany without incident but what awaited them upon their return was a great surprise, and not a good one either.

8. The TERRIBLE TRADE

In the middle of the Second World War (1939–1945) the Russians had successfully fought off the German Army at the Battle of Stalingrad, thus turning the tide of war in the Russian's favour. By the middle of 1944, the Red Army had pushed the German Army westward into Poland, continuously weakening Germany's military strength as it went.

Meanwhile, until the middle of 1944, the Western Anglo-American Allies were bogged down in Italy and completely absent on western European soil. At first it appeared the Russians, who had been conquering vast swathes of territory from the German Army over the previous three years, might occupy all of Germany before the Anglo-American Allies arrived on scene. The Russians would be able to set the terms for Germany's surrender and reap all the plunder they wished to extract.

The Anglo-American Allies—the United States, the United Kingdom, Canada—launched the successful D-Day invasion onto the beaches of Normandy on June 6, 1944. They were back.

With a toehold on the western shores of the continent, they moved quickly. By winter they were in western Germany.

Prior to these events, in February of 1945 at the Yalta Conference, the top three Allied leaders—Prime Minister Winston Churchill, President Franklin D. Roosevelt, General Secretary Joseph Stalin—agreed to a Demarcation Line from which the Russians would control everything to the east and the Anglo-American forces, everything to the west. In the heat of battle through April and May, however, the Anglo-American Armies advanced so quickly they often went beyond the Demarcation Line by as much as 320 kilometres, deep into the German states of Brandenburg, Thuringia, Saxony-Anhalt, Mecklenburg and Saxony. The state of Saxony just happened to be where the Hecht family had taken refuge on a farm in Oberdorf near Chemnitz and was living in 1945 as the war came to an end.

Germany surrendered unconditionally on May 7, 1945.

Here the Allies then had to determine precisely who, how, where and when each would occupy the defeated nation. They agreed to divide Germany into four sectors—American, British, French and Russian. There was also a desire to split Berlin in a similar fashion.

The Americans and the British proposed to share control of Berlin. The Russians had captured the city and physically occupied it. They had enormous sway over these negotiations and they were against the idea of shared governance but they did agree to the general concept of having each of the four major Allies—the Soviet Union, the United States, the United Kingdom, and France—occupy and independently administer their own sectors of the city in the same way they had done with Germany itself, but it would involve an act of faith on the part of the Americans.

The various states occupied by American forces, such as Saxony and Brandenburg, had actually been promised to the Russians at the Yalta Conference. The Americans would have to move their troops out and let the Russians in. Winston Churchill did not trust Joseph Stalin and was against the move. He thought the American troops should stay exactly where they were instead of giving up the territory in the hope that the Russians would cede West Berlin in exchange.

Roosevelt suddenly died on April 12, 1945 and Harry S. Truman became the US President. Truman ignored Churchill and agreed to make a trade with Stalin. President Truman cabled Joseph Stalin on June 14, 1945 to inform him that he was preparing to withdraw American troops in a week, on June 21st for the agreed upon transfer into Russian hands. Stalin unexpectedly asked Truman to delay the troop movement for one month. The Russian General Georgy Zhukov needed to attend the Parade of Victors in Moscow on June 24. Stalin wanted to wait until such time as Zhukov could return to Germany to fully oversee the trade.

It was in this brief moment that Alfred's mother Susanna and his older brother Franz had gone off to find Suza in Czechoslovakia.

While they were away, for nearly two weeks, the Americans and the Russians made the swap. On July 3rd Soviet troops entered Saxony's main city of Leipzig and effectively controlled the entire state, so that when

Susanna, Franz and Suza rejoined the rest of the family in Oberdorf, the Americans had left and the Russians had arrived.

"We were in the American zone before we left. When we came back, we were in the Russian zone!" Franz said.

"My mother was really disturbed by that because we were born Russian citizens. Russia like Canada, if you're born in Russia, you're a Russian citizen," Alfred explained.

Unlike Canada, anyone perceived to be a traitor in Russia faced deadly consequences.

Many in the Russian-occupied zone moved to one of the other three zones—American, British or French—as soon as they could. The Russian Mennonites with Soviet citizenship were not permitted to cross. If they tried, they would almost certainly be 'repatriated' back to Russia—a fate that had to be avoided at all costs. The fear was not unreasonable.

Alfred explained, "They caught twenty thousand Mennonites around Brandenburg. When they changed the boundaries, all of a sudden they were in the Russian zone. Russian trucks were in the next day."

News spread of what was happening.

"My mom actually heard from her cousin...what happened to this territory where we were. 'Get out of there. Go further to the West,'" Susanna's cousin had told her.

"But it was too late," Alfred said.

The infrastructure of control was quickly closing in on them. The Soviets were not interested in letting former Soviet citizens leave their grip. The Russian government was determined to repatriate their former citizens, yet the infrastructure of large-scale geographic imprisonment would take time to build. In that brief moment lay a glimmer of hope but the opportunity to escape was limited. Border guards were already in place. Barbed-wire fences had gone up. Guard towers with machine-gun mountings were being erected. The family would have to find a way to get out of the Russian sector, and fast. As bad as it was, Susanna being all alone with her six children and newborn baby, things were about to get even worse.

"That's when Mom hired this lady," to help escape to the American zone. The lady agreed to help, Franz recalled, and took the money from Susanna. Maliciously, "she never came back. The 2000 Marks (equivalent to US$10,000 in 2024) were gone!"

The clock was ticking. They were now out of money. Food was gone and the Russians were rapidly building the Internal Border between the freedom of West Germany and the totalitarianism of East Germany.

9. NIEMANDSLAND

Franz Friesen remembers it well.

"That's the only time I was really scared," he said.[2]

The Americans and the Russians had swapped territory in July, 1945 while Susanna and Franz had gone off to find Suza just on the other side of the border, inside Czechoslovakia. When they returned, the territory they thought was securely controlled by the Americans was now under Russian control.

"Dumb thing, (the Americans) all of a sudden traded part of it to the Russians so they could get part of Berlin because the Russians had conquered Berlin. So all of a sudden, we were back in the Russian zone!" Alfred explained.

It was the worst nightmare imaginable for the family and the thousands of other Russian-born citizens fleeing the Soviet Union who were now caught in territory they thought was safe. Without the security and adherence to basic human rights under the American Army, there was only one thing to do—get out of there. Their options, however, were closing quickly. The Russians had immediately begun fortifying the border between their zone of occupation and the other Allied-occupied zones to the west. The Russians were forcing people to stay and the one person that falsely offered help, had stolen their money. Fortunately, Susanna learned of a farmer who lived near the border and was secretly known to help people cross over to the West, for a price. Susanna travelled to the farmhouse by train with her seven children as fast as she could. When they arrived, they stayed the night with the farmer who explained to Susanna where she would need to go and exactly what to do.

Franz remembered "that farmer was so good. He let us eat plums" from the trees in his orchard. It was all the farmer could provide to the half starving family, not because he was short on food, but because the Russian soldiers stationed at the border would regularly come by the farmhouse and check up on him to see if he was harbouring fugitives. They would also take inventory of how much food the farmer had on hand in order to ascertain whether excess food was coming in or going out. The one thing they didn't consider was the fruit on his trees.

"We were so hungry," Franz said. "We had nothing to eat really up to there."

That night, they hid at the farm until the time was right to go.

Susanna gave the farmer the gold watch that Leonidas had left in Susanna's care for a moment like this. At 5 o'clock in the morning they set out on the dirt road that would take them either to freedom or death.

Franz was ten years old at the time. In 2023, he recounted in a cantered English, but without doubt or lack of clarity, what the farmer had said. "You go along the fence and there gonna be a hole cut out there. You go through that hole at exactly that time because the Russians had those towers not far away. They were looking always. They were exactly changing the guards, on those towers at that time." It had rained overnight. The road was muddy. Susanna had baby Johanna inside a baby carriage and Franz was in charge of pushing it.

At first, it may seem strange to some readers that Susanna would haul a baby carriage through a fence, forest, and danger instead of being extraordinarily mobile, yet, attached to the lower frame of the carriage was Susanna's economic freedom, her independence. Attached was Susanna's sewing machine and her ability to earn an income wherever she went. It would prove more valuable than gold later on. The sewing machine would go all the way to Winnipeg, Manitoba where it would continue generating an income and feeding her children. It was the last item Susanna would ever part with, even now as they fled through the guarded forest of mud, fear and uncertainty.

On the road that night, once they left the farmhouse, it was tough going right from the start. The darkness was deep and impenetrable. The fence they were told to follow, couldn't be seen. They were grasping in the dark.

"We had to drag (the baby carriage) through the mud," Franz remembered.

They struggled as they went, dragging the carriage and then, "suddenly she fell."

The baby carriage tumbled down a small incline and became lodged against something stern and solid. Baby Johanna was tossed out and came to a rolling halt.

When Franz stepped down into a small dry ditch, to collect the carriage and put baby Johanna back in, he realized he'd found the fence they'd been looking for. "I said to Mom, 'Here is the barbed-wire fence already.'"

It was a stroke of pure luck. If they hadn't found the fence at that moment, they would have gone too far and walked straight into the Russian guard tower. Instead, they followed the rest of the farmer's instructions. They made their way along the fence methodically until they found the small hole.

"Mom helped us all through the hole because it wasn't that big."

Once they were on the other side of the fence, they had to cross an open field inside No Man's Land where the guards would have a clear shot at them.

In the darkness, the family had the advantage but the rising dawn had begun to crack flecks of low light on the horizon. One's eyes could begin to make out shapes in the distance and at that moment they were now standing in the most exposed and dangerous place they could possibly be.

The guard tower, overlooking the forest below and the open strip of land beyond, was perched in such a way as to be slightly hidden up in the tree canopy.

"The forest kinda hid the tower but somehow it was higher up," remembered Rudy *(b. 26.6.1934)* who was only a few months older than Franz *(b. 8.9.1934)*.

The early wooden guard towers were of a square design with a long ladder taking the guards up to positions of power over life and death below. The early models with low half-walls around an open square parapet, with a simple four-sided pyramidal hip roof, looked like something skilled fathers built for their sons in backyards where countless hours are spent in mock-war play. But this was real. Armed guards were ready with rifles, machine guns and had been ordered to shoot to kill.

Later, enclosed guard towers with sophisticated monitoring devices, motion sensors and bright spotlights would be erected here, making escape a virtual impossibility. At this brief moment in time it was still possible to escape, although by no means guaranteed.

They carried on. In the middle of No Man's Land they came to a creek they would have to traverse without being noticed. No one spoke a word.

At the creek, "Mom put herself in," Franz recalled. It was July and the spring freshet had subsided so it was not at full height but it was still waist deep for Franz and almost over the heads of his youngest siblings. The youngest children, including Alfred, crossed over with the help of their mother and Franz. Franz was the last one to cross, taking the baby carriage with him to the other side.

Once they forded the creek without incident, they crossed the rest of the open field undetected and came to the base of a steep hill covered in forest.

"We hid quickly," Franz said.

So far, so good.

The trees of the forest helped hide them but they still had to make their way up the tree-covered embankment to a height of around eighty feet. The steep hill would be a challenge but more treacherous was the direction in which it faced. The slope faced toward the Russian guard tower.

While they were now technically in American-controlled territory, American soldiers were not standing guard at that precise location. There were soldiers atop the bluff but not down below at the edge of the forest overlooking No Man's Land. With the forest hiding them to some degree, the Russian guards could not easily see them. However, if given a clear shot, it would not be unheard of for the soldiers in the tower to shoot.

Susanna hurried to help all the children get up the hill but left Franz behind with the baby carriage and baby Johanna inside.

"I was still sitting on the edge of that veld (forest) waiting for Mom to come pick me and Johanna up, with the baby carriage, and the sewing machine," Franz remembered. While he sat alone, the summer morning still crisp, "Suddenly I hear tata-tat-tat. Machine gun going off."

Another group of people had been attempting to escape the Russian zone via the same route but the guards spotted them. They opened fire.

"That's the only time I was really scared," Franz said. "Then there was a couple guys come running towards me," as he sat at the edge of the forest overlooking the open field devoid of vegetation and the creek in the middle they'd just crossed. The thing that stood out for Franz, was that these two young men in their twenties were running furiously in a panic and "They had suitcases. I don't know why they still carried the suitcase." They came running toward Franz and in a short conversation, he learned that the two young men had been trying to help bring people through but the Russians had just caught the families as they tried to escape.

"These two guys got away. They caught the families there. I don't know if that was Mennonites or Russian Germans, or what. Maybe they let them go. I don't know. Then Mom came down and helped me up."

Franz and his mother climbed the hill and once they came upon the rest of the children, they carried on through the forest but became a bit lost. They were trying to find their way to the main road when miraculously, they came across "a guy picking berries." They asked the man if they were going in the right direction.

"Yes, this is the right way to the highway," the man replied.

Susanna, Franz, Rudy, Elsa, Suza, Alfred, Helene and Johanna carried on until they found the road.

"We came to the highway and there was a truck. I'm not so sure why there was a truck, actually (but) we got loaded onto that truck. Seems to me there was still somebody shooting. I don't know. At us? Or some gunfire there. But we got away from there."

"That was so close!" Franz said with a measure of disbelief when recounting the story seventy-eight years later, in 2023 at the age of eighty-nine.

As he pondered his own harrowing tale, the fate of good timing, miracles and the help of God, he added, "The others, they caught. We were just at the right time. God was with us all the way...otherwise we would have never made it."

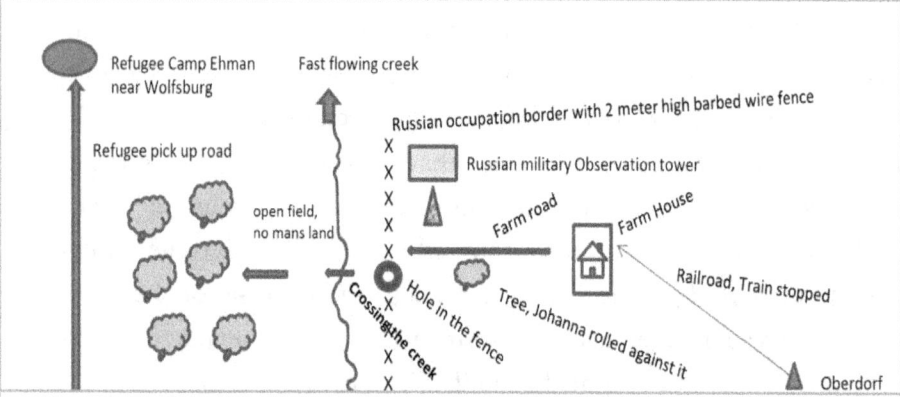

The map is from a presentation given by Alfred Hecht at Dr. Marlene Epp's CGUC class, January 19, 2017.

"My sincere 'thank you' goes to my siblings for reconstructing some of our flights; Susa Dueck (Friesen), Franz Friesen, Rudolf Hecht, Elsa Dueck (Hecht) and my uncle Bernhard Krause." - Alfred Hecht

10. REDISPOSITION

More than a year before Germany surrendered it had become apparent that Germany was going to lose the war. The Allies anticipated a looming problem—the responsibility of caring for an incredibly large number of Displaced Persons (DPs) across Europe.

The DPs would include forced labour, prisoners of war, and refugees who had fled their homes for various reasons. Plans for dealing with the future 20 million DPs were articulated in the "Outline Plan for Refugees and Displaced Persons," issued in June of 1944. Responsibility for carrying out the Plan was given to the United Nations Relief and Rehabilitation Administration (UNRRA) under the command of the US Military's Displaced Persons Executive (DPX).

The Allies worried about a potential mass exodus of DPs from Germany once the German government collapsed. The chaos would hinder Allied forces as the DPs flooded onto road, rail and every other transportation network and they would also threaten the spread of disease, causing significant hindrances to military effectiveness, not to mention countless deaths.

In February and March of 1945 the US Military Command, by this time in control of most regions of western Germany, began to experience the Displaced Persons problem they had both anticipated and feared. Many DPs were Russian, Polish and eastern Europeans that had been slave labourers in Nazi Germany who, once freed, became aimless wanderers.

In response, the US Military Command closed the western border of Germany on March 12, 1945 to those Russians, Poles and other eastern European Displaced Persons. Dutch, French and Belgian DPs were free to continue across the border in order to go home.

By the end of March 1945 there were 145,000 DPs in processing centres inside the occupied zones within Germany. Around 45,000 French, Belgian and Dutch DPs had crossed the border and gone home. It was a small trickle in what was about to become an almost unimaginable number of Displaced Persons, as the Allies advanced further east.

Alfred and his family had left Poland and were settled in Oberdorf, Germany in March, 1945. With the Americans officially closing the western border, and as former Russian citizens, they could no longer move west, out of Germany.

The US Military Command thought the most sensible thing to do with the DPs once the war ended was to send them back to their homelands.

For all ethnic Germans coming from the Soviet Union with Russian citizenship, including the Hecht family, this was a terrifying prospect and it was about to become dangerously real.

One week after Germany surrendered, on May 16, 1945 Major General Ray W. Barker of the Supreme Headquarters Allied Expeditionary Force (SHAEF) met with Russian General Golubev at Halle, Germany twenty miles northwest of Leipzig, which was ironically not far from where the Hechts were living in Oberdorf.

Barker and Golubev, unbeknown to the Hechts, were further deciding their fate and the fate of the other 20 million Displaced Persons. They were arranging a system upon which the prisoners of war, the forced labourers, the refugees and other DPs could be exchanged across the Demarcation Line.

The agreements made at Halle immediately resulted in the mass movement of people four days later on the 20th of May when the Russians handed over more than 2,000 liberated US and British prisoners of war in exchange for 60,000 DPs who went back to the Soviet Union. By the 28th all of the 28,662 liberated US soldiers under Russian care had been returned to the West.

The exchange of soldiers went well. The same could not be said for the movement of Displaced Persons.

Since the Soviet Union had lost a disproportionately large number of her population in the war, a loss that resulted in an economically debilitating labour shortage, they needed their former citizens to return home. Whether that was voluntary or not did not concern Joseph Stalin, although he was concerned with reputation.

International Soviet propaganda had touted the Soviet Union as a model of a successful communist society during the 1920s, 1930s and early 1940s. The propaganda held sway with most journalists in the West who gave favourable impressions prior to the war, after being given highly controlled tours inside the insular and secretive totalitarian state. Most in the West did not grasp the truly atrocious reality of living conditions and oppression within the Soviet Union between 1917 and 1945.

Yet, with millions of Soviet citizens now displaced and living in the West and telling their stories, there was the threat of uncovering the absolute failure of communism in the Soviet Union and exposing the great embarrassment this truth would bring to Joseph Stalin himself.

The dark reality, familiar to all Russian DPs, was the deeply cruel nature of Russian society at this time. Hell-bent on punishing so-called traitors, the culture of reprisal against those deemed disloyal was almost unimaginable to those in the West. It was so irrational that even Soviet citizens who were forced to work as slave labourers in Nazi Germany were considered traitors by Soviet society. When sent back to the Soviet Union after the war, in a great twist of cruel irony, they were then given decades-long sentences to work as forced labour, again!

The spectre of the irrational, bitter reprisals by the Soviet government resulted in many of its displaced citizens adamantly refusing to go back, even if it required violence to defend that position.

Regardless, "in June, the repatriation of Soviet DPs reached 250,000 a week."[7] By July 1, 1945, approximately 1,390,000 Soviet citizens had gone east. The Soviets "delivered 300,000 western European DPs and prisoners of war." Within less than two months, the number of Soviet citizens, including Susanna and family, who were still inside the defeated, Allied-occupied Germany, was under 700,000. Those former Soviet citizens that remained were becoming more violent in their refusal.

On July 8th, initially wishing to appease the Soviets, SHAEF ordered that "Citizens of the USSR identified as such by Soviet repatriation officers"[7] be sent home. The directive included force if necessary.

The Russians were also using nefarious means to steal back their unwilling citizens by going directly in to the refugee camps and taking people away.

By September of 1945, SHAEF had repatriated 2,034,000 Russian citizens voluntarily, and involuntarily. There was enough resistance among DPs, however, that SHAEF changed its mind and reversed the use of force policy on December 21, 1945. The policy reversal did not stop NKVD (Russian secret police) and other state agents from continuing to infiltrate the American, British and French zones, going directly into refugee camps, and continuing to kidnap and forcibly return people to the Soviet Union.

At this point, Susanna had escaped direct Russian control when she took her family through No Man's Land in the summer of 1945. The American military had driven Susanna, Franz, Rudy, Elsa, Suza, Helene, Alfred and baby Johanna to be processed at the Ehman refugee camp near Wolfsburg. And now, at the end of 1945 they were housed in the Grönau refugee camp so close to the Dutch border that freedom was literally in sight.

With the Soviets kidnapping refugees and others, it was an uneasy place to be. Even though they were no longer in the Russian-controlled sector, the Americans were not always firm in keeping them safe from Russian agents.

Of the 37,000 Mennonites that originally fled Russia, around 23,000 were repatriated back to the Soviet Union through 1945. Most were sent to Siberia where many were put in labour camps with as many as half dying of starvation and exhaustion. The same grim statistics were in fact true of all people wishing never to return to Russia.

At the end of 1945 and the beginning of 1946, a million people of Russian and eastern European origin were still in West Germany and by this point, they simply refused to go home.[6]

This is when Alfred's "own personal recollection starts."

ii. GRÖNAU

At the Grönau Displaced Persons refugee camp the Hecht family had a chance to rest and contemplate what lay ahead. The immediate concern was food.

"There was very little to eat in the Displaced Persons camp," Alfred remembered.

Not only was there a food shortage in post-war Europe, there was also a general shortage of food in America. At the end of the war, with around 5.2 million Displaced Persons, all but a million in the two US Army-controlled territories, the average basic ration was less than 1,000 calories per day.

Two million DPs were Soviet citizens. While the bulk of them were eventually repatriated to the Soviet Union and would suffer various fates, all of them first had to face hunger and malnourishment in the American-controlled DP camps immediately after the war, including the Hecht family.

Inside the refugee camp Alfred's mother had to physically bring her children to the food ration centre to prove she actually had seven children who needed the meagre food stuffs that were available. If there was a better option for survival, Susanna was going to find it.

"I was farmed out to distant cousins," Alfred said.

Alfred's father was the child of a second marriage of his grandfather Karl Hecht. Alfred's grandfather's second wife "was the nurse-maid that came from England. So, we have so-called British blood in us (and) my dad had half-brothers and sisters from an earlier marriage. (One of them), Tante Frieda, had two sons and one daughter. Frieda somehow got to Germany and (she and her husband) lived not far from our DP camp. They farmed me out to them because...the DP camp was pretty rough."

"When they were eating dinner the first time, I noticed all of them were licking their plates clean. There were five adults and me (sitting) at a big table that had not been destroyed during the war. One of them, right beside me, saw me looking and sensed that I didn't approve. He grabbed his dentures and snapped (them) at me."

Shocked by what happened, Alfred "crawled under the table. Everyone thought it was funny. 'It's gonna bite you, it's gonna bite you,' they said."

I laughed out loud at the image and Alfred quickly shot back, "Remember, I was five-and-a-half and had never seen dentures before! That was the first scary incident that I remember. The next one was on the ship. It was not the best."

Meanwhile in Grönau, while little Alfred was staying with distant relatives, the rest of the family was still threatened with the possibility that Russian agents would kidnap them in the middle of the night. The continuing lack of food, however, was far more concerning.

The great irony was that across the border in the Netherlands, food was relatively plentiful and the Grönau camp was so close that from the second floor of the two-story brick building used as a schoolhouse, the starving children could see the border gate. They were not allowed to cross, on pain of being shot.

With food so close, it was tempting to make attempts to get some of it. Naturally, that's exactly what some did including Suza and Franz. They would crawl under the border fence, sneak through the woods and cross into the Netherlands at night, find food at nearby farmhouses, and come back before dawn.

Fall turned to winter and eventually SHAEF ordered that living conditions be improved to "a standard as high as resources permit and without adverse consideration of the Germans." That order resulted in rations increasing for all DPs, equal to 2,000 calories per day, "even if it meant reducing rations from US Army stocks."[8]

The refugees stopped losing weight, not that there was much left to lose, by the time food rations increased.

Their living accommodations improved as well. The Mennonites were given their own quarters in a renovated building that came about through the care and help of the Mennonite Central Committee. It was spearheaded by Peter and Elfrieda Dyck from the United States. Donations also started coming in from America and Canada as well.

The refugees eventually had enough food that ribs no longer showed, lethargy dissipated and a new sense of joy began to fill the camp. The young, brave and overly hungry no longer had reason to sneak into the Netherlands.

They also learned at this time that they were going either to Canada or to Paraguay.

Alfred lived in the DP camp from the summer of 1945 until 1948.

12. PARAGUAY

During the Great Trek out of Russia, through Poland, and into Germany, of the 35,000 Mennonites who originally departed only 11,000 were still alive in the West at the beginning of 1946.

Over a thousand were hiding in West Berlin. Four hundred had been able to cross safely into the Netherlands. Five thousand were at the Grönau Displaced Persons refugee camp and the rest were in various other refugee camps across Germany.

The plan was to move the surviving Mennonites to a new home. The trouble was, finding a place for them to go.

Germany was war-torn.

The Netherlands was pressured by Russia not to let in anymore.

Nowhere else in Europe was open to them.

America flat out refused to take them.

Canada would let in families but only those with a male breadwinner, or a financial sponsor in Canada, and only upon the successful completion of a rigid medical examination.

The only country in the world that would accept them unconditionally was in South America—Paraguay. The odd, almost cathartic twist of irony for this country's openness had to do with experience.

After WWI the Dominion Government of Canada had begun implementing policies of cultural assimilation directed at all immigrant and non-Anglo communities. They legislated the mandatory use of English in all schools, outside of Quebec, and put restrictions on religious teachings. A large group of existing Mennonites in Manitoba, displeased with the loss of their religious freedoms and choice to school their children in their Low German dialect, packed up and left Canada. Some went to Mexico. Seventeen-hundred went to Paraguay and started the first Mennonite settlement there called Menno Colony.

The Paraguayan government was willing to let the Mennonites test their farming skills in the otherwise inhospitable Chaco region of northern Paraguay. Paraguay was very pleased to find these Mennonites were a highly productive, hard-working, industrious people and as pacifists, did not pose a threat to the government itself.

A short time later, another group of Mennonites who were fleeing persecution in Russia were let into Paraguay. They too established a settlement, in 1932, located near the original Menno Colony and called Fernheim.

Then, during the 1932–1935 Chaco War between Paraguay and Bolivia, these Mennonites in the Chaco helped thwart the Bolivian Army as it attempted to occupy the region. The loyalty shown to Paraguay by the Mennonites, along with their ability to generate wealth from successful farming practices in the poor country, left the Paraguayan government even more delighted. Paraguay, naturally, was willing to welcome even more Mennonites if the opportunity arose.

That opportunity came after World War II when the European Mennonites were in need of a new home. Paraguay agreed to officially take 2,000 Mennonite refugees from war-torn Europe. Over 5,000 arrived; Paraguay did not object.

Most refugees had actually wanted to go to Canada, not Paraguay, but Canada was strict and Paraguay was not.

Several members of the Hecht family failed the Canadian Immigration health exam and without a financial provider, the family was refused entry. They would have to go to Paraguay.

It was actually a common outcome. In the end, 5,000 Mennonites went to Paraguay and an equal number went to Canada.

It would take three ships to transport all the people to the South America continent. The plan was for the ships to sail to the port of Buenos Aires in Argentina. From there, they would transfer to smaller ships in order to sail up the shallow Paraguay River to transfer points at Asunción and Puerto Casado in Paraguay where they would then go overland to the interior of the Chaco.

Things didn't go according to plan.

There were three sailings aboard two different ships. The first sailing was aboard the Dutch-owned transatlantic liner, the S.S. *Volendam*. It sailed out of Bremerhaven, Germany on February 1, 1947 bound for Buenos Aires, Argentina with 2,303 Mennonite refugees aboard. Three people died on the voyage and four were born.[9]

At the same time, Paraguay was simmering with civil unrest. When the transatlantic ship arrived on February 22, 1947 into the port at Buenos Aires almost all the passengers had to be temporarily housed in large canvas tents near the Immigration Hotel.

The civil unrest in Paraguay went from bad to worse, erupting into a full-blown revolution that lasted from May to August, 1947. The little Mennonite tent city became less temporary than expected as they waited.

Meanwhile, Alfred and family went aboard the second ship—the S.S. *General Stuart Heintzelman*. There were 860 people on board. It was here, on the transatlantic journey, that the first emotional scars of childhood were incised. It was noticed that pox-like marks had formed on Alfred's belly.

He was quickly isolated.

"With eight other children I was locked in a steel room because I had the same little bubble on my tummy." He remembered, "the isolation on the ship going to Paraguay was one of the most terrifying."

One day his sister Elsa snuck down to the room, opened the door and said *hello* before quickly slamming the steel door shut and running off. It only deepened Alfred's sense of isolation. That wasn't the only source of isolation and feelings of abandonment.

"I never remembered my mother giving me a hug," Alfred said as he talked about what happened aboard the ship. He spoke affectionately of a young volunteer woman who took care of them. He well remembered her holding him against her chest, the affection even more so. The contrast between the affectionate caregiver and the coldness of his mother was apparent to Alfred even as a child.

After the civil war, of the 5,000 Mennonites that had gone to Paraguay, 1,723 started a new settlement in the lush region of East Paraguay, affectionately naming their new home Colonia Volendam.

The rest went to the northern interior of the dry Chaco, but it took time to get there.

Alfred's family left him behind in the refugee camp and sailed up the Paraguay River to the capital city of Asunción. There, they waited. Once Alfred, and the other infected children, were cured of what was probably measles, and deemed fit to leave, they did so.

Alfred reunited with his family in Asunción and together they took a riverboat to Puerto Casado, in January 1948. There, they rode a narrow-gauge railway for 145 kilometres west before transferring to ox-drawn wagons that took them to the Chaco Mennonite colonies.

In the hot scrubland of the Chaco this group of refugees built the settlement called Neuland.

It is in Neuland that the Hecht family began a new life of subsistence farming.

The Hecht family in Neuland Colony, Boquerón Department, Paraguay, 1948 with oxen, cart and house.

13. NEW LIFE IN THE CHACO

"It was dumb that they sent us to Paraguay." That's how Alfred's older brother Rudy, a young teenager at the time with aspirations for excitement, recalled the time he endured in Paraguay. When the family emigrated to Canada, Rudy was twenty-one years old. He never once went back to Paraguay and one gets the sense that for Rudy, Paraguay was synonymous with confinement.

Alfred, being almost eight years younger than Rudy, still in his early formative years as a boy, remembered it quite differently.

The family had a one-room, mud-brick house with a thatched roof. Inside there was space for seven beds against the walls and one in the middle. A primitive kerosene wick-lamp lit the interior.

"Looking back, there were times in Paraguay that were rough (but) it was also a time for some of us kids (where) it was pretty good. On Sunday we went to church in the morning and then in the afternoon we had about three hours that were free. There were four boys in our village. We would go hunting for pigeons with slingshots. Pigeons are usually at the top of a big tree. Three sizes. One was easier to capture. As long as the (dead bird) was still warm you could pull the feathers off easily. We built a fire, put it on a stick" and then roasted it over the open flame. "Tasted good," Alfred added although there was "no salt and pepper, but the burnt part was like peppery stuff. It was a great experience as kids, you know."

For a young boy among Mennonite farmers in the wild lands of the Chaco, surrounded by various hunting and gathering tribes at what seemed like the end of the world, it was undoubtedly like a German version of the English adventure novel *Robinson Crusoe*. Like all good adventures there was hardship, challenge and triumph.

"The first year in Paraguay, it was bad," Alfred remembered.

When they first arrived, they stayed three weeks among two families—the Wiens and Hildebrandts. Mennonite officials then took them to their new village site where the land still had to be surveyed, cleared and prepared for farming.

"Before we could plant anything, there was a time when all we had was beans and lard" and the beans had worms. Alfred distinctly remembered his mother putting the beans in a pot of water. Those that had air inside from the worms, floated to the top. It displaced most, although not all of the worms.

The second year they planted sweet potatoes which took a full season to grow. They also had cassava, but it took a couple years to grow that crop. If there had been little rain during the growing season, the cassava was quite dry and in order to swallow it down they heated up lard and added it to the cassava.

He remembered the food menu vividly. The first year was, "beans, beans and beans. Second year, sweet potatoes." The food was dull but they were no longer hungry the way they had been in the DP camp back in Germany.

As subsistence farmers they ate only what they could grow.

Two threats to their food supply were always present. The first was ants—they cut off the sweet potato runners.

"So, we had to put poison on the plants. The only problem was you could taste the poison."

The second problem was locusts. "You would see a whole cloud come over and they'd drop right down when they saw the green stuff. Oh, that was bad."

After devastating the young crop the locusts would lay their eggs in the adjacent wilds of the unplowed scrub brush. Young locusts would hatch two to three weeks later, come out of the bush "like an army, and devour everything. We had to throw poison on them. I think DDT was common. The worst part was chickens would eat the dead locusts (and) you could taste the poison in the eggs."

While hardship and challenge pushed everyone to their limits, they triumphed, with some help.

"The natives were always happy (when the locusts came). They first catch them in a cactus-fibre bag, put them on a stick and roast them over a fire."

"You know, we could have done the same thing," Alfred said, explaining that sometimes the Mennonites imitated and learned things from the local Indigenous people. The biggest was taking up the habit of drinking the naturally caffeinated plant called yerba maté (*Ilex paraguariensis*). And sometimes they called upon local knowledge with respect to traditional medicine.

A tree called Ironwood is so dense that if one hits it with an axe, "you hardly ever made a dent in it" and worse, the axe often bounced off the trunk, having a tendency to throw the axe back against the feller. It happened to Franz. It hit him above the ankle.

"Infection set in pretty rapidly," Alfred recalled. "Our native guide Cazzicky came by and Mom asked what to do. You gotta pee on it," was the advice given by the Indigenous man.

So, Franz followed Cazzicky's instructions and urinated on his own leg.

Meanwhile, Cazzicky left and returned later with the fibres of a piece of cactus that exuded a juicy milk. He laid the juicy cactus fibres on Franz's infection and sure enough, the wound healed rapidly within a couple of days.

On a more personal and primitive note, because the Mennonites here lacked toothbrushes and toothpaste, after eating a meal, the kids would get their domestic house chicken to pick at their teeth to clean out debris stuck in between. The kids loved it but "Mom really didn't like that," Alfred said with a faint chuckle.

Many things were learned from the Indigenous people. Many practices were adopted, but not all. The one thing the Mennonites never did was eat the locusts.

And like all good adventures, Paraguay was also the place that Alfred became a man.

Young men are eternally tasked with learning to stand up for themselves and protect others. The Mennonite pacifist religion with ideals rooted in "turning the other cheek" was in some ways a contradiction to the masculine drive. Consequently, it proffered an eternal source of internal tension for all Mennonites but especially the men. Many Mennonites have chosen not to follow the pacifist teachings of their religion, especially when faced with the reality of having to defend themselves or protect their families.

All men that eschew pacifism are inevitably forced to confront the paradox of violence, namely, its potential use to bring about peace. How will a man use violence? That is the most important question. Will it be honourably, judiciously, maliciously, or not at all? The answer often comes at a young age in a moment of righteous anger. For Alfred, that was exactly what happened.

It was the moment he went from being a boy to a man. It was one of his top three memories from childhood.

He remembered, "My sister being bullied by 'Big Willy Reimer.' One day when he pushed my sister Elsa...onto the hot sand, that was enough! I grabbed him in a head lock and flipped him over my hip and buried his head in the extremely hot sand. He never bullied my sister again."

Of course, sometimes the tables are turned. Revenge, a pleasure received in spades by young men, also meant that sometimes Alfred was on the other end.

"The first couple years in Paraguay, there was no electricity, no refrigeration." There was only one clean water source—a well that was one and a half kilometres away, which made it difficult to carry more than the minimum needed for cooking, cleaning and bathing.

"We had to bathe in one big pot. We couldn't just pour it out; water was scarce" those first years.

Once they dug their own well the situation improved. Water access was better but in the dry season they could barely get three or four buckets a day from that well. The situation worsened as demands grew. "By the third or fourth year, we had fifteen cattle and four horses (and) a number of pigs. The consumption of water was getting high," Alfred explained.

Thankfully, they had a second option for water.

"Between our village and the main village was a lower-lying area where water accumulated." The clay prevented water from draining through the soil and so the depression held some shallow water, but it was filthy. Cattle would bathe in it but the boys loved it nonetheless.

"I learned to swim there. On one occasion Willy Dueck, Dave Martins and me, we were swimming in there and someone said, 'Hey, what's that? Is it a branch floating on the water?'"

It was a snake. A big snake.

"Let's get out of here," one of them yelled.

It turned out to be a cousin of the primordial and fearsome Anaconda, "a species cousin in the Chaco but not quite as big. Still two metres long, curled, and could rush prey. I don't think it would crush us big guys but it could do a lot of damage," Alfred said with a tightening fist.

Yet, it wasn't the snake that snarled Alfred's clan of boys. "The problem was, this puddle, we thought, belonged to our village. But the guys in the next village thought it was theirs! If we got there after they did, we grabbed their clothes and soaked them!" He smiled with glee.

Revenge can be sweet, and short-lived.

Alfred needed to have his appendix removed, which required a week-long stay at the only hospital in the colony, at Neu Halbstadt.

"Dr. Ratzloff was the only doctor. I think he was an ex-Nazi," Alfred said.

At the end of his stay, his mother and Franz came by horse and wagon to pick him up. Alfred stood at the back of the open wagon. As they rode through one of the small Mennonites villages three young guys were walking on the opposite side of the road toward them. Alfred recognized them.

"I had a bad feeling," he said.

All three pulled out their slingshots and nailed Alfred in the back of the head as the wagon drove past.

Franz pulled the reins hard and brought the wagon to an abrupt halt, "but by that time the guys had crawled under the fence and gone off. There was no blood but I did have a little bulge (on my head)," Alfred said.

It was a minor battle in the skirmishes for dominance of the puddle, or as Alfred explained, "It was a continuation, of competition, for the puddle."

With a coy smile that hides essential details he added, "I'm pretty good with a slingshot...getting pigeons."

With the formative years spent in Paraguay, it is perhaps not surprising that as an adult and a university professor of economic geography, Alfred would return numerous times to officially study Paraguay's economy, and unofficially return to a land he loved and that was filled with fond memories.

The last time he returned to Paraguay, he took his entire immediate family in 2022. He was eighty years old. Unlike his brother Rudy, one gets the sense that Alfred felt a deep love for the country and land that shaped him as a child. When the Hecht family left Paraguay the year was 1955.

The future looked bright with opportunity in Canada for those willing to leave an imaginary utopia behind.

14. UTOPIA

Many people dream of living in a utopian society where all are equal, life is simple and a sense of belonging is guaranteed. Those who go looking for it, or at least a close approximation of it, are bound to make a long proverbial stop at the doors of the Mennonites.

As Anabaptist Christians, the Mennonites trace their roots back to the radical Reformation period of the 1500s when a great upheaval in religious beliefs swept across European society, in part due to the teachings of Martin Luther. As an influential Catholic priest, Luther rejected many of the tenets of the church and began to teach a new philosophy. Luther was not alone. The teachings of Menno Simons (1496–1561), his contemporary, also gathered followers who later became known as Mennonites.

While many Mennonites arose in what is today the Netherlands, some of the earliest ones actually originated in Switzerland with the first baptism in Zurich in January of 1525 marking the official beginning of their existence. The two geographic lineages remain today and many refer to themselves either as Swiss Mennonites or Dutch Mennonites.

The Anabaptists were known primarily for their belief in adult baptism, as an initiation rite into the Kingdom of God, that should occur consciously as a believer in Christ. Without the conscious will of the soul, child baptism did not make sense and they chose not to do it. This, and other beliefs and practices, infuriated the church and state leaders who set about persecuting the Anabaptists.

Anabaptists believed in serving God through tolerance and missionary ventures as well as refraining from violence especially on behalf of earthly governments. In other words, the Mennonites were devoted to pacifism.

The unfolding variations in interpretations of the Bible through time led to different offshoots of Mennonite groups. The different groups are categorized into three broad categories. The most traditional are the Old Order and Amish who practice a simple lifestyle that rejects most modern technologies. The middle path belongs to the Conservative Mennonites who believe in a theological purity, tend to wear plain black clothes but use modern technology and conveniences. The least orthodox are Mainline Mennonites who are indistinguishable from the general population in terms of appearance, although hints of who they are manifest in lifestyle and interaction with the rest of society. The latter's identity and faith, most often noticed by others, comes through their actions in community service, or lack of action, as per the refusal to military service. Alfred and his family are Mainline Mennonites.

The three groups exist in both Canada and Paraguay in one form or another. Intriguingly, the three groups appear more cohesive in Paraguay than they do in Canada where fracturing is common. There is a reason for this.

Unity in Paraguay is tightly connected to the maintenance of a communal and independent economic structure outside state control, as well as an exclusive membership system.

Alfred began the explanation by pointing out that "the Mennonites in Russia had understood that in order to be successful they needed to work together."

This required physical and financial structures that naturally provided a certain level of equality and communal access to resources. For example, each village was originally constructed with a long Main Street for houses. Behind each house was a lengthy piece of land large enough to grow household crops for domestic consumption such as lettuce, cucumbers, tree-fruits and other similar garden foods. At the end of Main Street "was communal property where they would send their cattle and horses to graze and they had a guy who was looking after them—the herdsman."

Other communal property for firewood and extensive crops such as wheat, cotton or peanuts, existed beyond this immediate area. When the population increased, a new village site was founded and built according to the same pattern.

The physical layout of the village ensured relatively equal access and sharing of resources while providing enough private lands for personal control over immediate family needs.

Ironically, when Russian Mennonites immigrated to Canada in the late 1800s, the government initially permitted the same communal organization system that was in some ways similar to the organizational structure of Indian reservations. These Mennonites became very successful farmers from the outset but the government eventually forced the Mennonites to disband their communal structure. Only fee-simple title (private property) was permitted, which of course nullified all the benefits that a group of people could accrue through the sharing of land and resources.

"When the Canadian government made the Mennonites in Canada disband their communal system, some from Manitoba and Saskatchewan left and went to Paraguay. They knew the only way to survive there was to act together in common," Alfred explained.

In Paraguay, those who went received a charter from the national government that allowed them to operate their communal system.

Their entire operation was registered as one single business which in essence was "based on the economic structure in Russia." The villages in Paraguay today are a virtual carbon-copy of the Russian Mennonite villages from the Ukraine in the 1800s.

The isolated Paraguayan Mennonites had to build and pay for everything themselves. Roads, sewers, education and virtually everything else was financed completely through the fruits of their labour. The Paraguayan government didn't have money to help.

And while initially beyond the reach of civilization, the Paraguayan Mennonite colonies were not alone in their isolation. "There were two tribes, Lengua (Enxet) and Chulupi (Nivaclé). At the end of our village was a Lengua group of about thirty. They would stay three months and then migrate to another village, and then come back. They were hunters and gatherers to a large extent. I do remember they could not read and write," Alfred recalled.

Aside from their Indigenous neighbours, each colony operated as an independent unit, a single business. The land was owned in common and supplies were all bought and sold through the colony's store, the co-operative. Every Mennonite had a membership in the co-operative. That community-owned store was the central economic hub for the buying and selling of all products coming in and going out of the colony.

"When we were living there, when we sold something, we had to take it to the co-op. They would give us credit on the co-op account and we could buy stuff from the one co-op store. That way there was no money involved. In one sense, it was great (because) at one time Paraguay had high inflation. If you dealt with actual money, it was not good, but having this kind of accounting system, you traded, basically."

It was a complete ownership system with its own autonomy as an independent economic unit and perhaps even more importantly, something rarely emphasized, yet a critical component, was exclusion.

Memberships are exclusive to the Mennonites only. And to get a membership required being a member of the local church. To be a member of the church requires acceptance into it from the approval of the congregation and that is how the gatekeepers keep the undesirables out.

The whole system operates the same today as it did when Alfred was a boy.

Each has its own governance system. "An Oberschulze is head of it (and) for each village, a Shultze, like they had in Russia. These are elected guys. In that sense, it's pretty democratic. Even the Schulzes at the top get elected. He's a full-time employee. I remember the Oberschulze in Neuland had a Mercedes (with a driver). He frequently had to meet the Oberschulzes of the other colonies (as well as) the Paraguayan representatives in Asunción. That was a status symbol (but) it was not owned by the Oberschulze. It was owned by the co-op."

While some may argue there is a similar co-operative businesses structure in Canada, it is not accurate to say this. "We don't have a similar co-op here," Alfred said bluntly.

There are co-ops in name only, in Canada. They are businesses with a limited shared membership which is different than the Paraguayan

Mennonites' system of full, communal ownership over the entire business including land and assets, regulated through a closed membership system linked to a set of values and beliefs.

The co-operative store is the face of the Mennonite economic system. Their churches are the gateway into the exclusive social club.

In Canada, the co-operative system lacks the unifying socio-economic-religious ties. Even more detrimental is the use of an inclusive membership system, open to anyone. *Kindred* for example, is a small credit union in southern Ontario with seven branches originally set up as a Mennonite community bank. Its membership system and economic ownership were not tightly linked.

"Originally, you had to prove you were a member of a church," Alfred explained. "Then they opened it up (and now) you have to (only) say you believe in ten key principles" and then one can have a membership. "So, Kindred Credit Union has people now that are not even Christian." It was a dilution of the theological in favour of economic expansion.

By comparison, in the Chaco region of Paraguay, there are three independent Mennonite settlements—Menno, Fernheim and Neuland.

"In Neuland...all the land is owned by the Neuland co-op," Alfred explained. People don't have private property with state-recognized private property documents. The Paraguayan government instead sees the co-operative, its land holdings and its members, as a single business. This is different than the rest of the Paraguay.

"Paraguayans have their own system. Mennonites have their own system."

Since the Mennonites operate almost entirely on their own, including paying for roads and other infrastructure, each year the co-ops have an annual meeting to examine how the business is doing.

"Expenses are this. Income is this. Given the present tax rate, they must vote on suggested increases. When inflation was high that was a big problem," Alfred said. Nevertheless, because they had their own tax system, "which in part supported their own private high school, as well as part of the elementary school because the government wouldn't give them the same for elementary, because half was taught in German and half taught in Spanish and some religious education. The Catholic country would not support Protestant or Mennonite religious studies. In Paraguay the government doesn't pay for anything anyway." So, each co-op would raise enough money to cover the expenses from infrastructure to education. Banks were not involved. It was a great success.

Some of this, I must admit, is a simplified version.

There was in fact a failure, of sorts, at the very beginning.

When the first 1,700 Conservative Mennonites from Canada arrived in Paraguay they re-established the private property structure they had become familiar with in Canada. That was in 1926. Then the group of Russian Mennonites arrived in 1932, established the Fernheim colony, and set it up based on the communal system in Russia. This second group, the communal group, became more successful than the private property group.

"In one sense the communists in Russia had forced them to be communal. And then they used that model in Paraguay because they were so far away (from markets). You know, it doesn't make sense to individually take one cow to the slaughterhouse in Asunción" over five hundred kilometres away. It makes more sense to pool resources and have all the local ranchers take their cattle in one shipment to cut down on costs, for example.

The same economic philosophy made sense when applied to virtually everything in the Chaco. With this philosophical approach, governed through a co-operative system, Fernheim was economically successful right from the beginning while the Canadian Mennonites in Menno Colony struggled.

Eventually, "the Menno Colony looked at Fernheim and wondered, 'Hey, why are those guys flourishing?' So, the Menno Colony adopted the Fernheim co-operative system," and it worked very well ever since.

Which again brings up one of the most overlooked elements that keeps Mennonite communities tight—the exclusion of everyone else. The *Us* and *Them* approach is critical to success. Creating difficult access points into the exclusive club helps maintain social cohesion. Anyone from outside wishing to become a member must overcome numerous hurdles.

They must be baptised, first and foremost. Being able to speak Plautdietsch is helpful. They must also become a member of the church in good standing, be accepted by the rest of the community socially, financially and to a certain degree, ethnically. Even then, a person not already born into the community will most likely be rejected.

"You know, Hecht is not a Mennonite name," Alfred began.

"Whenever I went to Paraguay," as an economics professor who was doing research, there was a need to meet with officials in the Mennonite colonies. "I would try to make an appointment. Usually, the secretaries were suspicious. I switched to Low German and then the secretaries would say, 'Oh, okay.'"

When Alfred would then meet the official of each colony—the Oberschulze—"they always started in High German with me because they would think I was German. They would start with, 'Guten Tag Herr Hecht. Wie geht es ihnen?'" (*"Good day Mr. Hecht. How are you?"*)

Alfred would respond by saying, "We can talk in Low German," which surprised them, in a favourable way.

Alfred would then explain that his father "was German but my mother was Mennonite from way back in 1785. East Prussia. Moved to the Chortitza colony in Russia." With this explanation came acceptance. Alfred belonged to the unofficial family club. The economic club, however, was more problematic.

When Alfred and Linda were revisiting Paraguay a decade ago, he went to see his grandmother's grave. It was unkempt and lacked a proper tombstone. Alfred found the caretaker and ordered a new tombstone but when he went to pay for it in Paraguayan Guarani he was told, "No, I can't accept Guarani. You must be a member of the Fernheim colony with a co-op account."

But Alfred no longer had an account from the time he was a little boy.

The caretaker asked, "Do you have relatives, or a friend, here?"

Alfred knew "someone that used to be the head of the Teachers College here in Fernheim, Jacob Warkentin."

"Oh yeah, he still has an account. I'll charge it to him and you fix it with Jacob."

Jacob Warkentin, who'd unwittingly covered Alfred's expenses, went to Canada a couple years later and paid a visit to Alfred and Linda.

"It was funny. I had to pay him back (then)," Alfred chuckled.

The economic-social-religious-ethnic connections to the Mennonite community, wherever they exist around the world, are all important, even mandatory, if one wishes to join this exclusive utopian club.

Membership offers community, trust, stability and a strong sense of belonging. Membership can also bring its own problems, too. For some, it compels them to reject the insularity and move away.

Among those who leave, an intense questioning of identity seems to overcome many. The inner turmoil over identity and meaning happened to one of Alfred's good friends who not only left the Mennonite faith and went to Hell, but later returned to accept an imperfect Heaven.

We put on our winter jackets and headed out to meet him.

15. WARKENTIN

"We are close to the Warkentins," Alfred said as he, Linda and I drove over to meet Marv and Karen Warkentin for dinner at a local restaurant. They first met in 1975 through the Mennonite Brethren Church.

Marv Warkentin, a tall and wiry man with a piercing stare of inquisitiveness, dug into the conversation right away as soon as we sat down. "I have to ask, is my friend giving it to you straight or is he embellishing things?"

"Oh, he's definitely embellishing things!" I replied with a coy sarcasm.

Alfred retorted. "This is eighty years of history. You think you're going to get it all on that (audio recorder). Nah, you can only get part of it."

Marv and Karen met in California where they both grew up. While they came from different religious backgrounds it seemed not to matter. Karen is Baptist and her family lineage harkens back to Sweden. She retains the blonde hair, cute smile and the mild-mannered demeanour of her Scandinavian roots.

Marv, by contrast, grew up in a staunchly traditional Mennonite community. "Southern Cali," he said in a carefully articulated speech with a slight twang that gave away his American roots. The place where he was raised, close to Fresno, was a small town of "mostly farmers, one or two businessmen (and) a couple of professionals." It was rural, Mennonite and highly conservative. At the age of sixteen "I rebelled against all of that," he said.

He joined the US Navy and became an officer, which took him off to the Vietnam War. He spent almost three years aboard a navy destroyer and one year on the ground. During that ground year he was stationed in the ancient city of Hué where he found himself embroiled in one of the 20th century's most epic battles.

It was 1968. The Tet Offensive erupted and Marv Warkentin was in the middle of it all and not in some minor sideline capacity either.

"The city of Hué...was completely overtaken except the compound I was living in. I managed to repel that attack."

He said it in such a casual way while we waited for our steak and potatoes that the enormity of his experience did not hit with the intensity it warranted. I assumed his statement "I managed to repel the attack" was some form of American braggadocio. I sluffed it off until later when further investigations revealed much more than expected.

It turned out, he wasn't exaggerating.

On January 30, 1968, the Viet Cong and North Vietnamese army launched a massive surprise attack at targets across the country. The scale of the attacks and the sheer surprise initially shocked and overwhelmed the American and South Vietnamese defences.

The American-controlled city of Hué had been completely unprepared for the attack. Most soldiers were on leave during the Tet Nguyen Dan holidays, which allowed the entire city to be quickly overrun. The ancient palace grounds at the centre on the north side of the Perfume River contained the airport. It was captured by the North Vietnamese. Reinforcements couldn't be flown in. The situation looked hopeless but when the North Vietnamese troops attacked the command-and-control centre of the American and South Vietnamese armies at the Mang Ca compound on the south side of the river, inside a small fortress originally built in 1812, their attack was repelled.

The outer ring area of the compound was breached but the inner compound, ringed by a perimeter of gnarled barbwire and not much else, held a small group of men inside who resisted every attack the North Vietnamese threw at them. The small garrison of soldiers and supply clerks put up such a ferocious fight that they alone held tight onto what was left of Hué. The "ad hoc 200-man defensive force of staff officers and clerks staved off the assaults."[15]

Marv Warkentin was one of the men inside that compound.

The Battle of Hué lasted a month and two days and was considered by many historians to be one of the most gruelling and intensely fought urban battles ever witnessed.

"It got a bit lively for me," Marv had said dryly before picking up his fork and knife and carefully parcelling his dinner into tidy portions.

Alfred, drawn to stories of showdowns between men, the challenge of rivals among equals, and attempts to see who can cut the thin difference in capability in order to outwit the other, listened intently. One of Alfred's favourite movies is *The Hunt for Red October* starring Sean Connery. It pits two Cold-War submarine captains against one another in a battle of strategy, bravery and death. Alfred, perhaps in an attempt to cut through Marv's brooding seriousness with a light-hearted humour said, "Don't shoot until you see the whites of their eyes, eh!"

But Marv answered with seriousness. "It was dark so I couldn't see the whites of their eyes. The perimeter wire was from here to the bench," he said, pointing from our restaurant table to a bench seat at a nearby table—a distance of no more than fifteen feet. "They were under the fence." Marv added in his carefully crafted communication style of hallowed tone and depth, "I had my fill of war."

He had gone from the quiet, restrained, non-violent life of a deeply religious Mennonite farming community to the frontlines of the Vietnam War. The war had given him a taste of violence in his youth. Later in life, age had given him the wisdom of contemplation.

"When you're sixteen, maybe you don't know enough to make these announcements about who you are," Marv suggested.

After the Vietnam War, Marv returned to his religion and dove in. He went into the seminary. After his studies he led the congregation at Alfred and Linda's Church—the Waterloo Mennonite Brethren Church in Waterloo. It wasn't quite his calling. A tumultuous internal coup occurred which Alfred, as chair of the Church board, still has misgivings about. The result was that Marv moved onto something else.

"When that was done it seemed like I was better suited to investment advising. So that ensured we had a stable life...then we kind of re-affiliated with a church. It was a more open congregation, so that's where we are now."

"So, you passed back and forth your whole life between Mennonite traditions and war. Both extremes?" I proposed.

"That's right," Marv exclaimed with a perked-up interest in the philosophical backdrop and timeline of his own life. "I've been pulled ultimately between the centripetal and centrifugal forces of being drawn back to my tradition and being thrown away from it."

The conversation shifted.

With age an important question arises among men. What is my legacy? It seemed to be a topic occupying a lot of Alfred's energy. Marv's, too.

"We were talking today with a lady in Recruitment (at Wilfred Laurier University)," Alfred said after listening to Marv's story. Alfred recalled his conversation with Cec Joyal, the head of Laurier's Legacy Giving department. Alfred was curious about the reasons that alumni donate to the university. Some leave a little and some leave a lot and Alfred wondered if it had anything to do with children.

The answer he got from Cec was that it comes down to how memorable the donor's experience was during their studies at the university. The more they enjoyed themselves, the more likely they were to give back to the university.

"Is there a difference between those who have kids and those that don't?" Alfred had asked.

"There's no difference. There are just as many with kids that make a donation to the university as those that don't," Cec had replied.

With the legacy question top of mind, Alfred and Marv began discussing the nuances of trusts, foundations, charities and other ways of leaving a financial legacy.

Alfred suddenly suggested, "Maybe we should leave nothing to our kids?"

Linda added, "Oh, I don't think they would be very happy."

"I don't think they would mind. I don't think they need it," Alfred replied pensively before turning to books. "On Fisher-Halman Road there is a library box. I have picked up a number of books there. The last one was Margaret Atwood, *The Handmaid's Tale*. A classic, great, but this one, I got to page 30 and (then) put it back in the box."

Marv said with the pleasurable grin of a book lover, "I got (*The Handmaid's Tale*) a year ago. It's such a classic that I thought I should have some passing acquaintance with it."

"You know, I met Margaret Atwood," Alfred said with a spark.

Wilfred Laurier University bookstore, since October of 1980, had put on "Meet the Author" events. Many prominent Canadian authors made appearances. They would speak about their work, do readings and interact with their fans. Norman Levine, David Suzuki, Peter C. Newman, Edna Staebler, Pierre Berton, Alice Munro and of course Margaret Atwood, had all made appearances. Atwood was known to show up at the pub in Laurier's Student Union Building to packed crowds and to enjoy a good drink with everyone. This was *not* where Alfred met Atwood.

It happened in Berlin, Germany at the John F. Kennedy Institute of North American Studies.

"I was just getting (to my new office). The caretaker for the building was talking to me about what name he should put on my door. Was it 'Dr. Hecht' or was it 'Professor Dr. Hecht'? And all I remember is Margaret Atwood coming down the hall and screaming at him! She said, 'I wanted to have my room darkened and you haven't done it yet. My child can't sleep.' Boy did she give him a lecturing."

"I guess her sense of entitlement had grown pretty big by that point in her life," Marv Warkentin suggested with a grin.

"It was obvious. It was obvious," Alfred replied with the frowning of moral judgement.

Conversation shifted back to legacies.

Alfred had arrived in Canada sixty-nine years prior. It was a long time ago and he had accrued a significant amount of wealth and stories to leave behind. By the age of thirteen Alfred Hecht had already been a war refugee, the child of subsistence farmers among a highly religious people in one of the most remote regions on the planet, and an immigrant. When the family moved to Canada in 1955, Alfred still had more than seventy years ahead of him.

He was bound to make an impact, and some mistakes, too.

16. CANADA

"My mom was by far the most dynamic," of her siblings. "When they had to plow the fields, Mom had to drive the horses—six horses in front. Dealing with horses in Russia, she knew how to" tame and manage them. "She grew up on a farm. My dad (on the other hand) couldn't keep a plow straight. She admired him for his teaching abilities but certainly not for his handiness. In Paraguay my mom was asked, 'Why are you migrating to Canada?'"

Alfred smiled widely as he recalled the answer given by his mother. "My younger kids are like their father. They don't know the difference between a horse and a cow."

By early 1955, Paraguay had occupied seven-and-a-half years of Alfred's childhood years but he would be going to Canada soon. The coming change would coincide with the transition from boyhood to manhood.

Alfred grinned as he explained that "Most boys go through puberty at twelve. Near the school there was a farmstead (where the) Klassens lived. There was a woman about eighteen. She was a beauty (and) I remember feeling like, 'I'm in love with her.' They moved to Saskatchewan." At the age of thirteen the Hecht family moved to Canada as well, although Alfred never saw the lovely Klassen girl again.

An aunt and uncle sponsored the family's immigration. They arrived in Winnipeg on June 25, 1955.

The sights, sounds and behaviours of Canadians were strange and unusual. On the second day, as Alfred was walking down a street, "a fifteen-year-old girl in shorts approached me and blew a bubble in my face. I thought it was spit. How disgusting! Only later I learned you could do that with bubble gum."

It was a time of adjustment and getting to work.

He took a summer job at a local gas station as a gas jockey. Working among men in the banter of a blue-collar environment taught him a little bit about customer service, a lot about sex, and a few new things about Canadian culture. He also learned that he hated being called Alf.

"The manager of the service station always called me *Alf*. I really resented that! If you go beyond Al go all the way to Alfred." As an adult, faculty and students usually called him *Al*.

At the end of summer that first year, Alfred started grade six in elementary school. "My sisters were in grade four and three."

The principal at the school would have Alfred and his sisters come to his office for an hour each day in order to help them with their English. Alfred begrudgingly noted that "German is a phonetic language. English was quite different. Unfortunately, I never learned how to spell properly."

They say good teachers are the ones who struggled themselves.

Alfred was bound to make a good teacher. He just didn't know it yet.

In the 1950s, Canada as a country was also coming into its own. It had slipped off the reins of British control over foreign policy in 1934, distinguished itself in both World Wars and had the rest of the 20th century ahead of it.

Canada was reaching its reputational peak on the world stage as an ambassador of enthusiasm and common sense with a calm and reasonable approach to internal and external relations. She'd come through the Second World War as a major player. The D-Day invasion epitomized Canada's up-and-coming standing on the world stage. Five beaches, five landing groups. Two came from the Old World's last empire—the British Empire. Two came from the emerging power full of braggadocio and confidence— the Americans. And like a young boy given the chance to join the adults, Canada was given its own role as the fifth group that landed on the beach in France. Her men did not disappoint.

And like Canada's growth as a nation, Alfred too was growing from a boy into a man. His mother had a strong hand in cutting a proverbial path forward and giving direction until Alfred was on his own. But the first thing they really needed was a house.

17. The FIRST HOUSE

He hadn't made a big deal about the house, which only deepened the essence of his character.

Nearly every day in March, Alfred and I walked from his house to a local strip mall two kilometres away that contained the usual accoutrements of a grocery store, bank and something for pets, plus a Starbucks. At the age of 82, he was perfectly capable of walking but his pace had slowed over the years, his energy had waned but his care for his community had not waivered one bit.

On that walk, he told stories about his life but what I often noticed were his actions, actually, one action in particular. We would meander from his house through a set of suburban streets before descending onto a path that cut through a local wooded area. The path soon spat us out onto a four-lane arterial road full of suburban traffic and the din of rumbling tires. A wide meridian of grass down the middle of the road split four lanes into two. On each side was an equally wide meridian with wide grass and narrow sidewalk. Being March in southern Ontario, the drifts and crust of snow had thawed to expose the debris of winter.

Garbage lay strewn about. Mostly its was empty cans, random bits of cardboard and unrecognizable scraps. Some of winter's debris had been picked up by city crews but new garbage was added every day by disrespectful and disdainful attitudes toward the environment.

It was here that I saw a side of Alfred's character that in some ways is quintessentially Canadian, quintessentially Mennonite, and unabashedly caring. He picked up plastic bottles and aluminum cans dominated mostly by the sugar water and power drink varieties. Sometimes, the smallest items of tinfoil wrap or other debris were also pecked from the ground.

"You know, when the mowers come along here, it's hard for them. They can't cut the plastic up."

He carried the garbage until we came to a bus stop with a garbage can. It was approximately one kilometre away. No one else seemed to care about the garbage. They all walked past it. Even his son Marvin had scolded him once. Apparently, Marvin felt it was dirty to pick up garbage and he was concerned that his father could get some random disease. But Alfred's actions reminded me that this small act of service used to be normal in Canada. It was instilled in most people including myself yet somehow, even I found myself no longer picking up garbage that I easily could, as though believing it's the responsibility of someone else. Yet, here was Alfred with an unwavering sense of duty to his community and an underlying level of care.

Perhaps it's his Christian upbringing that instilled a sense of virtue through acts of service. Although, it could just be the common-sense thing to do if you care about your community. So, at the age of eighty-two Alfred carries on caring for the beauty and cleanliness of his community.

We did the walk numerous times. I joined in. We picked up garbage along the way and continued on with the stories. In the meantime, Erb Street West was a little cleaner, a little nicer, and unbeknown to many, Alfred Hecht had a lot to do with that.

Looking out for others and working together, that's how Alfred's mother and his siblings also bought their first house in Canada.

"We pooled our money. That's how we bought our first house," Alfred said.

Alfred's mother was a single mother with seven children who raised them through war and refugee camps, cared for them in one of the most isolated and harshest places in the world, and once they came to Canada her first goal was to buy a family home. To do that, she put out a basket into which everyone in the household had to put their money. It was inherently understood that everyone had to work, including weekends, and all their earnings, all their income, went into the basket. Everyone understood they were collectively working toward buying their first house, as a family, in Canada.

"Whenever we needed money, we took it out. Of course, none of us would buy things we didn't need so soon we had enough money in that basket for Mom to buy a house," Alfred explained.

They bought their first house at 69 Noble Avenue in Winnipeg, Manitoba.

The communal pooling of money is a common behaviour found among some Mennonite families and communities. It harkens back to the earliest traditions and understandings of how people could thrive in harsh environments through shared works of service, the pooling of resources, and a sense of trust. Group buying is still a common practice among those of Mennonite backgrounds today, often making them successful in areas of business and finance that others fail at. It's inherently understood as normal that Alfred doesn't dwell on it as being anything special in the same way that cleaning up his community isn't out of the ordinary.

To buy that first house, the kids worked and pooled the money. Alfred worked at a local gas station. It was a time when he learned about money, community, and began to contemplate his own path in life.

"I once tried to join the Cadets," Alfred mentioned. The Cadets had an allowance and the outdoor activities were appealing. He was in his early teens and still under the auspices of his mother's approval. He hadn't considered how his mother would react to the idea of him joining the Cadets.

His mother, of course, had experienced the horrors of war firsthand. She had lost her second husband who had to become a soldier and never came back. She knew many more that had died in the Second World War and she'd witnessed the bodies of the dead, soldiers and civilians alike, often mutilated in ways unimaginable. Anything having to do with war, such as her son joining the Cadets, an organization not too dissimilar from the Hitler Youth, was not something she was going to approve.

When Alfred told his mother about his desire to join the Cadets, it did not go well.

"Oh, she was not pleased!" Alfred said. He didn't join. He would need to find a different path in life, and a wife, too.

18. LINDA

Alfred has an impatience for those that speak indirectly. Beating around the bush, some might call it. I noticed his wife Linda has an uncanny propensity for indirect communication. While opposites can attract, they can also repel.

I sat down with Linda in the living room at their suburban home in Kitchener-Waterloo on March 12, 2024. They've lived in the same house for the last forty-three years.

It was time to find out more about the woman behind the man.

Linda Agnes Huebert Hecht sat with a relaxed pose in the middle of a flower-patterned chesterfield. A slight nervousness seemed to come over her as the voice recorder was turned on. She normally stands at around 5'3"—somewhat shorter than her husband. Stationed in the middle of the chesterfield, she held a firm and upright posture.

Two days prior she had celebrated her 80th birthday at a local restaurant. In attendance were her two adult children Marvin and Melinda, their respective spouses Deborah and Albert and the grandchildren Rebecca, Joseph, Elizabeth, Max and Dylan. Albert and Melinda's youngest daughter Elizabeth stayed home that night.

There is an indecisive perfectionist quality to Linda's personality. The room where I am staying is spotlessly clean but Linda admitted that immediately prior to my arrival, it had been full of stuff. Having glanced earlier at her office across the hall, I had an idea of what my guest room looked like prior to my arrival with papers piled in various places.

"When you are gone the first thing that'll happen is stuff will be put on the bed. It's a nice place to put things," she grinned. "I have to spend some time and sort but I can't, somehow. They say downsizing is a bit of an emotional job."

'Perfectionist people-pleaser' might be used to describe Linda. It's a side that seems to be in a state of contention with the need for balance.

Perhaps it's why she gravitates toward a masculine assertion of identity, as I was about to find out.

Linda was born March 10th, 1944 and raised in Winnipeg, Manitoba. She went to a private school, the Mennonite Brethren Collegiate and graduated in 1962, "and that's where I first saw Alfred."

"How did you meet?"

"This fellow that I had a mad crush on in grade eight, finally in grade ten, asked me to go home from a party. He was together with Alfred who was taking somebody home too. They took her home first. Then I was in the car up front and Alfred was stretched out in the back. He wanted to take a good look."

Linda shifted ever so slightly in the chesterfield and carried on.

"Later on, I found out that fellow was doing this just to make his girlfriend jealous. I thought, when I saw Alfred later, 'Why doesn't a guy like that ask me out?' Well, he did…in grade twelve. He asked me to go with him to a banquet. Again, it was a double date. And the guys had to fix a flat tire," she said in a humorous tone recognizing the age-old tactics that young men will use to get women alone, stranded and in need of their help. She smiled fondly as she remembered the event. "But anyway that was an official start, I guess. Once we got dating, we were often at A&W."

A&W was Canada's first fast-food chain restaurant. Winnipeg, coincidentally, is where the company first began in 1956 with its ubiquitous drive-ins. Their buildings with their V-shaped carport roof supported by narrow metal posts and angled parking stalls that allowed large cars to easily drive in and park came with carhops—pretty young women in unforgettable orange and brown skirts—who came out on roller skates to take the order and deliver the food. It was the place to go on a date and if you ask those who remember, many will mention that a lot of root beer was spilled down the side of car doors, and those were some of the best times of their lives.

"At the drive-in? With the roller skates?" I asked.

"Yes, you had to roll your window up half, and they put the tray there. They developed a drink and Alfred always called it *dishwater*," she recalled him saying with a confident voice.

A&W was a stepping stone in the courtship and eventual marriage in 1965 but the dating ritual was not always smooth and easy.

Linda recounted a moment when she was about to finish her education at United College, which later became the University of Winnipeg. The final exams took place down the road at the University of Manitoba. And she spent long hours at the library with its long rows of tables that happened to allow one to see who was coming and going through the front doors. From that vantage point Linda saw Alfred taking another girl to coffee a couple of times. "So, I guess he was not set on (our relationship) yet."

"Oh?" I asked.

"He graduated one year earlier than me and went to teach in Oakville, outside Winnipeg. That meant we were separated and we had time to think about this, I guess."

The courtship was not a simple case of boy chases girl. Alfred wasn't the kind of driven male who chased a girl like a ferocious fox. One might say he had a wandering eye but for a male of his age, it wasn't unremarkable. Linda had to do some of the chasing, like the time she got on a bus on a Sunday afternoon to go visit him at the garage where he worked.

Alfred remembered it all a little differently. "Linda took pity on me, I guess," he had once said.

A pressing question, especially in a tight-knit religious community, concerned the approval from others.

"Did your parents approve of Alfred?" I asked.

"That's a good question. The church where I grew up had five hundred members—South-End Mennonite Brethren. At one point they split because some wanted to keep the German language and some didn't. So they built a new church and the majority went there. The people that wanted to keep the German language had come to Canada in the '50s." She paused with consideration to her wording and then added slowly, "They had a different way of thinking."

The negative impressions of the 1950s German immigrants brought consequences.

"One day my mother said to me, 'I don't know if we want you to marry Alfred.'" Linda looked as though she wanted to shake her head but held a firm pose instead and said, "By that time, what my mother said didn't matter anymore. They got to know him after we got married and they liked him very well. In the Hecht household everyone worked on the weekends. The girls did babysitting and Alfred worked in the garage. Everybody had to work to help pay for the first house and so on."

Linda pondered for a moment in silence before explaining that "My grandparents on both sides came in the '20s (when) Russia first let out landless people. My Grandma Huebert had land that she could sell and pay the family's journey (to Canada). Most immigrants couldn't pay for their journey."

The Mennonite Central Committee sponsored immigrants with the understanding that the funds were to be paid back to the religious support organization.

"That's one reason my mom went to work in the city, to help pay that back. But when the '20s people came, they headed right into the Depression era and on the Prairies the Dust Bowl and they couldn't make a go of it on the farm. Grandma and Grandpa Kroeker went out West and later bought a farm in Alexander (Manitoba). By the time I was four or five they moved to Winnipeg and Grandpa got a job at the Mennonite Brethren college as a janitor so they had something to live on. The '50s people would ask, 'How come you didn't make it? Why aren't you wealthier?'"

Three significant waves of Mennonite immigrants came to Canada. While they are associated with being ethnically German, their migrations were not always synchronous with those who came from Germany directly.

German immigrants came to Canada around 1900, establishing a strong presence in the Kitchener-Waterloo area. A large wave of German immigrants also came in the 1950s post-war era when skilled labour was needed.

The Mennonites, by contrast, were mostly fleeing difficult conditions in Russia where they had settled in distinct German-speaking communities since 1789. The first group to leave southern Russia was in the

1870s. The second wave was in the 1920s. The third wave came in the 1950s but many of these were refugees that had first fled to Paraguay right after the war. Because Germans and the Russian Mennonites all spoke German, although of vastly different dialects, they were often lumped together by Canadians as *Germans*, even though many were technically Russian citizens.

While Alfred was one of the 1950s Mennonite immigrants originally from Russia, Linda's family was from the 1920s wave of Mennonites who'd gone straight from Russia to Canada and begun integrating into Canadian society.

Linda's reference point had more to do with the 1920s Mennonite immigrants of her grandparent's generation than the 1950s Mennonite immigrants her husband came from. She distinctly noticed, "the '50s ones didn't integrate as quickly. Alfred's mom was always concerned that our children could speak German and keep the culture."

Linda shifted her thoughts again to her own grandparents who experienced Canada during the 1920s. Their experiences pushed them toward becoming more Canadian and relinquishing their Germanic heritage. "My grandpa learned English by going to town and shopping in the hardware stores. My grandmother learned English by helping her children with homework. They were eager to learn English. I can still hear my grandmother in my head speaking broken English, reading the paper."

The split in allegiances to the new country was contextual, and understandable.

During the mid and late 1800s, large numbers of Germans had immigrated to Canada, many to Kitchener-Waterloo. They built their own churches, public schools and were known as astute business leaders and industrious farmers. They took immense pride in their traditions and openly celebrated them through festivals including Saengerfest, Turnvereine and Oktoberfest. So large was their influence in southern Ontario that it was reported to be necessary to speak German if one were to live, visit or do business in the region's main city of Berlin.

Immediately prior to World War I, there was a general air of fondness toward German-Canadians that radiated throughout the country. That all changed with the outbreak of the First World War when Germany became the enemy. Mistrust, fear and animosity arose toward anyone and anything seen as German. As the war raged on, a purge ensued. German language classes were erased from school curricula. German newspapers were shut down. Speaking German in public was simply asking for trouble. Those of German ancestry in Canada quickly downplayed their Germanic background. A similar thing happened in the United States as well.

"So they no longer wanted to be German," I said to Linda. "They wanted to be seen as Canadian."

"Yeah, that's right. The Mennonites started to talk about their background as being *Dutch*."

The anti-German sentiment became official policy. The City of Kitchener in which Alfred and Linda now live had originally been named Berlin but its name was changed at this time. Other German-sounding city names were also changed including Kaiser, Carlstadt and Dusseldorf. But Berlin, Ontario had been the most prominent German city in Canada. Renamed in honour of an esteemed British military figure, Kitchener replaced Berlin and has remained the city's name ever since. The city's German history has faded under the erasure of time but has never completely disappeared.

Which led to another common theme of Canada's history—sometimes, instead of assimilating, a group of people will turn inward and become even more insular. Sometimes derision leads to entrenchment, which leads ironically to an even more prosperous community than before, albeit one that is more fundamentally religious and exclusionary to outsiders.

Some Mennonites, for example, continued to speak their own variety of German, kept their own schools and religious traditions and intensified their own in-situ culture at that time. The Amish in Canada, for example, proud of their German heritage, at the beginning of the 1900s numbered only four hundred people. Today, the insular community has grown to six thousand.

The corollary to insularity is high birth rates. Amish communities are not easy to define precisely but some researchers have estimated the birthrate to be as high as seven or eight children per couple, well above the

2.3 needed for replacement. In a sense, the war created a wedge that split the Germanic community into those who became more religious and those that became more Canadian.

Also, one of the defining tenets of Mennonite and Amish society is an adherence to a pacifist lifestyle. It was a cultural policy strictly at odds with the greater Canadian society, which saw it as a duty for men to sign up and go off to fight the Germans.

External geopolitics brought tremendous tests on internal identity.

Cultural splits within the German-Canadian community would be repeated by many others throughout Canada's history, including Japanese Canadians during the Second World War and more recently among Cantonese Chinese and Mandarin Chinese as well as South Asians to a certain degree.

The topic of immigrants and their experiences, especially in the immigrant-rich country of Canada, offers eternal lessons around identity but we had gotten off track.

"Was there a defining moment in your childhood that influenced you?"

"Yes, there was a very important one. When I was nine years old, I left home for the first time to spend a week at our Mennonite church camp. After one of the evening chapel services I wanted to become a Christian. One of the councillors prayed with me and it happened. The next day I clearly felt God personally protecting me as I jumped in the high waves of Lake Winnipeg with the other campers."

"And?"

"In the '50s seeing movies was one thing forbidden for Christians. I was in grade five when my friend was having a birthday party…and we were going to see a movie. I thought, 'Oh boy, this is my chance to go to a movie and my mom won't even know about it.' This movie was about a famous band; nothing bad or sinful. It was a fun thing with a lot of music."

Of course, her mother found out.

"I came home and I went straight in the house to the vacuum and I started doing my cleaning jobs like you've never seen before. That was funny when I think back but I guess I must have felt a lot of guilt."

After some silence Linda also confessed.

"I cheated on a test."

I leaned in.

"The teacher found out. Boy-o-boy, I sure remember that talking to. I made sure I never did that again."

One gets the sense that guilt carries a heavy weight on Linda's conscience. Perhaps it ties into the most monumental moment for a mother.

"After you were married, how long was it before Marvin was born?"

"Four years. We were on our way to Worcester."

The drive to Clark University in Worcester, Massachusetts was 2,600 kilometres. It was where Alfred's PhD supervisor was waiting for him with an aggressive impatience. The journey was going to be a problem and it had nothing to do with distance. Linda, now pregnant, was still one and a half months away from her delivery due date, or so she thought.

"He was born in Windsor, Ontario. It was really not an easy time," Linda admitted.

It had begun with a car and trailer full of their belongings and a long drive toward their new life at Clark University. Alfred had been accepted as a young PhD student to the prestigious geography school. Linda was an expectant mother. They had stopped in Windsor along the way and it was here that their first baby, Marvin, was born.

Alfred and Linda were having a late supper in Windsor after crossing back into Canada following a hectic drive on the Chicago Expressway, when Linda got the first sign of what was to follow. They made it to a hospital and Marvin was born.

He was underweight and the hospital wouldn't let him go until he reached six pounds.

At the same time, Alfred and Linda had no accommodations in Windsor and there was serious pressure coming from Clark University for him to get to Worcester as soon as possible or risk losing his position as a PhD student. Education and getting to the top of academia were paramount in Alfred's mind. The pressure from his mother, who emphasized hard work and education, hung over him. Alfred himself, having grown up as a teenager in the far reaches of a poor South American country after leaving a war-torn one as a child, knew that education was the ticket to a life that would allow him to never again face the deprivations, poverty and fear of his youth.

Linda was a young married woman following her husband's ambition and direction. So when the baby came at the Windsor Hospital halfway on their journey to Massachusetts it seemed there was only one thing to do—leave the baby behind.

Linda recalled, "I wasn't really attached to that baby. I believe there is no such thing as mother instinct."

She reconsidered her statement and then reframed it. "A maternal instinct. That developed with me over time. Caring for Marvin and having him and seeing him grow. I got quite attached to him but not at first. I couldn't have done that the second time though, when Melinda was born. I didn't want to leave her anywhere!"

But they did leave Marvin at the hospital in Windsor so they could get to Clark right away to appease the PhD supervisor. They returned, of course, to pick up baby Marvin once Alfred was settled at the school and they'd found a place to live.

It all happened so fast. The premature birth, a temporary abandonment of the baby, an unknown city and travelling for the first time well beyond what Linda had known before.

"I had taught high school for three years so I had a professional life but what hit me was, we were living in this third-floor attic-apartment with Marvin. We didn't have any real cupboards. It was really makeshift. There were just some shelves in the kitchen. I had to care for Marvin and there wasn't anybody I could talk to, no friends, no relatives. That was the hardest part but we gradually got to know one family in particular, in the (university's geography) department and we would do things together on the weekend."

Both Alfred and Linda placed a heavy emphasis on educational achievement.

The spouses of prominent academics are often, rightly or wrongly, cast as supporting figures in the life of an academic one, unless they themselves have their own careers.

Later in life Linda chose to go down her own academic path. She had a curiosity for the 16th century Anabaptist movement. "I got really interested in Anabaptism, which is the beginning of the Mennonite Church. I really enjoyed learning about the changes for women that were taking place. I would say I am interested in the equality issue but not in an extreme way." Following her MA she worked in the local Mennonite Archives.

A feeling of being minimized as a woman came early for Linda. "My brother came into our family when I as three years old. See, there had to be somebody to carry on the name—*Namentrager*. That always got to me a bit. That's why I used Huebert as my middle name in the title of my Master's degree. That was hard for Alfred to accept but I was determined to do that."

Linda published a book in 2009 called *Women in Early Austrian Anabaptism: Their Days, Their Stories*. A second edition was published while I was there. Over time, pride in both career ambitions and being a mother, grew.

"I am proud of Marvin. He worked hard to get a degree and then he wasn't able to become a professor because they were only hiring women. Melinda did a degree in geomorphology and I really admire her for that. Now her joy is sewing. She's an excellent seamstress. I'm glad she's doing what she wants and she's very good at raising the children."

"Marvin has a harder time I think with the boys because when they lived in Hawaii, he had to work in the evening from 4 p.m. until twelve midnight. He didn't see much of the boys but then he bought himself this older car and got the boys involved, so they did things together."

"We are fortunate to have a very nice son-in-law, Albert and a very nice daughter-in-law."

Linda looked about the room.

"Growing up in Winnipeg, I was always surrounded by family. I never thought we would stay here at the first job but that's what it ended up being." Forty-three years in one house, 2,000 kilometres from family in Winnipeg.

She came to enjoy travelling more than she first let on.

"The highlights of our years in Waterloo were the times we lived in Europe. The small kids went to school there. We'd do little trips in the summer."

They spent a total of six years in Europe, non-consecutively. The first time was in 1976 when Alfred was asked to teach an urban geography course in West Berlin at the John F. Kennedy Institute for North American Studies, at the Freie Universität Berlin. "The last time was in the '80s. During the '90s, Alfred had a half-year sabbatical and we spent time in both Australia and Paraguay. Those were very good times."

All told, "I'm very happy that Alfred and I can be together in old age. That's really special to have grown this old, past eighty, and we can still be together and relatively healthy."

And with that, the conversation came to an end.

I turned off the audio recorder, realizing there was something that stood out above all else. I was left with the impression that Linda Huebert Hecht would never want to be described as the woman *behind* the man. A more appropriate description, one she stood for her whole life, would be closer to the woman *beside* the man.

19. DECISIONS

"I graduated with a BSc after three years and was out of money."

The year was 1964 and Alfred was twenty-two years old. He didn't have to look very hard for a job. The Manitoba Provincial School Board came to him. There was a job available in Oakville, an hour west of Winnipeg, that the Board needed to fill.

"The school had hired a French teacher, an English teacher, and an ex-Army Sergeant to teach in the high school." The French and English teachers were fairly good but the former military sergeant had "walked into the grade twelve class, handed out the textbook and told the students to learn. The students and parents rebelled and the sergeant was fired. The board asked me to take over teaching grade twelve chemistry, physics and math."

Alfred went off to Oakville in 1964. The courtship with Linda was put on hold as he focused on this new potential path in life. That year gave him a taste for teaching and he realized he actually quite liked it, but his ambitions were grander.

"I enjoyed it but university was better," he said.

Being a high school teacher was something he could always fall back on if needed but teaching at a university was the role he saw for himself. He enrolled in a Master's degree program at the University of Manitoba and started it in 1965. At the same time, he got a better paying job in Portage la Prairie with the federal government at the Department of Manpower and Immigration. His task was to find jobs for people. "The first year at university I was hired by the Canadian government to be an Employment Advisor in their Portage la Prairie office."

Mostly, it was matching day labourers with farmers in the area who needed temporary workers during the harvest season. It was fine, but Alfred's real focus was on his education not moving up the government ladder.

Meanwhile, in 1964 Linda was studying at United College in Winnipeg and so with Alfred going back and forth between Portage la Prairie and the University of Manitoba in Winnipeg, the courtship resumed.

20. MASTER'S DEGREE

Anyone who has travelled across a large, flat, rural landscape such as the North American prairies, the Russian steppe or the northern plains of Europe has probably noticed there are many small towns, a few mid-sized cities and only one or two large city centres, all equidistant apart. The German geographer Walter Christaller (1893–1969) introduced Central Place Theory in 1933 as a way to explain the spatial distribution.

Christaller proposed that urban centres exist as market centres and each market is related to the products it can offer and the distance its customers are willing to travel. Daily goods such as milk and bread can be bought each day and few customers are willing to travel far for those items. Higher-end products such as complex machinery and luxury goods are purchased less frequently and by fewer people. Customers are willing to travel further afield for those and thus, those items are only sold in the largest markets.

In terms of market capture area, it will be larger for larger centres and smaller for smaller centres. Since customers have a distance threshold for how far they are willing to travel for any particular item, the multitude of transactions across the landscape eventually leads to a predictable spatial distribution of urban settlement sizes spaced at predictable distances from one another.

From its introduction in 1933 until late in the 20th century, researchers working with Central Place Theory were mostly attempting to see if Christaller's theory worked in the real world. It required the accumulation of a lot of case studies from around the world. By the end of the 20th century it became apparent that Central Place Theory was a reasonably sound concept although it needed some refining for real-world usage.

Central Place Theory continues to be used for economic and urban geographic modelling. It is taught in geography classes around the world at all respected universities. The odd thing is that while Central Place Theory was introduced in Germany in 1933 it wasn't until after the Second World War that Christaller's work was fully translated into English. For at least two decades German scholars, students and academics had the advantage of working with the theory long before the Anglo-American world took notice. When the English-speaking academic institutions finally took notice, they had to furiously catch up.

Even by the 1960s, as an economic geography student Alfred was one of those that maintained a certain advantage through his ability to converse with German academics.

By contrast, Alfred's thesis advisor at the University of Manitoba was an urban geographer from England. When Alfred first proposed the idea of working on a thesis involving Central Place Theory his advisor agreed in person but admitted later that he had never heard of it.

"My advisor told me later, when I told them this is what I want to do for my thesis, as soon as I walked out of the office he got on the computer and researched this thing...and he said, 'Oh, there were stats involved too!'"

So, Alfred set off on his Master's degree at the end of the 1960s and like most researchers in his field at the time, he wanted to see if Christaller's theory was applicable outside of Germany. He turned his focus to the Canadian prairies. His working hypothesis was that Portage la Prairie in western Manitoba was a market centre that should align with Christaller's Central Place Theory. To find out if his hypothesis was accurate he needed to do one major task—ask everyone in town where they shopped.

"I asked the high school students in Portage la Prairie to take the survey (questionnaire) back to their parents." The parents of Portage la Prairie were more than willing to oblige. "There were about nine hundred returns."

Land ownership on the Canadian prairies and the American prairies during the mid to late 1800s was organized through a land survey. The solution in Canada was to use the Dominion Land Survey System which demarcated the entire prairie landscape into six-mile x six-mile square plots called Townships. Each township was further subdivided into thirty-six squares, one mile by one mile, called Sections. Further subdivision of each Section into increasingly smaller pieces of land continued down from there including the quarter Section, Legal Lot, and so on.

This grid structure helped Alfred immensely.

"When I got the information back, I knew the address in terms of township (and then) I had to plot them. I had to do a lot of mapping. I even got my sister Elsa involved. I had her help me draw these maps."

Once all nine hundred shoppers were plotted on maps, "Then I had to determine the areas (and) the connecting points. Let's say 30% came to Portage la Prairie to shop and then closer to Portage la Prairie it was 90%. And only for a few items did they go to Winnipeg. So, I tried to find out if there was a market area hierarchy that would correspond to Central Place Theory Hierarchy."

It was a huge endeavour but his research did add to the existing body of knowledge, just as all good studies do, and all good scientists do.

"I think it was 268 pages," he said as we both quickly drank down the last of a Labatt low-alcohol beer on the back porch. The early afternoon had been warm although the leafless trees were barren and the buds still absent any signs of spring.

While his sister Elsa did not get a university degree out of her work, Alfred successfully completed his Master's thesis with her help, not to mention the help of most of the high school students in town and their parents. He completed his Master's degree from the University of Manitoba in 1968.

He wasn't quite sure what he then wanted to do. Maybe go into business? [The answer would come to him in a fitful moment of serendipity on a bus in the middle of the South American continent.]

A few things happened that made him realize "If I'm going to stay in this area, I might as well go to the top (of academia) and that meant I had to get a PhD."

The next big question was, *where?*

Linda wanted to stay in Winnipeg.

Alfred wasn't so sure.

"The problem came when I got the Master's from Manitoba. We were still living in Winnipeg," where Linda had all her relatives.

I gave him a questioning look.

"I couldn't get along well with her mom, but her dad was very good. The other thing is also all the friends from high school, (there were) no new ones."

21. AMBITION

Alfred had high expectations of everyone. His son and daughter were no exception, nor was the biographer.

Within the first few days of staying at their house it was clear that Alfred rewarded good work but I also noticed through his facial expressions in numerous conversations that he had a disdain for weakness and indecision, and something else.

Alfred and I had gone off in his Volkswagen SUV one day to meet a friend. Along the way he commented with the inflection of disapproval, "I expected you to come with questions."

I had interviewed academics and published their stories in magazines. I read their papers, knew their stories intimately and had guided the interview with questions formulated to capture both their work and personalities. That process required me to show up with the formality of preplanned questions but Alfred's biography actually required an organic approach. I wasn't fazed by his questioning of my methods, but I could see how others, especially if seeking his approval, might find his expectations *tough*.

I replied, "Are you impatient with people who are incompetent?"

A puff of anger pushed out immediately, "I can't stand incompetence."

I waited.

"You know, my mother (would) hit me. I was—" he paused while he turned a sharp corner before continuing. "It taught me that you should do a good job at whatever you are doing. Carry through on things."

I wasn't sure if ambition was innate or beaten into him but regardless, it appeared that ambition was now in Alfred Hecht's genes the same way a dog can't help but chase that which runs.

Important decisions about one's future must be made early. For some, the decisions surrounding career, future and life come easily. For some they come after terrible hardship. Some fail to choose any path at all and let life crash around them. Alfred looked with glowing approval upon those who are decisive early in life, and forever after, as well.

After teaching high school the idea of becoming a university professor crossed his mind. Then again, maybe he would open a business in Winnipeg? He was uncertain, undecided. That indecision didn't last long. As already mentioned, the future trajectory of his life came in a fitful moment on a bus in the middle of the South American continent and it shaped the trajectory of his entire life.

By the time he retired, Alfred Hecht's academic credentials were long and deep: a Master's degree from the University of Manitoba, a PhD from the acclaimed Clark University in Massachusetts. He became a geography professor at Wilfred Laurier University for his entire career. Not one to be confined to one place, he also taught in Canada at the University of Waterloo and the University of Guelph. For twelve years (three terms x four years each) he was chair of the Geography Department at Wilfred Laurier University.

As a visiting professor in Germany he taught at the John F. Kennedy Institute for North American Studies at the Freie (Free) University in Berlin, Philipps University of Marburg, Fachhochschule as well universities in Cologne, Hof, Giessen and Kiel. Alfred Hecht was designated a Canada Council Doctoral Fellow, a Clark University Fellow, a Fellow at the Alexander von Humbolt University in Berlin and a fellow at Conrad Grebel College. He was also President of the Ontario Division of the Canadian Association of Geographers from 1992–1994.

This does not even scratch the surface of the influential scientific papers and studies he conducted and wrote nor the many international field schools he undertook with students. There were the meetings with dignitaries, projects with business leaders and forays into places that others were forbidden to go, such as the Soviet Union and East Germany prior to the fall of the Berlin Wall. It is perhaps these last points that are of greatest intrigue.

Alfred would return many times to the lands of his birth and childhood in a time when most Westerners were excluded.

One gets the sense that Alfred Hecht's ambition was born in a quest for answers and reconnections with a childhood amid the ruins of war, refugee camps and subsistence farming, all before the age of thirteen.

"So, where does your drive come from?" I asked.

"Mainly from my mother's side. Even in Paraguay if we had horses, they had to be the best."

Alfred turned slightly toward me. "You know, I never forgot my past when we only got beans. Poverty is not my thing."

"You don't need to do that again?" I replied sarcastically.

"Yeah, lard and beans, that's it. Even the bread, we couldn't have a normal white bread. We had to have sorghum. It would stick to...even the dog's mouth. You can imagine what it did to humans."

After the war, the refugee camp, a transatlantic voyage and years spent in the Chaco, they were able to come to Canada in 1955 to take advantage of a country that offered opportunity for those willing to work hard. He was still a teenager in 1955 but it wouldn't be long before he would have to make important decisions about the future trajectory of his life and the army wasn't on the list of options.

He noted his mother's brother Bernhard Krause had worked in a factory all his life. Alfred thought, "I'm not so sure I want to work in a factory."

Ironically, one summer Alfred got a job in a factory working for General Electric making electrical circuit breakers. The company offered him a management position off the factory floor, "but it meant staying in Winnipeg."

He didn't stay long at that job.

His mother had been pushing Alfred to become a teacher. "Mom kept saying, Dad had been a teacher, your uncle had been a teacher, your aunt had been a teacher." As persistent as Susanna was, it wasn't his mother that solidified Alfred's decision to go into academia.

He had completed his undergraduate degree in Winnipeg and was then working on his Master's degree in the late 1960s. The question at the time still remained; what was he going to do in life, after the Master's degree? Would he go into business? Would he go on to higher education and get a PhD? And of all things, where would he and his young wife Linda, live? (They had been married in June 1965.) He still wasn't sure at this point what he wanted to do with his life, let alone answer the basic questions of why, where and when.

"Of all things," Alfred said, "on a research trip to Paraguay, Linda and I flew to Asunción, then took a bus to the Mennonite colonies. There was a couple ahead of us on the bus, a couple of years younger. She introduced herself," and when Alfred introduced himself by last name, the woman asked, "Are you thee Hecht?"

Alfred was a bit confused as to what this woman meant by, "Thee Hecht."

It turned out the woman, when she was young and living in Poland during the Second World War, had a special teacher she remembered fondly. The teacher left such an indelible impression on her that she never forgot him. That teacher was Alfred's father.

Leonidas Hecht was drafted into the German Army shortly after teaching this woman in Poland in 1944. Alfred was not old enough to know his father but the woman on the bus certainly remembered Mr. Hecht with great affection, although she had not learned the fate of her favourite teacher. She said to Alfred, "If you are thee Hecht, you have aged properly. Do you remember Poland?"

The woman was remembering Alfred's father, not him. The reputation of his father seemed to follow Alfred wherever he went and he didn't like it. The reputational shadow was especially overbearing in Winnipeg.

Since many immigrants from southern Russia and Poland had settled in Winnipeg after the war, there were many who knew Alfred's father from back in the old countries.

Alfred explained in an unusually soft tone, "Whenever we saw somebody they would say 'I knew your dad,' and then they would ramble on (with great affection)."

On that bus in the middle of Paraguay, Alfred suddenly knew, "If I want to be my own independent person and not my dad's son per se, I gotta get out of (Winnipeg)."

"I learned a lot about my dad indirectly, but nah yah, I became a teacher."

He would be a professor. That he knew. He just didn't know where.

His wife Linda was less certain about the path forward. Perhaps she had a sense of the troubles that lay ahead.

22. SPRING MEMORIES

The spring air had warmed as though winter had picked up camp and departed the night before. The temperature had risen into the mid-twenties. That afternoon, Alfred and I walked to the local strip mall a couple of kilometres away.

At the corner of two busy roads on the suburban edge of Waterloo, the strip mall contained a Starbucks, a no-name bank and a grocery store chain with an equally forgettable name. The local bank used to have free coffee but in the Covid era that little perk vanished. So, we paid full price at the Starbucks and went outside to sit on a bench that overlooked the asphalt parking lot.

"Even my own advisor said, 'Don't come here (to the University of Manitoba). We don't have a good record at producing and our graduates don't get good jobs,'" Alfred recalled.

It suited Alfred just fine since he wasn't particularly interested in staying in Winnipeg to do a PhD anyway.

The next choice was the University of Minneapolis-St. Paul. It was roughly five hundred kilometres from Winnipeg and Linda was pushing for where Alfred could get a PhD and eventually a teaching position. She saw it as a place they could settle down, raise a family and still be within a day's drive of their families back in Winnipeg.

"I looked at the program," Alfred said of the Geography Department at the University of Minneapolis and concluded, "It was not that good in my area. They were pretty good in historical geography but not in urban economic geography."

Alfred took a pass on the University of Minneapolis. The next option was the University of Wisconsin at Milwaukee. It too, had insurmountable problems that Alfred was not willing to overlook. When "that turned out negative, Linda was getting quite disappointed. She knew it would have to be further."

Two suitable options showed up.

"I got admitted to Ohio State which was very good. And then to Clark, which was ranked very high."

The decision was made to go to Clark College (later named Clark University). Located in Worcester, Massachusetts, the venerable college aligned with both his academic ambitions and his desire to be far enough away from Winnipeg that he could shine in his own way without the persona of his father or the expectations of family gnawing at him. He could be an independent man at Clark College.

The journey of 2,600 kilometres to Clark, delayed somewhat by the birth of their son, was arguably the beginning of Alfred's purpose in life.

He recalled the drive to the border. With their car towing a trailer behind, loaded with all their possessions and nervous excitement for a new life, the Canadian border guard looked at them and remarked, "Well, I see you're finally leaving home."

Indeed they were and perhaps in more ways than they understood at the time.

Once they left Winnipeg, they never made a home in the city again. Although they tested the waters of nostalgia it always failed to deliver, at least for Alfred that is.

"I went to teach in Winnipeg on a summer program. It just didn't feel like home anymore, you know."

Alfred's attachment to Winnipeg had been permanently severed and without so much as a whimper. He held no remorse about it. Linda felt otherwise.

"The last couple of times we went to Winnipeg, we went to hotels" instead of staying with friends or family as is often the custom among Canadians, Alfred began to explain. "Linda's sister wanted us to (stay) there but her sister is...dogmatic."

"If we go to Winnipeg I call my cousin Henry Thiesen. They have a mansion with room for visitors. He built a pretty big company. Over three hundred employees and expanding. They always drove a BMW, top of the line, not bottom." He smiled and continued. "He had a fantastic relationship with his employees. Even when he was retired, he frequently went in to the office and brought them cigars and a bottle of Glenfiddich."

The rapport between the two was very good.

Alfred recalled, "I was into rentals. He heard I had some rentals and asked, 'Is that a good business?' For me, it is," Alfred had replied.

After that his cousin partnered with some other businessmen and bought an entire apartment tower.

"A whole apartment tower?" I asked incredulously.

"Yeah, a whole tower! He didn't do anything half-heartedly. And when Pizza Pizza first started, he lent them money at 10%."

"A venture capitalist!"

"Yeah."

"Did you go into that?" I asked Alfred.

"No. Financially, I'm conservative."

The more appropriate term, I thought, might be *calculated*.

In retirement, Alfred needed to keep himself busy, which coincided with making money. He went into buying houses and planned on renting them out for a tidy profit. His first purchase was a newly built townhouse in London, Ontario that came on the recommendation of a friend. The whole thing went badly and Alfred lost money. He learned his lesson. From that point onwards, he discarded friendly recommendations and put his analytical skills to use instead.

While it's common for real estate investors to look at market comparables and roughly judge which are best, Alfred went a few analytical steps further. He created an entire dataset of variables for each and every house that came up for sale in his market area. He then ran a regression analysis on the data to find those properties that offered the best variable-to-price ratio, and thus the best value. When the metrics pointed to a top-buy he would purchase it and rent it out. He never went wrong after that, at least on the purchase side. The renter side was a different story.

"Yeah, I knew (you were fiscally conservative) when you told me you did a regression analysis for your real estate portfolio," I said. "You're not the kind to just casually show up and say, 'I'll take it!'" We both laughed.

His financial approach to life was instilled into him by his mother. Susanna had always said that some debt, such as buying a house or a farm, is good. Consumer debt was bad although even that might not be so bad if it had a financial purpose.

"You need a good car to get a good woman," Susanna had told Alfred once. True to her word, after she bought their first house, his mother bought the family, but mostly with Alfred in mind, a sports car for getting groceries and catching a wife. Alfred enjoyed the car immensely.

Linda never mentioned the car once while I was there.

We shifted a little on the bench. The sun was beating down hard.

"Value structures have changed in terms of money," Alfred said.

He told the story of how one time he offered to sell a rental property to his son and daughter-in-law. "Between them they make good money. She even has a church pension and support. So, they're fine." But Alfred knew the rental property would also offer them a nice passive income stream that could help boost their financial situation. "But they didn't want to deal with renters." He returned to Thiesen again. "My cousin, he knows how to turn a dollar over!"

Ambition, money and the spectre of avoiding the poverty of his youth, while making a model citizen of himself through faith and hard work, were the values and principles that had moulded Alfred Hecht's character. In return, he looked for a free coffee wherever he could find it, a nice walk with family, friends, fishing, giving back and most importantly, the opportunity to tell a good story.

We both turned back to the warmth of spring and gazed out again at the comings and goings across the asphalt parking lot.

"Huh," Alfred said. "You see the girl with shorts and halter top. I'm always amazed how fast women adjust to warmer temperatures."

The sight made me smile, too.

23. PhD

The PhD itself was quite straightforward and in many ways an extension of the Master's degree but with a larger scope.

At this time, global outsourcing was leading to the loss of manufacturing jobs in North America. Some manufacturers, instead of relocating overseas, moved their factories instead to cheaper land on the outskirts of cities they were already located in. Alfred wanted to find out more about the economic effects of this move.

"If a manufacturer moves his plant from the downtown area," how would it affect the labour pool and labour costs for the company? A worker in a downtown area that used to walk to work is going to weigh the costs of having to commute to the suburbs for the same job they used to have. Many workers would find the cost of commuting too high; the company could find itself with a labour shortage. The managers of the companies, according to Alfred, had considered the land costs of moving their manufacturing plants to cheaper land far away but never really considered the labour situation. He studied this issue with great verve and curiosity for many years. Meanwhile, behind the scene Linda was taking care of Marvin, feeling alone and isolated.

As Alfred worked through the many hours of research involved in completing a doctoral degree, he was making new friends and was thrilled with his new life. It offered intrigue, challenge and the disconnect from Winnipeg that he'd been craving. Temptation briefly tested his resolve.

Just when he thought he'd left Winnipeg forever, he was offered a position by the chair of the Geography Department at the University of Manitoba, a man Alfred knew personally.

Alfred's reply to the offer was, "I don't have my PhD."

"No problem. I have a tenure-track position," the chair assured him.

Alfred considered it. It was a nice job offer but it was not everything he wanted and he'd have to live in Winnipeg again. Ultimately, "My advisor said, 'You're not leaving until you have a PhD in hand!'"

Besides, there were lots of jobs waiting for him at McMaster, Simon Fraser, University of Wisconsin and other universities. There was also political turmoil going on inside the Geography Department at the University of Manitoba that didn't bode well. Alfred didn't need to settle.

He finished his PhD at Clark College in 1972.

24. WLU

If it wasn't for the Vietnam War the rest of Dr. Alfred Hecht's story would have taken place in the United States.

He was offered a position at the University of Wisconsin in Milwaukee but the Vietnam War was on and it raised the question of conscription for Alfred and Linda. If their children were born in the United States they would be American citizens and with citizenship came the possibility of being drafted into the US Army in some future war.

By comparison, other than a brief stint during the Second World War, Canada had a history and attitude of voluntary military service only.

Alfred declined the offer from the University of Wisconsin.

In 1972, he instead took a teaching position as an Assistant Professor at an institution mostly unknown to anyone outside the local area. It was located in the Kitchener-Waterloo region in southern Ontario, Canada. The post-secondary institution was called Waterloo Lutheran University.

The City of Kitchener used to be the largest ethnically German city outside of Germany prior to WWI. Anti-German feelings at the start of WWI led the Canadian government to change the city's original name of Berlin to Kitchener. Its Germanic heritage remains noticeable to this day and it suited Alfred perfectly.

It was a risky career choice. Waterloo Lutheran University was undergoing metamorphic changes and was not guaranteed to survive. If Alfred could position himself well, work hard, get involved in helping direct the growth and success of the institution then there was a chance the risk would pay off. He went for it. He took a chance on *"last chance U"* as it was disparagingly called then.

One year after he was hired, Waterloo Lutheran University was renamed Wilfred Laurier University. It was a time when the small faculty, many of them new in 1973, had to make it thrive or die but to make matters more challenging, they had a herculean foe competing with them literally right across the street.

In a protracted recurrence of the twin city's historical machinations, Kitchener-Waterloo was bound to produce not one but two competing academic institutions. They were less like brothers and more like mother and daughter. One gave birth to the other, only to be dwarfed later in popularity and prestige by its offspring.

Wilfred Laurier University began as a seminary school in 1911, established by the local Lutheran Church officials. In 1914 it expanded its offerings to include non-theological courses and rebranded itself as the Waterloo College School. In 1925, it aligned with the University of Western Ontario and began offering honours degree programs in the Arts. In 1960, the Lutheran Church revamped its support and affiliation leading to a new charter and direction. But the provincial government, in lockstep with societal changes in the 1960s, lost interest in supporting religious colleges. A schism soon formed internally at WLU. From that internal division was birthed a new post-secondary institution—the University of Waterloo.

The upstart University of Waterloo, like a vigorous youth, grew rapidly and became one of Canada's most esteemed institutions of higher education especially in the areas of science, math and physics as well as its co-op education option. As Waterloo grew, and its reputation along with it, Wilfred Laurier University's future looked increasingly limited and dire. It would have to find its own brand and develop a unique reputation for excellence.

Arthur Stephen, who joined the institution in 1967 and eventually became Vice-President of Advancement (a.k.a. student recruitment), remembered that in the 1970s the quality of students was so low that "in '75 half the student body didn't have 60%" as an average grade coming out of high school. "Even if they only had 56% they were admitted on probation. We were near the bottom in the pecking order for Ontario scholars."[10]

It wasn't certain that WLU was going to succeed.

WLU had some soul searching to do and some wayfinding to make. In 1973, the university changed its name from Waterloo Lutheran

University to Wilfred Laurier University, which kept the abbreviation WLU the same. The seminary origins were branched off to Martin Luther University College.

When Alfred joined WLU's Department of Geography in the summer of 1972 as an Assistant Professor with a dedicated cadre of existing faculty and a fast-burgeoning troop of new faculty, WLU was looking to grow from a small religious college to a small university with a big reputation. It just had to figure out what that reputation was going to be and it wasn't at all certain it was going to succeed.

The school planned to take on Canada's top universities—Toronto, Queen's, Western, McMaster and Waterloo. With some extraordinary faculty, innovative approaches, teaching excellence, a lot of frugality and fabulous marketing, plus a collegial faculty, they knew they could do it. "By the end of the 1980s we were number three behind Queen's and Waterloo," Arthur Stephen reported in an interview with Robert Alexander in 2011.[11]

Then disaster struck.

In the 1990s, *Macleans*, a familiar Canadian national magazine, began ranking Canadian universities. The annual ranking became the benchmark upon which all Canadian universities strived to outrank one another. Most prospective students referenced it before choosing their school to enroll. Macleans, the first year, ranked Wilfred Laurier University at forty-two out of forty-five. It was a marketing disaster.

Arthur Stephen quickly lobbied Macleans to use the same criteria that similar American publications were using, which included a lower emphasis on financial metrics. Macleans agreed that the change in metrics would make the rankings more balanced and followed through on the changes. Once they did that, Laurier instantly rose again to gain the number three spot in its category. Student enrollment went up and Laurier began attracting some top students that would go on and make a name as WLU alumni such as Liberal MPP Herb Epp and Canadian Ambassador Paul Heinbecker.

The growing success of Laurier, however, did not mean they could ignore the herculean reputation of the university across the street—the University of Waterloo.

Laurier would need to do a strange juggling act of pooling resources with Waterloo when advantageous, while differentiating itself at the same time.

Internally at Laurier, the Geography Department had split in 1962 when the University of Waterloo opened. Some of the geography faculty migrated over to Waterloo and some stayed behind at Laurier. For some, such as Herbert Witney who was teaching in the Geography Department at WLU, it was the most ideal place to be.

"Most attractive to me was the size of Waterloo Lutheran University, about 1,800 students. My wife and I both had undergraduate degrees from small liberal arts colleges and preferred them to the large universities. In addition, WLU had a Geography Department larger than any in a similar-size college I knew of—an ideal combination!"[12]

John McMurray, the chair of the Department of Geography, Geology and Planning, along with Herbert Witney, are credited with getting the Geography Graduate program going but it would limp along until Alfred Hecht and a few others came on scene to really build it up.

"Over the years faculty came and went, especially at first. But there was also marked stability; the faculty of 1976—John McMurray, Gunars Subins, Jerry Hall, Ian McKay, Russell Muncaster, Alfred Hecht, Bruce Young, Grant Head, Barry Boots, Houston Saunderson, Helen Parson, Ken Hewitt—were all still there (plus four more) when I retired in 1993,"[13] Witney recalled. "What I particularly liked about the Geography Department over the years was its collegiality. Faculty members genuinely liked each other."[14]

The university was small, feisty and mostly unknown. The President, John Weir, wanted to change that but it required hiring the best, the most collegial and the most gung-ho academics of the time. Alfred Hecht was one of those who joined the team.

Alfred saw some opportunities and was keen to capitalize on them. He would build up the Department of Geography and the university simultaneously.

Yet there was a pause in his commitment to Laurier early on when his employment came up for review. After being there for three years, he didn't yet have tenure and he wasn't sure he was going to get it.

"In 1975, when the question of tenure loomed, I thought I should look around to another job, just in case," he said.

The John F. Kennedy Institute for North American Studies, Freie Universität Berlin had been advertising an Assistant Professor position in Alfred's field. He applied. While waiting to hear back from Freie University, he successfully gained tenure at Laurier and was promoted to Associate Professor. He then received an offer from Freie University to teach for six years. With his secured position at Laurier and the limited term at Freie, he declined the offer in Germany.

But they came back to him and said, "Come teach an introductory lecture on urban geography in the summer as a visiting professor. We would really like to have you."

Alfred accepted and that summer he took Linda and his two young children to West Berlin where he taught at Freie University from April to August in 1976.

"It was my first foray into German academia." And it was a bit of an eye opener, too. The free-loving, 1960s hippy-era had never really taken off in its fullest expression at the universities within the conservative region around Kitchener-Waterloo. Progressive Berlin, Germany was a world apart from conservative Kitchener-Waterloo.

Alfred described the setting of his first lecture.

The amphitheatre-style room with tiered rows, rising up toward the back, was filled with around a hundred students in attendance. It was not so much the crowd that was remarkable to Alfred as their behaviour.

"Students came in to listen to my presentation and rolled their cigarettes and in the first row sat a young woman breastfeeding her baby," he said with a grin.

The summer teaching session went well. In September he was back at Laurier but keen to go back to Europe again.

"Being a faculty member, you had to teach but you also had to do research and to do research you needed money. You had to apply for grants. Alexander von Humbolt was one of the ones that if you were an established scholar at a Canadian university under forty, you could apply for an Alexander von Humbolt grant for twelve months. They paid equivalent to your normal wage. In fact, you could double your wage. Frequently, when summer session was on, I would go abroad."

Not only was Freie University especially good for his career and pocketbook, so too were other offers in Germany. He would go on to teach as a visiting professor or fellow at other German universities including Marburg, Kiel, Cologne and the Giessen Fachhochschule.

"I was better known in Europe in the geography field than in Canada because I spent so much time there," he noted.

In fact, Alfred's work in Germany turned out to be very good for himself but also beneficial to Wilfred Laurier University as well. WLU wanted to offer students expanded opportunities to study abroad. Through contacts in Germany, Alfred Hecht helped make that happen. But before Alfred could create new opportunities for students there was one thing he needed to do for himself in 1976.

He needed to confront his past and there was no guarantee he was going to come out alive.

25. RETURN to STALIN'S EMPIRE

It was a watershed moment for Professor Hecht.

His career was in its fledgling stage. He had been given the security of tenure but now he needed recognition from his peers. An opportunity arose but it could not have been a worse offer. In 1976 he was invited to go to the Soviet Union to give a presentation at the International Geographical Union conference that year.

Every country has their own independent national geographical society that together form the International Geographical Union (IGU). The IGU holds a conference every four years. It is absolutely mandatory for any aspiring geography professor to attend if they are looking to rise up the career ladder. Meeting and networking with international peers, officials and diplomats was crucial for Alfred's career and having an invitation, no less, would have been career suicide to turn it down. But he was worried about something much worse than a career fumble.

The international conference was to be held in Moscow. The young Professor Hecht couldn't afford not to go. He needed to be there. Yet, the Soviet Union—the same country he had fled as a child—appeared to still be the same country that thirty years earlier had labelled him a *traitor*. While the nefarious dictator Joseph Stalin had died in 1957 it wasn't clear that things had changed much inside the Soviet Union in 1976.

Hecht was worried.

For most people, travelling inside the Soviet Union at that time, as long as all paperwork and visas were approved, was of no real concern. Alfred Hecht, unlike others, worried his past would catch up with him.

Born a Russian citizen, he worried the traitor designation still hung over him. He worried about the possibility of imprisonment or worse. It wasn't an unreasonable worry either.

Alfred's family had suffered through the mental convulsions of the Russian nation's bitterness, anger, ideological delusions and subsequent outburst of internal violence that had climaxed with the Russian Revolution in 1917. A depressive paranoia seemed to linger inside Russia ever since, but maybe the country's psychological health had improved?

Alfred really didn't know. The internal psychology of the Soviet Union at that moment was difficult to judge although he was still very familiar with the ugliness of her past.

Alfred's grandfather had been a wealthy upper-class landowner prior to the Russian Revolution. Landowners in Tsarist Russia had formed a distinct and privileged social group which included some of the original Mennonite settlers such as Alfred's grandfather.

Large land holdings were mostly acquired in the mid and late 1800s when land was cheap and large acreages were needed to pasture flocks of sheep. As population increased, pastoral lands were converted to more lucrative arable farmlands. By the end of the 19th century southern Russia was almost entirely cultivated farmland. Modern machinery combined with peasant labour became the foundation of the economic structure which resulted in a small but wealthy landowner class and a large but mostly poor peasant class.

By 1914, over 500 private estates owned by Mennonites existed in southern Russia. They varied dramatically in size, some as large as 110,000 hectares although most were less than 550 hectares. The latter was still large enough to require hired hands.

The landowners and their families lived separate lives from the rest of the population. Intermarriage within this upper class was common and the exclusive practice only facilitated an increasingly stratified society. The upper class included not only landowners but also industrialists, businessmen and high-ranking politicians. Their lifestyles were vastly different than the rest of the population with large houses, servants, well-educated children, international travel and socializing among the Mennonite and Russian intelligentsia. They had direct ties to the Russian Tsar and aristocracy.

From family accounts, Alfred Hecht's grandfather, Karl Hecht, was a member of this social class. He was a landowner with perhaps a hundred to two hundred workers. He was the epitome of success.

Yet bitterness was ripe within the general population due to economic inequalities. That bitterness exploded during the communist revolution of 1917 and suddenly the upper social class came under violent attack.

The Bolshevik revolutionaries went to Karl Hecht's estate one day. He and his wife were forced to watch as the Bolshevik gang took their five sons out to the barn, lined them up against the wall, and shot them all.

After the devastating murders, details of which are vague, a mix of stories told to me indicate that Karl Hecht's wife disappears from the scene, perhaps through ill health, and he marries a second woman—Loise Waechter, whom Alfred affectionately labelled, "The British Governess."

The British Governess, Loise Waechter, had been a lady-in-waiting for the Tsarina. Her position as a *Hofdame* in the Royal House of Russian Emperor Nicholas II would have given opportunity for her and Karl Hecht to cross paths. She was slim with wavy blonde hair, full lips and high cheekbones. Her narrow face would later carry an innocent sorrow but Karl would have first known her as a beautiful woman of great intrigue.

Karl Hecht first hired Loise Waechter as a nanny to educate his children. Loise would give Karl's children the opportunity to learn the social etiquette and manners of the dominant global empire at the time. Manners, etiquette, morals, sophistication and a command of the English language were the necessities for maintaining social and economic status among those connected to the global economy. The nanny, of course, could not be from the working class. Details lack clarity at this point in the story but it appears from various family accounts that Loise was originally connected to the House of Lords of the British Parliament.

It was an imperfect time and their love was caught in a dangerous world of turmoil and change. Together, Loise and Karl had three children. One was Leonidas Hecht (Alfred's father).

All of it goes back to the land. While the wheat and other cereal grains produced on Karl Hecht's estate had been sold on international markets, it was the shared culture of the global elite that had allowed Karl Hecht and family at that time, as it does today, to remain in the upper ranks of the social hierarchy, that is, until the Russian Revolution changed everything.

Russian Tsar, Nicholas II, the Emperor of Russia, was executed by Bolshevik revolutionaries on July 17, 1918. His wife, five children and members of the imperial entourage that had accompanied the Tsar were also murdered. The landowning class across all of Russia, including Karl Hecht, would face relentless attack from this moment onward. The executions of his five sons against the side of the barn were only the beginning.

When Joseph Stalin came to power as General Secretary of the Communist Party a few short years later in 1922, the landowners had been given the nefarious label "Kulaks." This epithet applied to anyone who owned a farm, cattle and horses and had the wealth to hire labour. As a derogatory term in the eyes of the communists, Kulaks were seen as leaches on society. Joseph Stalin considered the Kulaks to be of three types, all of which were to receive varying degrees of punishment for being successful. The Active Kulaks opposed collectivization openly and vociferously, were usually the wealthiest and had the most to lose. They were targeted for arrest and execution. Karl Hecht was in this category.

Unfortunately, the Hecht side of the family was not alone in the suffering. On Alfred's mother's side, as Alfred had noted earlier, "during the Stalin persecution era, both my grandfather and great-grandfather Krause died by forced drowning, by the communists."

The other two categories of Kulaks were less wealthy and less active in resisting collectivization but still suffered hard labour and banishment.

In 1976, with the invitation to return to the Soviet Union, an invitation he couldn't refuse, Alfred was worried.

The Soviet Union represented a haunting past that hadn't fully faded away with time. The same Soviet apparatus that had murdered his grandfather, great-grandfather and other family members was still very much alive and well. The same bureaucrats and leaders and their descendants were still in control.

If Alfred entered the Soviet Union, would he be arrested upon entry and thrown in prison? There wouldn't be much that Canada and its diplomats could do about it. The Soviet Union was far too powerful to worry about appeasing the West over some academic that had allowed himself to be arrested and thrown in a Soviet prison to languish indefinitely.

So, was the Soviet Union of 1976 still the same Soviet Union that Alfred had been born into? Maybe the passing of time and life in three different countries had given Alfred enough distance?

When Alfred's family fled the Soviet Union in the Second World War they were given German citizenship in 1944. Then Paraguay had given them permanent residence status. When they immigrated to Canada in 1955, five years later he became a Canadian citizen.

"When I started teaching in Portage la Prairie, to teach at that time, you had to swear allegiance to the Queen and you had to give up all other citizenships. According to my documents I was listed as German, so I had to give up that citizenship."

That didn't mean the Russians saw it the same way. Although Joseph Stalin was no longer the leader of the Soviet Union, and detainment would not be of any benefit to the Soviet Union—Alfred certainly wasn't needed for manual labour in a gulag—he inquired with the authorities to make sure he wasn't entering a trap.

"I've been invited to give a paper over there (in Russia) and I am a little worried," Alfred admitted to the Russian embassy contact person with whom he was dealing. The embassy agent reassured Alfred that he would have no problems leaving Russia.

"Can I get out of my Russian citizenship?" Alfred asked over the phone while he was at it.

It would have cost $725 dollars. "At that time, it was no small fee," Alfred recalled. Besides, it may have already been rescinded de facto, although he couldn't be certain. He did not inquire further and never pursued the application to officially relinquish his Russian citizenship.

In the summer of 1976 Alfred returned to Stalin's Empire on a promise from the authorities that he could freely leave.

The same authorities said nothing about entering.

Since Alfred was in Berlin that summer as a visiting professor, a colleague who was also going to the IGU conference in the Soviet Union suggested they take the train together. And since Alfred was going to the Soviet Union anyway, he hoped to do a side trip down to the place where he was born. That request was denied. The region was off limits to foreigners.

However, there was a sub-conference of the IGU occurring in the Black Sea port city of Odessa, which was somewhat close to his birthplace and seeing as how he was permitted by the authorities to go to Odessa for the conference, and because his own father had studied at the university in Odessa in the late 1920s, Alfred decided he would go there before attending to the main conference in Moscow.

Like a hopeful proposition, they would go by train from Berlin to Warsaw and then transfer to another train bound for Odessa. Total journey would be almost 3,000 kilometres. What could possibly go wrong?

"I was flying from Odessa to Moscow but had to go by train from Berlin to Warsaw and then Odessa. When I started in Berlin in the morning, the temperature was going to be horribly hot. The train was leaving early (so when I) got to the train station I didn't have a chance to change money."

The summer heat did in fact swell to record temperatures. "The train could only go about forty kilometres per hour because the rails had warped. Instead of arriving in Warsaw where I was gonna meet some people which I knew from Clark (University)" the train arrived more than a day late. "Then, I had to catch the train south to Odessa."

There was so little time that again he didn't have a chance to officially change money.

"Then we got to the border and we had to get out of the train. They searched my bag. They kept saying, 'Where are the rubbles you bought illegally?'"

Alfred replied that he didn't buy illegal rubbles off a street hawker and he didn't have time to change money legally, either. "I didn't have time," he argued. After a while they believed him.

"Finally we got on the train with a sleeper" for the 1,200-kilometre journey from Warsaw to Odessa. When the train finally arrived in Odessa, the city was in a jubilant mode for a national holiday.

"I get out on the platform, it's full of people!"

Alfred had been expecting a quaint little station and someone from the IGU to be waiting for him holding a sign with his name on it but it was crowded and the train was more than forty-eight hours late. No one was there waiting for him. A woman helped him onto a bus instead and instructed the driver to drop him off at the hotel.

Everybody in the bus heard the woman giving instructions and ever helpful as Russians are, they were all determined to help this poor lost traveller.

A shorter guy, with a leather patch over his shoulder, carrying a ring of barbed wire, pinched Alfred and signalled, "Follow me." He walked through the crowded bus with everyone jumping to get out of his way.

Alfred followed close behind.

They reached the back of the bus where the rear doors allowed easy exit when the time came.

As the bus drove on, Alfred peered out the window, not understanding anything that was being spoken. But every time he looked out the window, wondering if the stop was his as the bus came to a halt, everyone else watched him. "I looked out and the whole bus said, 'Nyet!' Then...all of a sudden, everybody in Russian says 'Now!'"

With barbed wire wrapped over his shoulder, the human porcupine shuffled out the back door with Alfred in tow. The bus drove off and Alfred and the man shook hands, before silently turning and going their respective ways.

Alfred arrived at the IGU sub-conference reception and announced, slightly exhausted, "I am Alfred Hecht."

"We have been looking for you, for two days!"

"Well, I was...delayed."

He still made it on time to present his paper at the conference.

The paper was on "Regional Development in Canada in Terms of the Agricultural Frontier." In other words, it looked at where agricultural cultivation stopped in Canada once poor soils, climate and other factors made it unviable. Theoretically, if the government gave unlimited subsidies, the entire country could be awash in agricultural fields even into the Arctic. Left to the market, however, there's a distinct geographic tipping point beyond which it no longer makes sense to engage in agriculture.

Of course, countries and their academics compare notes all the time on how much land is under cultivation and they typically want to know where, how much and why.

Professor Hecht showed that in Canada, the Atlantic provinces had actually lost 60% of total agricultural acreage since first being settled.

"At the beginning everyone was a farmer (that) cleared the land. Once the prairies and southern Ontario came into production, it didn't pay (in the Atlantic provinces) so they let it grow back wild. Too expensive to produce wheat. I showed how much it collapsed in the East and expanded in the West."

After his presentation, academics from other countries followed but one in particular caught Professor Hecht's attention. A Russian colleague, "gave a paper on 'The Great Expansion' of agriculture under the Russian Soviet Union regime right into Siberia. (It was massive) in terms of acreage."

On paper the Russians had put more acres under cultivation than existed prior to the Russian Revolution. Alfred thought it odd. "I asked during question period with everyone sitting around, the chair in front and a couple other guys, 'In Canada we are retreating. You are expanding in marginal areas. *Why?*'"

The Russian presenter gave a vague and terribly ambiguous answer.

When the presenter finished, he casually walked over and sat next to Alfred and whispered in his ear, "We gotta go for a walk."

They went outside and took a stroll down the street at which point the Russian presenter said to Alfred, "I couldn't tell you the real reason. We economists and agriculturalists all know it's dumb (trying to grow crops in these marginal areas) because you get one crop out of three at best. The growing season is too short."

Alfred looked at him, "And?"

"The chair is a KGB agent! I could not tell you the truth."

Alfred returned to Canada, thankful to be in a county that valued freedom of inquiry, open debate and that didn't lie to itself or do silly things such as attempt to grow crops in the sub-Arctic just to appease a jingoistic leadership. Alfred was also glad no one called him a *traitor*.

"The British Governess"
Loise Waechter
Died: 1921
(Also known as 'Luise Warter')

Alfred's Father
Leonidas Hecht
Died: 1944
(Shown in German Army uniform)

26. MARBURG

It was 1979, more than three decades after the Second World War ended, and Alfred was in the homeland of the defeated Germany. With American aid she had quickly rebuilt herself but evidence of her past had not entirely disappeared. The war generation had mostly turned their shattered ambitions into reconstruction. Work offered an emotional solace for those who chose to suppress honest opinions of the war; an entire populace had effectively swept aside, at least in public, their personal roles and feelings about their new position in the world. Often, for good reason.

Those most committed to the ideals of the Third Reich had been influenced during their youth and those that had survived the war were, by the 1970s, into their fifties and sixties, an age when self-censorship begins to wane.

Alfred Hecht remembered a brief moment when self-censorship had come off. He was a visiting professor at Philipps University in Marburg, Germany, the world's oldest Protestant-origin university. Founded in 1527, it was well regarded for its sciences. It not only ranked prestigiously among global universities but its earliest buildings also retained their architectural majesty, making it one of the most pleasing European university campuses. Many notable graduates have gone to Marburg over its 500 years including Alfred Wegener who first proposed the geographic theory of Continental Drift in 1915. Wegener's original theory is now referred to as Plate Tectonic Theory. It is the foundational theory to explain virtually everything connected with earthquakes, volcanoes and the shifting ground we stand on. The early 20th century German climatologist and geographer died in Greenland in 1930 just a few years prior to Adolf Hitler's rise to power.

Alfred spent a great deal of time at this prestigious university and on numerous occasions, "the local guides would show us around Munich, Regensburg, Cologne and so on." On one occasion, "we come to Nurnberg and the lady (tour guide) comes on board. 'Greetings,' she said. As the bus drove around and went through the former Nazi Party rally grounds the tour guide explained, 'That's the big square where Hitler started.' She then announced to the whole bus, 'I'm proud I was one of the Hitler Mädchen!'"

The Hitler Youth (HJ) originated in 1922 as the youth arm of the Nazi Party. It encompassed both male and female branches.

For boys, from 1936 until 1945 it was the only permitted youth organization. All boys 14–18 deemed to be Aryan were required to be members. A version for younger boys ages 10 to 14, called the German Young Folk, also existed. The Hitler Youth organization was modelled on the Boy Scouts Movement and originally included camping and hiking but over time, it morphed into a paramilitary organization focused on weapons training, physical fitness and indoctrination in Nazi ideology.

For girls it was similar. The League of German Girls, for those 10 to 18, promoted traditional family values and concepts of racial superiority.

Claims of being a "Hitler Mädchen" is a way of affectionately claiming to be "one of Hitler's girls."

Young and impressionable, many soaked up the ideas and ideology easily and never let them go. Others were averse to the whole thing but had no choice but to participate. Most were somewhere in the middle with a love of some aspects and indifference to others.

Those who held firm to the most radical Nazi ideas had mostly faded from German society by the 1970s but there were still a few around.

Alfred laughed out loud as he recalled the incident with the female tour guide at the front of the bus who announced her admiration of Hitler. He also recalled the reaction. "The bus driver slammed on the brakes, opened the door and said, 'Out!'" Alfred gave another chuckle. "I couldn't believe it! She was still a Nazi through and through. You could see it. (And that) bus driver decided, 'This one is not going with us.'" He shook his head a little more. "It was one of the first times I met one of those so-called Nazis."

Linda was listening in on the conversation. She turned to me and said, "Your father was in the Hitler Youth, you know."

"Yes," I replied, being well aware of this. It was both an interesting point and simultaneously unexceptional. Every boy under the age of eighteen that wasn't Jewish or deemed undesirable was mandated to be in the Hitler Youth during the war years in Germany and prior. That included my father Rudy, Alfred's oldest brother.

When I was a teenager myself, my father mentioned that the Hitler Youth was actually very good at promoting physical fitness. "The fat kids got bullied until they weren't fat any longer," he once said, or something to that effect. Not being physically fit was simply not tolerated and my father had a lot of respect for that. Whether good or bad, it was one of the core elements of the Hitler Youth—physical fitness.

I suspect most fitness coaches, yoga instructors, and ultra-marathon runners today would have felt quite comfortable in the early version of the Hitler Youth. It had a stern discipline, expectations, a fair amount of judgement and produced noticeable results. Rudy never talked about the rest of it.

Alfred, being too young for any of it, broached the topic with some empathy. He knew his older siblings had been mandated into the Hitler Youth while they were living in Poland. "The Germans organized all the boys to be in the Hitler Jungen," Alfred said, and explained that not all were happy about this. "Elsa's husband (Hein) was also in there. (He) was really concerned about the whole thing but he had no option, you know."

The rationale for the Hitler Youth morphed over time. It shifted from Boy Scouts into training the young for war and that too, was mandatory.

"Franz and Rudy were meant to march in one of these soccer fields. And then afterwards there was a little ditch in the hill and they were given rifles to practice shooting. They had to practice. One of the Youth Leaders made sure of it. He stood over them, watching." Severe repercussions would occur if the boys did not use the rifles. It was a tough position to be in for some that came from a pacifist Mennonite background. Since my father rarely spoke of the Hitler Youth and what happened, and had shown no interest in weapons, I assumed my mild-mannered father had never actually shot a gun.

Alfred added, "The war was basically over, you know."

Then he remembered another incident. "I was with a group in Germany and this guy from the University of Marburg, he was Assistant Prof, he says, 'Not far from here I want to show you how Hitler was able to hide production.' So we drove to the field; it was a little bit lower lying. They had dug into the hill, a big place. From the top all you could see was grass and trees." An older man from across the street came over and asked, "Where are you from?"

Alfred replied, "Canada."

The man invited them into his place. Down in the basement he had a vast collection of Nazi memorabilia.

"It was unbelievable," Alfred said.

"Like a museum?" I asked.

"Yeah, but private. I guess at one time he was in the army. He didn't show it as though he was a pro-Nazi." Instead, he offered everyone something to drink. "The students did not say, *no*," Alfred recalled with a giant grin before tabulating the amount of beer that was consumed that day. "Twenty-four times two was forty-eight bottles (for) twenty-three students (and it was) gone in no time!"

27. The GRADUATE PROGRAM

"Laurier is not known for its sciences. If you want to take a BSc, go to Waterloo."

When Laurier's math and chemistry faculty crossed the street to join the new upstart University of Waterloo in 1957 it became clear that Waterloo was going to be the science and technical institution going forward. Laurier would have to focus on its liberal arts tradition.

One of the challenges facing Laurier was the need to build strong graduate programs in each department in order to compete on an equal, albeit different, footing with Waterloo.

Alfred knew what had to be done. The Geography Department needed to be a leader, or perish. Inside the Geography Department and at Laurier in general there were a couple of possibilities for growth and leadership.

The first thing the Geography Department needed was a solid graduate program.

Wilfred Laurier University had only 2,000 students when Alfred joined in 1972. "Laurier wasn't big enough," he admitted.

Geography actually had a graduate program but it was minuscule and Alfred could see they were going to lose it if action wasn't taken.

"You need critical mass," Alfred explained. Geography had only four Master's degree students when he stepped in, as a newly appointed graduate officer. His plan was to not only expand the number of Master's degree students but also offer a doctoral degree as well. The first thing he needed to do was recruit some students.

Alex MacLean, who now teaches at WLU, remembered Alfred taking another fourth-year student named Bob Metcalfe and himself out to the Heidelberg Hotel for a beer.

"We were finishing our fourth year and we were applying for the Master's program. We applied other places, too. You were taking us out to the Heidelberg to persuade us to stay at Laurier," Maclean said to Alfred.

"Did I really do that? Sounds like a bribe," Alfred replied facetiously with a grin.

"Yeah, we had a beer at the Heidelberg Hotel and that was it; we both signed up."

"No, no, let me get you the full story," Alfred retorted.

When Alfred joined Laurier he taught with a specialty in economic geography, urban geography and regional development. With a desire to expand the graduate program he had fourteen students in fourth-year courses who showed potential for graduate studies. All were bright, smart and enthusiastic.

He had students in mind but what he desperately needed was money to pay the students. He went to the Dean and was told, "Give them all TA (Teaching Assistant) jobs."

Alfred then approached each of the fourteen students he wanted and told them they would get financial support through the teaching assistant job if they signed up as a graduate student. Alfred had excellent rapport with his students, and they with him. "It was a great group. They connected to each other really well," he said fondly.

Regardless, he worried not enough would actually apply. There were other schools with excellent reputations and great offers not least of which was the University of Waterloo right across the street.

Ian McKay, another graduate officer, disparagingly told Alfred, "None of them will come."

As it turned out, sixteen accepted the offer! Fourteen came internally from Laurier and two came from external applications.

"The graduate program went from four to sixteen!" Alfred said with a broad smile. Geography had never had more than four graduate students at any one time in the past. It was barely a program at all. Now, it was playing in the big leagues. Yet, Alfred still remained quietly uneasy. Once up and running, he was concerned about the long-term survival of the program. How long could it actually last? They had enough students, enough critical mass, but every seven years the provincial government evaluated programs at all post-secondary institutions and if a graduate program was not good enough, it lost accreditation and was disbanded. Everything hinged on the next hurdle—the review.

Alfred recalled, "The two Smith boys did the review. One from Edmonton and one from McMaster. Both last names were Smith."

Since Alfred had access to the resumes of all the graduate students, he knew what they were doing or more importantly, not doing. He worried that some were not publishing enough or not moving quickly enough through the program. Would the Smith brothers find his students lacking?

On the day the evaluators arrived Alfred sat down with them and began with an apology. The graduate program had roughly ten students who had been really productive in terms of publishing and getting grants, in Alfred's estimation. The rest were not performing up to Alfred's standards.

"The Smith boys said, 'Hey, if you keep that up, half of them publishing, that's fine. Even in big universities, that is the norm!'"

Alfred couldn't believe it. His program, and his students, were doing more than expected of them.

Now Alfred had the students, he had the blessing of the Provincial government, but there was still one more outstanding issue. He needed more money. He had a good idea of how he would get it, and kill two birds with one stone along the way.

28. PLETSCH

Professor Dr. Dr. (h.c.) Alfred Pletsch had a desire to go to North America. They say timing is everything and in 1982 Pletsch suffered a false start, which worked out well for everyone else. Pletsch, a tall man with a healthy physique, has an inquisitive seriousness in his eyes suggesting he is not easily deterred from his target. Fate seemed to agree.

At the Justus Liebig University in Giessen, Professor Dr. Gerald Romsa, knowing of Pletsch's desire to go to North America, had suggested he apply for a posted position at the University of Regina. Pletsch applied in 1982 but failed to get it.

Meanwhile, Alfred Hecht was serving one of his three terms as chair of the Geography Department at Laurier. He had a grand plan to offer someone in Germany a one-year visiting professor position at Laurier. Through mutual contacts including Romsa, Hecht and Pletsch were connected in the spring of 1983. The timing was perfect.

Alfred Hecht was going back to Germany in late April of 1983 for another summer teaching position at Marburg. Upon his arrival, Alfred Hecht met with Pletsch. They met at the Justus Liebig University in Giessen, a twenty-five-minute drive down the road from Marburg.

They hit it off right away. Shared academic interests were well matched and their personalities even more so. It didn't take long and an agreement was made. Pletsch would go to WLU as a Visiting Assistant Professor for two terms—Fall 1983 and Winter 1984 and Hecht would introduce him to Canada.

The Hecht family returned from Germany at the beginning of September and immediately began introducing the Pletsch family to Canadian life. Over the course of the following eight months this included the usual accoutrements of maple syrup, flap jacks and fashionable toques.

Pletsch remembered a night-time horse-drawn sleigh-ride organized by an Old Order Mennonite family and a baptism at Hecht's church.

At the time, Alfred Hecht was serving as chair of the Geography Department at Laurier and Pletsch recalled that "he did his job as chairman in an always responsible way and he was 100% reliable."

Pletsch also wrote about his time in Canada, "Although Canada and Germany belong to the Western culture, some ideas of how university is working, are different."

The Pletsch family first returned to Germany at the end of April 1984. Forty years later, in 2024, Alfred Pletsch, a Member of the Marburg Centre of Canadian Studies at Philipps University and Professor Emeritus in the Department of Geography, was still giving lectures at conferences and guiding local geography tours in Germany. Between 1984 and 2024 he had aged gracefully. Tall and thin, a receded hairline was marked by silver sides. Full eyebrows retained a brownish hue. He had square, metal-rimmed spectacles with thin arms. Wrinkles radiated to the sides of his eyes forming the frame of a deeply inquisitive, albeit friendly seriousness in his gaze. A chiselled, vertical jowl line stood sharp and firm with a weathered wisdom.

Between those years—1984 and 2024—a lot happened between Pletsch and Hecht. Back in 1984 when Pletsch had returned to Germany his teaching experience in Canada facilitated a promotion to a higher position at Philipps University. That gave him credentials which allowed the two Alfreds to go on to bigger and better things together.

At the end of the 1990s Hecht and Pletsch initiated a project called *The Virtual Geography Texts on Canada and Germany*.

Pletsch described it as "a kind of comparative regional studies textbook on Germany and Canada. The plan was to offer an information source for teachers and students on the internet, as a new information medium." It was translated into English, German and French.

Hecht remembered the trip he organized for Pletsch who wanted to take a group from Germany to Paraguay. "I came from North America and they (22 people) came to Asunción from Germany. We had rented a bus and we toured the Menno colonies in the Chaco." To get there, they had to drive from Asunción to the Mennonite colonies nearly five hundred kilometres north, over what is essentially a flat monotonous continental-sized floodplain.

"Once you cross the Paraguay River (heading out of Asunción), until you get to the Menno colonies, there is nothing. It's only scrub forest and very flat. If it rained the cattle grazed in the water," Hecht said.

Pletsch and his tour group were not fully prepared for the stifling homogeneity of the Chaco.

Hecht chuckled a little as he remembered that in Europe, when Pletsch and other academics did bus tours, everyone on the bus would switch sides so there was an equal opportunity for a good view. On this drive from Asunción to the Menno colonies, "After about 150 kilometres Pletsch gets on the bus microphone and says, 'We don't need to change today.'"

That unassuming first meeting in Giessen would foster a friendship between Hecht and Pletsch that would last more than forty years.

Pletsch's unwavering interest and research in Canada throughout his career was officially recognized by Canada itself. Alfred Pletsch was the first recipient to receive the John G. Diefenbaker Prize from the Canada Council for the Arts.

Strangely, Pletsch's interest in Canada forced Hecht to make friends with two other men—one, a billionaire boilermaker, and the other, a man who had never driven an automobile and wouldn't allow his picture to be taken.

29. The BOILERMAKER

It would be fair to describe Dr. Hans Viessmann as the boilermaker since his company was producing 80% of all the boilers and heating systems in the European market.

Hans Viessmann originally took over his father's boilermaking business after WWII when it had only two employees at the time. He introduced series production and modern manufacturing processes which expanded Viessmann Werke GmBH & Co. KG to an operation that had 1,400 employees by the 1970s. Branch plants outside Germany were built at Faulquemont in France and one in Waterloo, Ontario in 1987.

Expansion was good but Viessmann's boilers had a big problem at the beginning. They were rusting too quickly much to the chagrin of customers. Viessmann was determined to make a better product. He needed to figure out why his boilers were rusting. At the time, Krupp Stahl (Krupp Steelworks) was producing the boilers and Viessmann was getting frustrated with them. When Viessmann would ask why his boilers were rusting, Krupp didn't have an answer, only excuses. So Viessmann partnered with the Chemistry Department at Philipps University Marburg to see if they could figure out what was wrong.

"(The university) had a new device that took pictures of the steel in the boilers. They were able to show him all these little dots inside. There was either water or air trapped...and it caused them to corrode and start leaking. He took the picture to Krupp Stahl to talk to the head. He said, 'How much business do I do with you guys?'" Alfred remembered Hans Viessmann telling the story.

Viessmann produced the evidence from the university's research that indicated Krupp Stahl's facilities were contaminated.

In a stern voice Viessmann told the head of Krupp Stahl, "You're producing steel in an unclean environment. I insist you clean the environment."

Krupp Stahl's facilities appeared to be impeccably clean so they couldn't understand at first how there could be contamination in their factory. They suspected the air might be the problem so they draped a sealed covering over the entire facility, suctioned out all the air and put clean filtered air back in.

"That solved the problem," said Alfred.

Micro flecks of airborne material were contaminating the steel surface during the production process. Once they put air filters in place, "his boilers were never corroding," Alfred said.

The Viessmann company continued to innovate and expand its product line.

In Europe, heating systems ran hot water through pipes which give off radiant heat. It's efficient in terms of heat transfer but it's costly in terms of the physical infrastructure, with the vast network of piping that corrodes and must be replaced at great expense.

In North America, heating systems pumped hot air. It was not nearly as efficient in a thermodynamic sense as the European systems but it was much simpler. Viessmann looked at North America and realized his company could improve upon the system and then introduce it to Europe. He began producing free-standing heating units with a focus on making them as small as possible.

"For Germany, they developed a standing oven downstairs that radiated heat out and rose to upper stories. It got so good they condensed it down so it could hang on the wall. It worked perfectly. With all this technology, they have 80% of business for heating homes and apartments (but) the main thing was he always believed in cooperation between business and university centres," Alfred explained.

This is where Alfred Hecht and Hans Viessmann were introduced.

In the early 1980s, Hecht and fellow researchers received a major grant of 248,000 DM (C$176,600) from the Volkswagen Foundation of Germany to study "Ethnicity Problems in Central Canada." The research team included Dr. Alfred Pletsch, Dr. Ludger Müller-Wille from McGill University in Montreal and Gerald Romsa from Windsor, as well as a number of Canadian and German students.

In the same time period, Pletsch and Hecht had been organizing workshops and symposia in both Canada and Germany. At one of the early ones in Germany, Walter Kröll, President of Marburg University, who later become the head of the European Space Agency, asked if there was interest in setting up a partnership between Laurier and Philipps to foster increased cooperation.

When the idea was first proposed to President John Wier at Laurier, he stressed the need for money if anything was going to happen. He certainly didn't have any himself.

Kröll approached Viessmann, whose company was near Marburg.

Viessmann actually knew the city of Waterloo well, having set up a major branch plant there a few years earlier. It didn't take long for him to pledge money for students at Laurier to travel abroad. It was funding that satisfied President Weir's needs. The Viessmann pledge got the ball rolling.

By 2005, roughly seventy Laurier students had gone to Philipps University Marburg in Germany to study. A slightly larger number of Marburg students came to Laurier. Twenty faculty and staff were also involved in the exchange program. The Viessmann Group has honoured their pledge ever since.

Philanthropy went well but Viessmann's innovations and other business ideas weren't always as successful. At one point, Viessmann noticed that during the shipping process, wooden pallets, used as the shipping tray for everything from appliances to water bottles, would sometimes break, and often damage his products. He not only wanted to fix the problem, he wanted to revolutionize the shipping pallet industry. He wondered if the wood could be replaced with another material.

"He got the pallet suppliers together and explained that egg cartons are made of compressed cardboard. He wanted something similar instead of a wooden pallet," Alfred explained.

But when the research team reported back, Viessmann was not thrilled.

"I was there," Alfred said. "Viessmann asked me to come by one day (but) he was busy. I had to wait on the side (and) watch. Viessmann pushed these guys…pretty hard."

The two men said, "We tried different combinations. Either you can compress it or you can suck all the air out of it and it compresses itself, but we cannot give it the strength that is needed to be equal to a normal pallet." The meeting ended without any solutions. The next time Alfred saw Hans Viessmann he asked, "How's the pallet business?"

"We had to give up," Viessmann replied.

Technology was not up to the task of replacing the common pallet and even more importantly the Russian market had opened up. With vast forests in Siberia, pine lumber was not only strong enough to make pallets, it was cheap enough to do at mass scale. Pallet production with western European wood, where very little forest remained, was quickly undercut on price. Viessmann dropped his innovation plans for pallets and negotiated a deal with the Russians instead.

"It's interesting that the business world lives on innovation," Alfred mused. "If you can beat the competition by process and quality, you win. If you can't do it, stick with the old stuff."

Hecht was so impressed with Viessmann that he recommended Wilfred Laurier University give Hans Viessmann an honorary degree.

Laurier agreed.

Hans Viessmann already had an honorary degree that was bestowed in 1982 by Philipps University Marburg. Laurier give him the second honorary degree in 1993. At the WLU ceremonies, Alfred Hecht "put the hood and the scarf" over Dr. Hans Viessmann.

As far as German salutation protocols were concerned, Dr. Hans Viessmann could now call himself Herr Dr. Dr. Hans Viessmann. In fine German tradition he could demand that he be addressed as such, which he never failed to insist upon thereafter.

Viessmann wasn't alone. Alfred Hecht had also received an honorary degree from Freie University Berlin in 2000 and could thus technically, in line with German salutation protocol, call himself Herr Professor Dr. Dr. (h.c.) Alfred Hecht. But leaning on Canadian customs and expectations, he rarely referred to himself that way in Canada. In Germany, it was a different matter. Different countries, different customs, different greetings.

Alfred Hecht and Hans Viessmann became close acquaintances if not outright friends. Viessmann had the money and Alfred had the vision for how to spend it.

Alfred was extraordinarily grateful to have Viessmann paying for students' travel abroad but Hecht wanted more. He saw the need for a research centre so one day, he went to Viessmann's castle in Hof, Germany and over a few good glasses of wine, he asked for money.

Viessmann replied, "How much do you want?"

Alfred gave a number.

"Too high."

Alfred dropped *the ask* too low.

Viessmann countered by simply giving Alfred what he needed in order to get the research centre up and running at Laurier. *The Viessmann Research Centre on Modern Europe* at Wilfred Laurier University was founded in 2001.

Viessmann's philanthropic ventures extended late into his life although he handed company operations over to his son Martin, in 1991. Martin Viessmann took the family business to even greater heights. Hans Viessmann's grandson Maximilian Viessmann went even further and is currently the CEO. Maximilian Viessmann was ranked in 2024 by Forbes magazine as one of the globe's influential billionaires.

Hans Viessmann died March 30, 2002.

30. HORSE & BUGGY MENNONITES

Alfred is a mainline Mennonite not a horse-and-buggy Mennonite.

There are now at least forty-eight different branches of Mennonites in southern Ontario alone. The most traditional with horse-and-buggy are fairly numerous but also quite insular. They keep to themselves.

Architecture helps differentiate the groups. Conventional Christian denominations meet in churches. This is pointing out the obvious.

What's not so obvious is that the fundamentalist and most Orthodox Mennonites such as the Amish meet in the living room of someone's house or barn. The Old Order have meeting houses. Unlike the recognizable architecture of churches, meeting houses are easily overlooked. They are unadorned, plain, utilitarian and easily mistaken for a barn or warehouse. Inside a meeting house, one will find the more obvious markings of a congregation, albeit one beholden to the tenets of simplicity and sacrifice. They have hard pews, cold floors and long sermons.

Alfred and Linda belonged to the Waterloo Mennonite Brethren (MB) Church—a mainline Mennonite group. Alfred was a former Moderator at the church from 1983 to 1986 and a Board Member of the Mennonite Brethren Conference during the same period. Prior to that he was also a member of the Eden Christian College Board from 1980 to 1983. He did confess to me that he let his membership lapse. Even though he was a leading advocate to have one of the four Kitchener-Waterloo Mennonite churches built, the commitment to the church was sometimes more challenging than expected.

"Church politics is worse than university politics," he said.

Aside from politics, memberships and commitment, he could rightly call himself a true Mennonite.

Pletsch didn't agree.

After Pletsch had returned to Germany, Hecht and Pletsch kept in touch and one day, Pletsch said, "Hey, I'm scheduled to give a paper on Mennonites and need help."

Alfred replied, "I'm a Mennonite!"

Pletsch said, "No, not you." He wanted to talk to a horse-and-buggy Mennonite not a suburban mainline Mennonite.

Alfred would have to help his friend in a different way. He obliged and set off on a sketchy mission one Sunday morning. The plan was to find an Orthodox Mennonite that would be willing to talk to Pletsch. There were plenty of Old Order, David Martin, Amish and others in the area. Many were not more than a fifteen-minute drive from Alfred's house. The only problem was that Alfred didn't know any of them personally.

So, the next Sunday morning after his conversation with Pletsch, Alfred took Marvin and Melinda with him and the three of them went for a drive down country roads until they found a randomly chosen meeting house. They parked and went inside.

"We went to one where the service was just going to start. The usher said 'Come on in.'" The seats were wooden and austere, purposefully devoid of frivolous things including cushions or padding.

"Everybody looked at us," Alfred remembered. "We just followed. When they said it is prayer time, everybody (knelt down) and so did we. They had three preachers. It took nearly three hours. You had to be there by 9:00 a.m. We were out at twelve."

As they neared the exit a conservative Mennonite man dressed all in black walked over and asked, "Can I invite you to lunch at our place?"

"Sure. Why not," Alfred replied as they introduced themselves and walked outside. Alfred pointed and said, "My car is over there."

The man, named Amon Weber, replied with a grin, "Good. Follow my buggy. Marvin can come with us. We have room for one more person."

At Weber's farmhouse, "We got there and it was a day where people could come over. Among the Old Order Mennonites you don't know who is coming for dinner. It's self-invitation. So we went there and Amon's wife Mary was setting the dishes on the table. We had juice, mashed potatoes and white bread. They always bought white bread the day after it was due so it was half price."

"They had a visiting pastor, a cousin of Amon Weber," Alfred said describing the table setting. "I was at his end. Melinda on my right. We talked back and forth...the men. Nobody else said a word, you know, and then when we finished eating," Amon said, "Shall we go over to the visiting room?"

The men went while the women washed dishes in the kitchen.

"Their oldest boy came with us," Alfred added.

Alfred and Amon hit it off and from that time forward Alfred would drop in regularly at the farm. Sometimes Linda would join him, mostly to visit with Mary.

In fact, one day Alfred took me out to visit with Amon and Mary.

We took the VW SUV from Kitchener-Waterloo and headed north fifteen minutes where we went through the original Mennonite settlement of St. Jacobs and then on to Elmira, which was another fifteen kilometres up the road. Just north of Elmira, Alfred turned off the two-lane highway and into the driveway of an immaculate but spartan farmyard.

Out back was an aluminum-clad building with a small furniture-making business. We walked into that building unannounced and were greeted by noisy sanders and planers, operated by Amon's son Oscar and another youthful man named Luke.

Oscar took us up to a small loft office where the noise could be shut out and business discussed. We soon learned that economics were driving them out. They had sold the furniture business to Luke, who'd gone back to sanding.

Amon and Mary, plus Oscar and his wife Christine and their seven children, were in the process of moving their operations north. They were going to Kirkland Lake, Ontario which is almost 700 kilometres north and ten degrees colder. The growing season is so much shorter, in fact, that corn barely has a chance to reach full maturity.

"We can grow it for silage but not for cobs," Oscar reported.

Corn yields dominated the conversation and Oscar eventually admitted, "I'm still not sure it's the right thing to do."

After the hot coffee and mild confession we went over to the main house to see Amon and Mary.

Amon, at 86, looked young for his age. He wore dark suspenders that held up black pants suited to church and field. He had a moderate walk and an extroverted personality that paired well with Alfred's persona. The two bantered back and forth across the table.

Picture books filled with images of Mennonites in South America lay on the wooden surface of the table, which offered too much intrigue not to thumb through. Brilliant photos and imagined worlds of serenity captured my attention.

As the conversation came to an end, Amon proudly suggested we look at his new acquisition—a brand new buggy.

Out we went.

In the carport, there it was. A black, narrow, sport model buggy made for a single horse to pull.

Amon's religious beliefs did not allow the taking of personal pictures. The fundamentalist Mennonites can neither take pictures nor have their picture taken. Pictures of things including buggies were fine, so I snapped a few of the buggy and none of him and then we promptly left. On the drive back Alfred offered answers to the usual questions.

"What about inbreeding?"

"Yeah, sometimes it's a problem." There was a known propensity for Orthodox Mennonites to have a higher rate of problems with eyesight than the general population.

Back at Alfred's house, he pulled out a family tree diagram of the Mennonite lineage for the past five hundred years. There were the Old Order, the Old Colony, the Beachy, the Amish, the Mennonite Brethren, the David Martin group and more. Almost fifty in total.

It was interesting that here were Alfred and Linda who were more liberal and very much Canadian in the broad sense of that term. They had gone down the route of cultural assimilation while Amon and his family followed a path of isolation.

Like biological evolution that is in a constant state of divergence, it was all such a splendid example of the forces that are constantly underway within any nation. In one instance there is an ethnic creation *in situ*—the formation of new identities through the splintering of what exists. At the same time there is assimilation into the larger group. Divergence is how we ended up with French, Italian and Spanish from Latin. Assimilation is how Breton, Occitan and a multitude of smaller languages merged into French.

Kitchener-Waterloo was a perfect microcosm of all the cultural questions, possibilities, and relationships that could exist and that Canada has had to grapple with since the beginning.

For Alfred, the religious heritage his family had come from was all around him. Yet, in order to be re-acquainted with that side of himself, it took a man from the outside—Alfred Pletsch—to ask for a favour.

In the end, Weber talked to Pletsch and added information to the lecture but it was arguably Alfred Hecht who gained the most in the end—a life-long friend down the road, just a buggy ride away.

31. BERLIN WALL, 1989

It was the first week in November of 1989. Hecht and Pletsch were eating in the dining room at their hotel in Berlin.

"We'd brought our students to the Alexander von Humbolt Institution to give presentations." While eating and talking, "these guys overheard us speaking English and they came over." They were East Germans and they didn't waste time confessing their thoughts about the country they lived in. What they said startled Hecht. East Berlin was apparently on the cusp of a shocking moment that would change the history of the world.

East Germany had been a virtual prison from 1957 onward when the physical apparatus of containment—barbed wire and guard towers—was first constructed. It wasn't enough to prevent people from escaping in the early years. They began construction in August 1961 of a concrete wall 155 kilometres long, encircling the entirety of West Berlin. It was completed a short time later. For the next twenty years the Berlin Wall appeared to be permanent and impenetrable.

The division into East Berlin and West Berlin at the end of the war affected one of the world's great academic institutions—Humbolt University of Berlin. Generally regarded as the world's preeminent university in the natural sciences throughout the 19th and 20th centuries, it was originally founded in 1810. Named in 1949, it honoured German polymath, geographer, naturalist and explorer Alexander von Humbolt and his founding brother, German philosopher and diplomat, Wilhelm von Humbolt. The university was famous among geographers as the pinnacle of research and collections in all things geography related.

During the Cold War, Humbolt University was placed firmly under East Germany's control and as a puppet state of the Soviet Union, East Germany was under communist ideology.

Communist ideology strangled Humbolt.

Teaching at Humbolt University suffered so badly under communist control that it was concluded in the West, there was no way of fixing it. A mirror institution was set up on the free, capitalist side in West Berlin. Freie Universität Berlin (Free University of Berlin) opened in 1948 and was tasked with searching for truth.

The emotional heart of the German people remained attached to the splendour and history of the original Humbolt University campus located in East Berlin.

During Alfred Hecht's time as a visiting professor between 1976 and 1989, going between Freie University in Berlin, Philips University in Marburg and Justus Liebig University in Giessen, he spent a considerable amount of time in West Germany, he'd also spent time travelling back and forth between West Germany and West Berlin through communist-controlled East Germany.

Once, as Alfred and Linda drove back from West Berlin, they made a bad decision.

Westerners were supposed to stay on one of three designated roadways as they made passage through tightly controlled East Germany. This time Alfred changed his mind along the way. He wanted to exit East Germany close to his desired destination in the West, instead of exiting far south and then having to drive north again. Why not just cut off some distance through East Germany and cover ground along the short side of the triangle, he thought? His official permission slip did not allow it but it seemed harmless enough.

At the border, Alfred's change of plan was not well received by the East German border guard. As far as the guard was concerned, Alfred had driven through territory for which he was not given permission and for all he knew, Alfred could be a spy who was surreptitiously dropping off, or picking up, confidential information or maybe even weapons.

The 1976 Montreal Olympics were going on in Canada at that very moment.

After being stiff with stern questions, the East German guard mentioned that the German athletes were doing better than the Canadians at the Olympic Games, at which point he cracked a dry smile, and let the family go.

They carried on but it was a lesson that impressed upon Alfred the rigid character of the East German state and its iron grip and control over the most mundane things, such as deciding which public road one chooses to travel on. A decade later, restrictions to visit East Germany had begun to ease. Alfred took full advantage.

An International Geography Conference was organized and guests were invited from around the world to attend in the fall of 1989, in East Berlin. The East German government was cracking the door open to the world. Hecht, and Pletsch, were eager to go. Together, they took nearly two dozen students to the conference held at the famous Humbolt University of Berlin.

Erich Honecker, the leader of East Germany, was still firmly in control. The imposing Berlin Wall still divided the people with its razor wire, machine-gun posts, guard towers, trip wires, attack dogs and deadly snipers. Or, so it appeared.

"Two years before, (my colleague at Marburg University had) said it would never come down," Alfred commented.

It looked to many as though the state of affairs was fixed in place forever. But, like most historical events the transition from one era to the next often comes suddenly in a dramatic spasm.

The East Germans that came over to the table that evening said, "It's finished." East Germany as a legitimate state was coming to an end, they said. And they were right! A few days later, on November 9, 1989, the government opened up travel to the West so that East Germans could visit family on the other side. A trickle of people turned up at the border at first but it soon turned into a flood and suddenly, the government could no longer contain their people.

The Wall fell that night and the state of East Germany came to an abrupt end. Eleven months later, East Germany and West Germany were united.

Now, the cleanup began.

32. EAST GERMANY CLEANUP

After the fall of the Berlin Wall, Alfred Hecht witnessed the cleanup operation in which East Germany underwent a transition from communism to capitalism, and Humbolt University regained its reputation.

It was not an easy transition but a necessary one.

Alfred returned to Philipps University in Marburg in June of 1990 and again from May–July, 1997 when he taught Canadian Studies. In the fall of 1997, he was back again in Germany. From October to March 1998 he was in the city of Hof and taught at the technical school (Fachhochschule). Here he also spent time with one of Laurier's great benefactors, Herr Viessmann.

During this entire period of the 1990s, with the considerable amount of time he spent in Germany he witnessed the dramatic changes as East Germany was united with West Germany—communism with capitalism.

"Travelling through East Germany when I did my research, I stayed usually in smaller cities" where quaint places adverted with nothing more than simple signs saying, "Room for Rent."

He often garnered the trust of former East Germans and was thus able to find out how the changes were affecting them.

"I frequently had a chat in the evening wherever I stayed in the household. You'd be surprised; after sometimes a beer or two they said, 'All these ex-Stazi and ex-East German government officials are all back!'"

Honecker stepped down in October 1989 and one month later with the fall of the Berlin Wall, sought asylum at the Chilean Embassy but was soon sent back to stand trial. In ill health, Honecker never faced a jury for the deadly repression he had instigated against his own people. He died in 1994. Many other officials of high rank switched to become members of Western political parties and went right back into the upper echelons of government as though nothing had happened.

The protests that brought the Wall down had begun with the church pastors and the average person. They had marched in East Berlin, Leipzig, Dresden and elsewhere until the pressure forced the East German government to grant travel passes that turned into the overwhelming flood of people at the border.

While the visually dramatic change appeared to result in the destruction of the regime, the apparatus of government was, in fact, extraordinarily entrenched. In the following years, a similar reality and similar outcome would take place in other east European countries from Romania to Serbia as well.

"It made a lot of people very angry," Alfred remembered.

While many government officials simply swapped labels, Humbolt University saw things differently. They couldn't afford to keep the old guard. They needed qualified people if they were going to regain credibility and attract good students.

The unified German people also saw Humbolt University as a symbol of Germany's more glorious academic past and they wanted that reputation restored.

"After unification the Germans were saying the main university should be Humbolt because it had a far longer tradition" than Freie University.

The German government altered its funding formula whereby each university was given the same amount of money instead of giving funds on a per-student basis. It favoured Humbolt, which had fewer students at the time than Freie University. One of the first things Humbolt did was root out former communists and East German collaborators. Not so much because they disliked communists but because they were incredibly incompetent teachers.

Humbolt created a small task force that was meant to find and remove the existing low-quality professors and those associated with the former East German state apparatus.

"Eckart Ehlers was one of them," Alfred said of the three henchmen that were about to clean things up in the field of geography and environmental science. "I knew him from Marburg. Him and two other guys did the examination of the geography profs in East German states."

Alfred knew a thing or two about the situation. Prior to the fall of the Wall, "because I was in Germany, I went to many of the meetings of the German professors' association. There was always one East German guy. I (always) was surprised to see him."

How was this guy able to get permission to leave East Germany so often in order to attend conferences?

Alfred explained that "Eckart Ehlers got ahold of the Stazi list." Lo and behold, the man was a high-ranking Stazi member (East Germany's Secret Police), which explained why he was able to leave East Germany so easily pre-1989 and travel to university meetings in West Germany.

"Naturally he got canned right away. His licence to teach in eastern Germany was cut off." Alfred expanded by mentioning that the actions were less about retribution and "in large part because they didn't recognize East German graduate degrees—they were highly communist-indoctrinated."

It wasn't always easy to tell who was genuinely indoctrinated and sympathetic to the communist ideology and who'd simply gone along in order to safely march up the social ladder. Looking at someone's previous teaching credentials and their CVs didn't help either.

Among East German professors, "nearly all the CVs started off, 'We thank Karl Marx and his contribution to society…'" Alfred began explaining. "I talked to one guy (and) he said you couldn't get anywhere if you didn't put that in. It's like a subtitle after a name."

It was not unlike parallels with Western universities today where ideological statements are attached to CVs. Pandering academics at nearly every post-secondary institution in the West, with pronouns and land acknowledgements in their biographies, are reminiscent of those darker times in communist East Germany, not to mention the Soviet Union. Compared to the current culture wars in the West, East Germany was different only in detail and timing but certainly not in its ideological circus performance. Humbolt University in the 1990s wanted nothing to do with the rot of ideological propaganda. It sanitized things quickly.

Once the communists were gone, "Humbolt University pulled itself out pretty fast. Western profs got in and research went up," Alfred said proudly.

33. RECONCILIATION with MOTHER RUSSIA

All went well with Mother Russia upon Alfred Hecht's first return in 1976. In fact, the strained relationship, like two badly betrayed lovers reconnecting under a new and recommitted relationship, began to blossom in the 1990s.

At that time the Russians went looking for Professor Hecht. They needed his help. The Soviet Union had collapsed and was in need of economic assistance and professional advice.

"The Canadian International Development Agency (CIDA) gave $20 million to help Russia change from a so-called planned economy to a market economy. You couldn't use the term 'communist' because they would feel down-graded," Alfred grinned. "It was a planned economy. Unfortunately, they couldn't plan."

"Under that umbrella, I had five contracts to work with Russians. If they wanted to have something done in Siberia, for example, they would say it falls under 'Regional Development' (and so they had) to find a Canadian academic who had done something like this. I had done some in Canada with one of my students. In fact, we published that (at the) University of Marburg."

The person could work in Russia while Alfred could compare from Canada.

"The interesting thing is that for all the geography projects, I was the financial guy! CIDA did not allow us to pay the Russians directly. They set up an account in Germany, and I paid them in Deutsch Marks. It was a weird set up. I think it was highly corrupt in Russia and this was one of the ways the actual researchers got the money. When I worked with PhD students, the advisors got a chunk, that was fair."

"I got to know a number of PhD students. In fact, one of the donors to our charity who (now) lives in Washington State, I got to know at that time. We kept in contact; when he applied to the University of

Washington he gave me as a reference (and because) he was a great scholar he got in. That's when he got his PhD. He is now on the faculty there."

While Boris Yeltsin was the President of Russia there was, "a bright man of Jewish decent helping Yeltsin. But then he got fired because all the oligarchs were out of jobs," Alfred explained. "But Yeltsin gave him some money to set up the 'Institute of an Economy In Transition.' We worked through this institute and because of that I got to go to Russia: St. Petersburg, Odessa, Moscow, Novgorod and the big military complex southwest of Moscow. A military production base—tanks." Alfred clarified that "On this trip they said, 'No photographs!'"

The relationship with Russia was becoming friendlier. The past was the past. All was forgiven, at least for those who worked together in academia. But the military was another matter entirely.

Kaliningrad is an important enclave of the Soviet Union squeezed between Lithuania and Poland on the Baltic Sea. It is an ice-free port making it extremely important as a Russian naval base. It was occupied by the Soviet Army during WWII, and never relinquished. At the end of the war only Lithuanian citizens were allowed to remain.

For much of its history Kaliningrad was an important Old Prussian/German settlement originally established by the Teutonic Knights, which they named Konigsberg in 1946. All German citizens were expelled. Russians were brought in to repopulate the city and make it ethnically Russian, not German. The name was changed to Kaliningrad. It has remained an important Russian military outpost ever since.

"Kaliningrad, I went there twice," said Alfred.

He had been invited as an economic geographer to tour Kaliningrad with hopes Alfred might be helpful in the economic transition of the former Soviet Union to a more profitable system. Immanuel Kant Baltic Federal University in Kaliningrad asked Alfred to give a lecture.

"So, I come into this class of maybe sixty or eighty. The guy says to me, 'Most of them know English from listening to the BBC or Finnish radio. (Just) speak slowly.' So I did. They were well informed on what was happening in the West and yearning to go there."

But Kaliningrad exists in an awkward geographic dilemma.

"It was shut off from Russia. Consequently, they had to fly or go through Poland and Lithuania," so in many ways their interactions were more with the West than Russia.

"I talked to some of the senior people in government as well as in industry. In one case, he was the head of the Russian military establishment, with an interpreter. I asked him, 'You are partly in Europe already. Most of your commodities are sold from the West, not Russia. Are you ever thinking of separating from Russia and joining the West?'"

Alfred's eyes popped a little as he relived it.

"Wow! That hit a nerve. He said, 'We fought a big war against the Nazis. This is our payback. We will never give it up!'"

In spite of emotional sentiment, the economic situation of Kaliningrad was problematic for Russia. Businesses had to ship all commodities and foodstuffs from the West. Russia didn't produce enough nor produce it consistently. Consistency, being the backbone necessity to run a military operation, was wanting. The civilian population wasn't of much concern to authorities but the military personnel absolutely required consistent feeding to maintain loyalty.

"Eggs. There was no way you could get them from Russia on a steady basis," Alfred noted.

The Russian military commander did admit, "The West is very reliable. If they say they are going to give me twenty boxes of eggs, they will deliver."

Alfred prodded him. "How come not Russia?"

The reply he got was, "Russia does not have infrastructure. There are no connections between producers and consumers."

Alfred explained. "The Russian mentality is, you have an acre-and-a-half where you produce all the goods for yourself. No supplies. If you have extra potatoes, you could maybe do something extra. Perhaps make a little whiskey or vodka but otherwise the mentality is one of self-sufficiency."

The Russian landscape mirrored the cultural paradigm.

"The train from St. Petersburg to Volgograd was maybe thirteen hours. Watching the countryside, you could see these little villages and farms that were cultivated but the rest (of the landscape) was bush." The lack of agricultural production for profit was missing and it explained a lot to Alfred as he saw Russia through the eyes of an economic geographer.

It wasn't the only train ride through Russia. Hecht also went with a contingent of fellow researchers from St. Petersburg to Novgorod where a boat on Lake Ilmen, with Russian researchers, had been hired for a celebration.

"Our guide from Canada with CIDA organized it all. She could speak Russian." She told them to spread out and mingle with the Russians. "We gathered in little groups of five. One Canadian, four Russians and usually with a translator. I was talking to a group. They had been drinking already. Russians drink like crazy. It's an old saying, but I saw it firsthand. They can hold the liquor pretty good. They said, 'We really hate Gorbachev. I know you guys in the West love him because he got rid of communism but it meant we are no longer on the top of the pecking list. We don't get the high salaries anymore. We now have to do research.'"

"Wow, were they angry at him. They said, 'We were an empire but now we are dependent on a little country like Canada to get paid to do…research.'"

34. LAURIER INTERNATIONAL[16]

Living in another country, having to speak another language and meeting a cohort of fellow students from a different culture is an educational experience like no other.

Alfred, having experienced the reality of living in vastly different cultures and circumstances, some quite dire, understood this all too well. If he could find a way to help students have similar experiences, at least the positive ones, through a study abroad opportunity, he would.

On December 14th, 1984, President John Weir of Wilfred Laurier University and President Walter Kröll of Philipps University in Marburg, Germany signed a co-operative agreement that would facilitate an annual exchange of four students from each country. It was Laurier's first international co-operative agreement and Hecht had a lot to do with it.

As mentioned previously, in the summer of 1972 Alfred had joined WLU as an Associate Professor. Then in 1975, the question of tenure loomed and he wasn't sure if he would get it so he went looking for another job elsewhere, just in case.

He turned down an initial off from the John F. Kennedy Institute at the Free University of Berlin but in lieu of, went as a visiting professor during the summer semester of 1976, which set the wheels in motion.

The head of the North American geographic studies was Professor Dr. Karl Lenz, who happened to be a graduate of Philipps University in Marburg, Germany. He had introduced Pletsch to Hecht. The two hit it off and were soon organizing conferences and obtaining large research grants together. At one of the symposia, the President of Philipps University asked if they would be interested in creating a formalized partnership between the universities that would foster further cooperation. John Wier, President of Wilfred Laurier University, had responded by mentioning there wasn't money for that purpose.

So back in Marburg, President Walter Kröll went looking for money. He approached Viessmann. Since Viessmann had established a small branch plant in Waterloo in 1987, he was well aware of the city and its universities.

Viessmann agreed to "provide a travel scholarship of 1,500 DM (C$1,000) to the best Canadian student coming to Marburg on a student exchange. This pledge was good enough for John Wier, and the cooperation agreement went into effect in 2005. Around seventy Laurier students had studied for a semester or more at Marburg. A slightly larger number of Marburg students came to Laurier. In addition about twenty faculty and staff exchanges took place."

"Mr. Viessmann's generosity to Laurier was not restricted to travel scholarships for exchange students. In 1991 he donated $13,000 to support the work of the European Faculty Interest Group at Laurier" of which Alfred was the chair. In 1996, at Viessmann's castle in Hof, Germany Viessmann also donated another $9,000 during the day. And then in the evening, as Alfred remembered, "over a glass of wine in the castle library, he announced he was setting up two endowment funds at Laurier, selecting from a list of options I had given him, one for exchange students from Laurier going to Europe (C$100,000) and one for the Geography Department to upgrade software and hardware in campus renovations. At another meeting on January 30, 2001, again over a glass of excellent wine he asked me how much I wanted for further projects."

Viessman gave 400,000 DM (C$284,000) to set up the Viessmann European Research Centre at Laurier.

Collaboration with the universities led to Viessmann's company acquiring over 1,300 patents.

"For this achievement Laurier awarded him an honorary doctorate in 1991," Alfred explained.

The signing of Laurier's first international agreement also led to participation in two Ontario-wide student exchange agreements, "one with Rhone-Alps, France and the other with Baden-Wurttemberg, Germany."

During this period Alfred stepped in and administered the German exchanges while the French Department administered those in France. In the 1994–95 academic year, under the guidance of Vice-President: Academic Rowland Smith, the university created Laurier International (LINT).

Laurier International "inherited the institution-to-institution relationship with Marburg, as well as the Ontario programs, a study program in Nice (run by a number of Ontario universities), and a three-year Canada-EU multicentre program. The first staff person was Karen Strang and the first director was Frank Turner, followed by Anne Murray."

In the summer of 1999, Rowland Smith appointed Alfred as Director of Laurier International and International Liaison. Hecht got a new office, a reprieve from some of his teaching load, two staff members and the task of expanding the international component at WLU.

"According to Laurier tradition, the budget was small," Alfred said.

Sending students abroad was only half the equation. The other half was setting up the agreements with partnering and hosting universities. It wasn't always easy. Smooth relationships and big reputations played a significant role in determining who to work with and who to avoid.

"Agreement could be initiated by Laurier, but frequently we were responding to requests from institutions abroad. To come to an agreement required a good fit. Also important was the potential partners' academic reputation. In 2005, nineteen of our partner institutions were ranked in the top 500 universities worldwide (unfortunately we were not). Of our partner institutions, forty-four were in Europe, ten in the Americas, eight in Asia, two in Australia and one in Africa."

"By 2005 the total number of Laurier students studying abroad had increased more than eightfold, from fourteen in 1995 to 117 in 2005, an increase that far surpassed the doubling of full-time undergraduate students over the same period."

Laurier International was given the responsibility after 1999 of also coordinating international student recruitment. International enrollment increased from 224 students to 688 four years later in the 2004–05 academic year.

President Bob Rosehart stated, during meetings with President Lehman from the University for Applied Sciences in Hof, Germany and

Vice-President Mr. Yoshio from Akita International University in Japan, that Laurier's "goal was that 10% of graduating students would have an international experience."

In the 2004–05 academic year 2,580 students graduated from Laurier with 277 being involved in an international experience. That was 10.74% of all the students. In the last semester of 2005, on the cusp of Alfred's retirement from Laurier, that number had risen to 12.96% of all graduates. They hit the target, and more.

More students than the school had planned would gain the enormous benefits of studying and travelling beyond Canada. And as Alfred wrote in the book, *I Remember Laurier: Reflections by Retirees on Life at Laurier*, "as anyone who had studied abroad will testify, the effect of living and studying in another culture, often in another language, is incalculable and lasts a lifetime."

35. BEHIND the BACK of BUREAUCRACY

The graduate program was doing well. Laurier International was doing well. All seemed rosy but in truth a new threat was looming on the horizon that bedevilled the geography profession and threatened to undermine its very existence.

Technology was changing the world and nowhere was that more evident than in the realm of maps and geography.

Geography schools had been teaching cartography—the art and science of designing, reading and using maps—since the age of Aristotle. But at the end of the 20th century, new technologies were upending the entire profession of maps, travel, wayfinding, and geography in general. The age of the smart phone and Google maps was only in its infancy in the 1990s but those who could see the future, knew they had to change and do so, quickly. Those that didn't were going to be left behind.

In Germany, the Marburg Geographical Society, affiliated with the university's Geography Department, housed in spectacular architectural buildings used by the Teutonic Knights in the 15th century as their headquarters, was a leading institution in cartography and mapping.

Alfred Pletsch not only taught geography here, he was intimately connected to the Marburg Geographical Society. In other words, he had direct insight into what was happening.

"(Pletsch) was teaching map reading (and) he said no student was taking that anymore. GIS has replaced it," Alfred Hecht recalled.

Hecht had also noticed the same thing happening at Laurier. Student enrollment in the classic cartography and map-reading courses had fallen off a cliff. GIS was the new thing.

"Grant Head, our cartographer and map reader, when GIS came in, was too old to do it," Alfred said of a colleague that couldn't keep up.

From the outset, Alfred Hecht knew he had to move the Geography Department into alignment with the new technology.

"We switched from cartography to GIS. Poor Grant was out of a course but Bob Sharpe was very good with computers and GIS," Alfred said.

The switch from cartography to GIS wasn't as easy as it sounded. At the beginning, they needed to actually have GIS courses on offer but the administration, like most bureaucracy, was averse to change in the way a pauper is averse to wealth. Hecht had to get the new GIS courses through the back door somehow, without the administration noticing.

"We thought (maybe) some progressive high schools wanted their students to learn GIS. So we offered a course in GIS, Friday night and Saturday (and then) we created a phoney diploma." It didn't take long and "the Geography Department was making good money on this but we never informed the university."

It was just a matter of time before Hecht would get caught.

"One day the Dean calls me in and said, 'I hear you're running programs on Friday and Saturday. Is the instructor getting credit?'"

Hecht admitted, "No, he teaches his normal classes. This is extra."

"Well, maybe the university should get a cut because you're using university property," the Dean told Hecht without belabouring the point.

"We ran it for about five years. Bob Sharpe made extra money and the Geography Department made a fair bit but then we had to shut it down and offered a normal university course instead."

It was a brilliant move.

With technology changes came the need for the Geography Department to change as well. Hecht, as chair, offered something innovative behind the back of bureaucracy and once it was popular, the administration couldn't afford to shut it down. All they could do was make it their own.

In the end, Hecht got GIS off the ground, students in the door and a foot planted firmly ahead of other universities.

"Would the administration have really said no to you?" I asked.

"The bureaucracy would never approve it. They would say, if it's not in our calendar then we can't offer it."

Alfred Hecht found a different way; a successful way, but not every project he took on met with the same success.

At the end of the 1990s, Alfred Hecht and his good friend Alfred Pletsch created *The Virtual Geography Texts on Canada and Germany*.

"At that time it was a really progressive idea to use the internet as a medium for school textbooks," Alfred Pletsch said of their online textbook.

But search engines such as Yahoo, Netscape Explorer and Google superseded the benefits of their online reference textbook.

Technology sometimes advanced faster than their best ideas but the ventures had the benefit of being catalysts to even more audacious projects in the future.

36. CONSCIENCE

"Linda, she can't make a decision," Alfred said as we sat in his home office mulling about and getting ready to meet a friend at a coffeeshop across town in an older neighbourhood. Alfred looked frustrated as he made the statement. He then caught the questioning look on my face.

"It's not out of a lack of love. It's not that," he replied.

He shuffled some papers on his desk and then shut down his computer.

"You know the trailer at the back?" he asked rhetorically, referring to a single-axle, open-box, work trailer that's small enough to pull behind an underpowered econobox. It was currently tipped on its side against a railing on the back deck.

"We got that from Linda's father" who fabricated it himself about twenty years ago. It had seen a lot of use and a lot of wear and tear. "It's useful but I've replaced the wooden sides three times already. I keep wanting to get rid of it. I could buy a metal one from Canadian Tire that would last longer and never fall apart but Linda won't let me get rid of it. Well, this year, she finally said, 'Okay, you can sell it.'"

"After twenty years?" I ask incredulously.

"Yes," he said letting out a puff of exasperation.

"I'm more someone that likes to get rid of things that I no longer need. A simple desk, one computer, a coffee cup and nothing else."

He looked around and squinted as he recognized he wasn't being completely truthful with himself.

His office was not the minimalist reality he'd just described. A bookshelf against the back wall was full but without the tight, book-straight form of a minimalist organizer. The large office desk had small piles of paper waiting to be filed, or thrown out, and there was scant room on the desk top for a coffee cup.

Alfred looked around and slowly curled his lips back. He drew in a breath of air through the sides with a sucking hiss, as he realized his own contradiction. "Okay, maybe I need to clean up a little."

We got up and went off to meet his friend, a man named Dr. Barry Boots. He'd co-written and published a book called *Spatial Tesselations: Concepts and Applications of Voronoi Diagrams*. It had amassed close to 8,000 citations, which is a big deal in the academic world.

As we drove over Alfred went quiet. It was an odd silence from a man that usually loves to tell larger-than-life stories of which most are accurate. I figured he was about to tell a really long tall tale and wanted to give it a firm outline in his mind beforehand or he was about to admit something that troubled him and likewise, needed a moment to frame it with more care.

When he did finally start, he began by mentioning that he hired a new instructor while he was chair of the Geography Department and that student evaluations play a large role in determining whether to keep someone or let them go after a one semester probationary period.

"His evaluations came back and they were terrible," Alfred said as he drove on.

When Alfred met to discuss the matter with the new instructor a simple excuse was given. The man said he was sick and of course, that affected his performance but otherwise he would be a great teacher.

"Well, all I have are these evaluations to go on and they're not good, so I can't give you any more work," Alfred replied and then fired him the same way he would anyone else who didn't live up to expectations.

Rightfully so. Alfred was building a university department. The last thing he needed were instructors that drove students away.

But there was clearly more to the story.

The vehicle and a silence covered another block of asphalt before Alfred glanced over and said with a wince on his face, "The guy died seven months later from cancer."

"What! He was genuinely sick?"

"Yes, but I didn't know."

Another silence came over both of us for neither of us were willing to bring up the question of whether or not it should matter precisely because we were both wondering if it should. It's a tough question. How much leniency should be given for incompetence? What are reasonable grounds to give a person a second chance? There is no right answer and I don't think Alfred ever found one that could satiate his mind or his conscience.

Alfred Hecht was well respected by his colleagues especially as the chair of the department. He was kind but most importantly he was fair. He expected people to perform. If they didn't it was only right that someone more competent should take their place. That still didn't change the fact that this particular man had been telling the truth—he was deathly ill.

"That was hard," Alfred whispered.

I wondered about the eternal challenge of knowing when to mete out rewards and when to bring down punishment. Leaders often struggle with knowing when one action is better than another. Some people need encouragement. Some need punishment; carrot and stick. A bad leader mostly gets it wrong but even a good leader doesn't always get it right.

Somehow, holding the tension of two opposites brought me back to another story Alfred had told earlier. It had to do with tests of courage and cowardice. Courage requires facing death. Realistically, most don't want to put themselves in a situation where they would die early and needlessly even if their legacy might be one of honour and glory.

Alfred had told a story of an uncle with a missing finger. There was nothing but a stump and the reason centred around the uncle not wanting to go into the German Army during the Second World War.

He shot off his trigger finger and went to the hospital claiming it happened on the battlefield. Once the finger healed the army deemed him useless without a trigger finger and consequently released him from duty.

Having a finger shot off was suspiciously common at the time.

I asked if they changed the rules later.

Alfred replied, "Yeah, I think you would be court marshalled if they caught you later, especially under Hitler. It was like being a deserter. Hitler didn't waste (energy). Just shot them."

Alfred had then said softly and I suspect it weighed heavily on his mind when he mentioned that "My mother told me he was a coward."

Judgments can weigh heavily often without an easy answer. We drove on and came to Belmont Avenue where we turned onto a residential street and parked in front of Barry Boot's house. Like the other heritage brick houses dotting the street with their beaming authenticity and large maintenance bills, Boot's house was sweet, cute and endearing. A Mercedes-Benz SUV filled the short driveway in front.

Alfred mentioned that Barry Boots had a penchant for antiques generally and a collection of war medals, mostly Greek and British specifically. We got out and met Boots at the front door.

"I would invite you in but Chris (my wife) says our house is not in shape to invite anyone in."

Boots had recently had two knee operations and a hip operation. We pushed his limits by walking two blocks to the high street where we scurried inside a cozy diner for a cup of tea and two coffees. In spite of his physical condition that might limit exercise Barry was a lean man. He was also an academic superstar.

Alfred never had to fire him. In fact, Hecht and Boots became close colleagues, as academic equals. Both men came with similar pedigrees of respectable academic accomplishments.

37. BOOTS

At the diner, Boots cornered himself into the cozy booth opposite Alfred and myself. We, by contrast, sat upon a bench seat too small for two burley men.

Boots' straight and healthy but overly long hair made one wonder if he was an eternal fan of Pink Floyd, or just eternally British. A textured zip-up cardigan in sombre grey complimented the silver hair. Being British, Boots had the characteristic wit of the Isles. Full of subtlety and uniform cadence, his speech was devoid of overly articulated enunciations but his voice was soft.

Since Alfred was relying on reading people's lips and body language as his hearing was fading, he was having trouble fully understanding his friend. Nonetheless, the two bantered back and forth about old times.

Alfred shared stories with a deep and booming voice.

Boots shared with a quiet and reserved voice, affixed to a piercing stare.

Contrasts aside, it was clear the two had forged a long and enviable friendship through an era that rewarded meaningful research and expansion of knowledge. As academia changed parameters over time, however, basing promotion on the number of publications and the number of citations elicited by global peers, the metrics of reward skewed increasingly toward those who could write quickly instead of those that had something meaningful to say.

A metric called the H-index measures exactly this—papers per prof. It is neat and tidy but often misses the true value of the old-school researchers. Dr. Barry Boots scored a thirteen on the index. Not bad in the past but today it's not considered exceptional. If one digs deeper, however, it becomes apparent that Boots was a real pioneer in applying mathematical modelling to spatial data. In one case, he used real-world data to project how far and how fast the devastating Mountain Pine Beetle would increase and spread. It was the kind of useful information that forest companies needed to know so they could plan future harvests. And that was the type of information a provincial government, such as British Columbia, could use to determine how much money they would or would not have in their coffers over the following years from the forest companies. That knowledge would allow the provincial government to forecast how many schools, roads, hospitals and services they could afford to build without blowing their budgets.

From that perspective, Boots was a superstar in terms of doing meaningful research but his best-known work was *Spatial Tesselations: Concepts and Applications of Voronoi Diagrams* first published in 1992. It was co-authored with Atsuyuki Okabe from the University of Tokyo, Kokichi Sugihara from Meiji University and Sung Nok Chiu from the Hong Kong Baptist University in China. The 8,000 citations were a phenomenal number for an academic book.

In his self-deprecating humour, Boots mentioned that a Russian academic named Yuri Pavlic described the book as "the most brilliant theory of utter useless nonsense." He grinned widely at the compliment as he said it.

Boots had done a Master's degree at Bristol University in the UK, and that too, he affectionately referred to as trash. He did research at Rutgers University and then taught at Columbia University before the entire department was terminated and sent packing. Boots made his way to Wilfred Laurier University and found the pay to be almost double that at Columbia and the civility of Canadian society even better.

Boots and his wife Christine settled in as much as immigrants with emotional attachments to their place of origin could do. When Boots was not busy teaching and doing research, he and Christine went off on vacation as much as possible. That invariably meant going back to Europe, twice a year if possible, to spend their leisurely passions on barging and anything to do with slow boat tours that merrily punted, puttered and lazily drifted through the Old World's industrial canals, locks and waterways.

For all the world's stereotypical angst about dreadfully dull British food, Alfred and Boots turned the conversation to recall a culinary adventure they had in Japan.

Barry Boots' Japanese co-author Dr. Atsuyuki Okabe and his wife met up with Hecht and Boots in Tokyo one evening. The city was lit up with fireworks for a festival. Throngs of people had filled the streets. They managed to squeeze their way through the crowds and found their way up to the fifth floor of a hotel where a famous restaurant welcomed them. Okabe wanted to give his guests a superb and novel experience.

"There was a tank of huge shrimp with tentacles," Alfred remembered with eyes askew as he said it.

After choosing live shrimp from the aquarium, the chef placed them in boiling water and then immediately served them at the table.

Okabe demonstrated how to properly eat them, which included pushing the head in first and letting the tail hit the back of the mouth.

Alfred gulped. "I'm not so sure. I may puke," he said and remembered looking over at Barry who had the same ashen look on his face.

The server returned to spill coffee and then left in a squawking exit.

Barry and Alfred carried on reminiscing with gossip, names, places and faces. The tea and coffee cups ran dry and in a flash, time had pushed on so we walked Boots back to his house, said goodbye, and drove away.

In the car, Alfred recalled a time when they had been invited to China. While Alfred had gone to many conferences around the world in Germany, Russia, Israel and Nigeria, it was the one in China that came to mind.

"I met the President of Beijing (university and was given) a certain spot to sit to his right because I was a Full Professor. But before this, we walked by a glass container of fish swimming around. The translator said, 'You gotta pick out the fish you want.'" One looked similar to bass, so Alfred pointed at it.

"The guy scooped it out and (before) long it was on your plate. You know, the whole idea of taking a live thing and saying hey that's my meal, I mean, some people can take it easily but Barry had problems with it."

We drove down the street a little further to where Wilfred Laurier University was stationed on one side and the University of Waterloo down on the other.

Laurier and Waterloo seemed to be perfect symbols of the evolving changes in Canadian society, politics and government direction. Waterloo went in one direction with its own glory and its own unique sufferings.

Alfred Hecht was there to make sure Wilfred Laurier University excelled in its own way as well. And while Alfred was there, it did. But as I was to learn later, what goes up must eventually come down.

38. WENN SCHON, DENN SCHON

He prefers to be called Marv. Like his father, he spent a lot of time in the United States. He got a PhD at Boston College in Massachusetts less than an hour from Clark University where his father got his PhD. After Boston College, Marvin A. Hecht completed a post-doc at Harvard University. He then got a job as an Assistant Professor at Louisiana College. Things were looking good as an aspiring academic just like his father but this was a different era.

At Louisiana College Marv had not been promoted into the security of tenure. There was an increasing societal obsession with diversity, equity and inclusion which of course meant excluding white middle-class professional males. There wasn't much employment opportunity for him as a man attempting to be a tenured professor at a university. He picked up an IT job with Oracle instead. His wife Deborah worked at Oracle as well.

A few years in and a transfer later, Marv and Deborah with their two young boys—Max and Dylan—found themselves living in Hawaii.

The move suited Marv. He found his true love in the Aloha State—the ocean. He became passionately obsessed with surfing, health and fitness and began losing the weight burden he'd carried his whole life. Of his tall frame over six feet with his short dark hair, the slimming physique suited him well. In more ways than one he became a new man in Hawaii.

Deborah didn't like it.

"She told me she married a nerdy computer geek that liked food and that man was now gone," Marv said half-jokingly. Deborah was not thrilled with the Aloha State either and so they eventually returned to where they first met—Kitchener-Waterloo. Marv continued working in IT and Deborah got a job with the Waterloo Mennonite Brethren Church.

Now living just down the road, it didn't take long for Marv to drive over one night and take me out for a burger, beer and insight.

"I sold my other car," he said as we both crawled out of his current low-slung sports car at Morty's Pub. As we headed inside, a heavy rain battered down a sharp chill that caused our breath to condense in the air like mist.

"As a Christian, I was honest about what was wrong with it," he reported but then lamented about having told the truth, knowing it was used against him by the purchaser to bring the price down. He struggled with the morality of the American cutthroat culture he spent a lot of time in—a culture which favours taking as much as possible from others even by hook or by crook versus the morality of honesty in which he was brought up. As though trying to take a definitive stance, he said, "My father is too nice. Like when those renters took ten thousand dollars to move."

It is a common rift, not just between father and son but also in the Mennonite faith overall. It's one of the many philosophical divides that has split the Mennonites into at least fifty different branches in Ontario alone.

Strict pacifism, like strict honesty, is a major tenet of the religious belief as well. It leads to dilemmas that run deep in faith and family.

"As a Christian, I used to be a strong pacifist but now I'm not so sure," Marv ruminated as we neared the front door and went inside.

Morty's was packed with energy, the warmth of orange incandescent lighting, casual friendliness and the jostle of university students who dominated the space. Light wood abounded with framed memorabilia that filled lower wall space. Pennants hung high and gave a sense of community connection and a history permeated in soft mystique.

We sat near the bar at a small table with two free-standing chairs.

When our food came, I shovelled the hot wings down quickly while Marv ate less than half. He'd been a very overweight man at around 300 pounds but today, he was lean and athletic looking.

"How did you do it?" I asked of his weight.

"Overeaters Anonymous," he replied.

He realized his weight problem was like a drug or alcohol addiction and he needed to control it in the same way.

Marv liked to talk in an almost incessant way, not without purpose but also not without pause. I barely said anything and for doing nothing, Marv gave me everything.

"My dad has a saying. The same one Arnold Schwarzenegger used to say. Wenn schon, denn schon." Roughly translated it means, "if you are going to do something, do it fully, don't go halfway."

On Saturday mornings when Marv and his sister Melinda were young, they were tasked with washing the family car, a Mercedes-Benz; for this job three hours was normal. The smallest speck of dust was removed, multiple layers of polish were applied and the wheels shone immaculately. A showroom would have been proud to display it.

After cleaning the car properly, there was always the reward of a thick and juicy barbequed steak for dinner. In fact, rewards for a job well done were a mainstay at the Hecht household in virtually every aspect of life.

"We were paid for getting good grades. I tried to make as much money as possible," Marv said with a grin. Good grades were also rewarded with a trip to the local BMW dealership. Marv loved cars, especially anything German—BMW, Mercedes, Porsche. He seemed to have no trouble successfully meeting his father's every expectation. It was perhaps even a little bit more than his father had planned on.

Having spent large dollops of time at the BMW dealership, in 1986 with Marv having recently obtained his driver's licence and the family about to go off to Germany so Alfred could do another teaching term as a visiting professor, Alfred was pretty much obligated to do the obvious—buy a BMW.

Linda hated the thought of having a BMW. "It's too showy."

"It's black like the Amish buggies," Alfred had said with a bemused smile trying to insinuate it wasn't that showy. Regardless of the conflict between Alfred's sense of status and Linda's sense of humility, the BMW four-door 3-series sedan was purchased.

They picked it up at the factory in Germany and Marv loved every chance he had to drive it during that year they were in Europe. It spurred him on to do even more and continue living up to his father's expectations.

"They were high standards that we had to live up to. It got me into Harvard!" Marv exclaimed.

In fact, the immense pressure pushed Marvin through his education so quickly that he had a PhD by the age of twenty-five and became a young professor.

As a professor, "I was a hard marker," he admitted.

His students disliked it at times but many came back to him later to say that once they left his classes and went to other universities, they often found themselves at the top of their classes. It pleased Marv to know this, yet what he really wanted to know, as all sons do, is where he stood in his father's eyes. Was he good enough?

"How am I doing, Dad?" he asked his father one day.

"You are doing alright," Alfred had replied.

It was the most nonchalant answer a father could give. It was not disappointment but it certainly wasn't encouragement or support either, at least not in Marv's eyes.

His mother told Marv that even though his father had given a lacklustre response he was actually very proud of his son. Alfred had been bragging to the neighbours that his son went to Harvard but a mother's indirect praise is not the same as that which comes directly from the father.

Alfred himself had grown up in a household where praise and encouragement was seen more as a weakness than a strength—too much encouragement was bound to produce laggards and misfits. His own mother had beat Alfred when he did things poorly and certainly had never given encouragement when he did things well. Physical affection was out of the question.

Marv, like his father, didn't do things halfway but there was a cost to that. Marv had been vastly overweight through his schooling and teaching years. Then one day, while chasing after his young son, Marv's knee gave out and he tore his meniscus. His doctor told him, "I'm not going to operate on you. Just lose some weight."

So again, Marv went all in. Wenn schon, denn schon.

He lost one hundred pounds in eight months and kept it off ever since. Ironically, by doing something for himself, without the underlying ulterior motive of seeking approval from his father, the praise came on its own.

After noticing Marv had lost a significant amount of weight, Alfred, without prompting, said the very words Marv had been looking for his whole life. "I'm proud of you, son."

The benefits of trying to please his father had been immeasurable, but the costs had also been high.

Marv still looked up to his father, of course.

He vividly remembers spending a lot of time with him at work, especially in Germany and going to conferences across Europe where he saw him in action as a lecturing professor.

"When I saw my dad giving lectures, teaching, he was tremendous. He gave all his energy to it. When he got home…there wasn't much energy left for us."

It was a pattern that may have been inherited; a family trait that runs deep and one Marv could understand, and forgive.

After a conference in Dublin, Ireland, Alfred had been invited to the ambassador's house. Marv went along with his father to the ambassador's mansion where the ocean views were gorgeous, the building was other-worldly but the dry martini, Marv commented, "Was terrible." Still, it was his father's world and other than a bad martini, Marv loved being with his dad.

When sons break free from the father's will, they find their own way in life. High expectations from Alfred drove Marv to great heights but over time he was able to set his own path, on his own terms, as an independent person. His focus now is the ocean and it has nothing to do with his father and everything to do with himself, and for that, he seemed genuinely happy.

Marv recalled one more thing. "I remember, we also had to cut the grass perfectly"—sharpen the blades, clear the debris, single pass, diagonal pass, back pass and finish with a perfect edge trimming. Having broken the will-of-the-father and become his own person, Marv said with a reflective grin, "You know, maybe the grass doesn't need to be cut perfectly every time."

39. RETURN to PARAGUAY

"Last time we were in Filadelfia there was actually a bank, the National Bank of Paraguay," in a little unassuming building. "I didn't see anybody go in or out," Alfred said.

The Chaco was still an isolated place even in 2022 when Alfred took his immediate family back to his childhood home. The bank was unusual, or noteworthy, depending on perspective.

The main industry in the Chaco was cattle ranching, mostly done by Mennonites. And the Mennonite community had always had an autonomous banking and monetary system where virtually all financial transactions operated through the central co-operative, not a bank. Yet, as Alfred pointed out, "even the co-operative would have to deal with the national bank, sometimes."

The co-operative had an effective financial and market monopoly. They would decide which goods and services would be sold through the co-operative, essentially the general store. With a religious temperance guiding sales policies there were certain things absent from the shelves such as sex, drugs, tobacco and definitely not firearms.

As more non-Mennonites moved into the Chaco, independent stores moved in as well to meet market demand where the Mennonite general store was unwilling to do so.

"For example, the co-operative would not sell tobacco so an (independent) guy sells Paraguayan-made cigars," Alfred said with a smile, having enjoyed a few of the local cigars himself.

The Mennonite general store also worked on a credit system with membership requirements that precluded non-Mennonites. The independent stores by contrast were connected to the Paraguayan economy and used the national currency—the Guarani. Anyone could buy their goods and services, from milk to cigars to sex.

In the past, the independent stores were virtually non-existent. The co-op was quite literally the only store in town. The tightly controlled economic system operated by the Mennonites had significant benefits not the least of which was massive financial success. It was by no means a socialist or communist-type economic structure but the unified, albeit exclusive system, did help the Mennonites become much more economically successful than the rest of the country. By controlling the entire community's finances they could bypass inflationary problems, the banking middlemen and unregulated profit outflows.

However, the Mennonite economic system hit a demographic wall.

Since their economic activities are largely agriculture-based, a lot of cheap labour is needed. With Mennonite birthrates hovering slightly above replacement levels there weren't enough children to meet labour demands. They had to look elsewhere for people to fill lower-level jobs and fierce judgements on economic status, plus a streak of independence, among Mennonites didn't help the situation either.

"The mentality is quite independent," Alfred explained. "Run your own farm, your own estancia, then you are somebody! If you are just typing on a computer, you are not (important)."

The sentiment led to very few Mennonites willing to fill manual labour or administrative positions. Consequently, the wage-rate for labour and administrative positions went up.

Paraguayans, including everyone from manual labourers to the laptop class of accountants and administrators and even doctors, responded by migrating into the region in such large numbers they soon altered the regional culture and demographics.

"Even in the Fernheim co-op there was a supervisor that could speak Low German but the rest of the workers were all Spanish," Alfred reported.

In some ways, the Mennonites are victims of their own success.

Even the first time Linda went with Alfred to Paraguay in the 1970s, things were already changing.

Linda remembered, "The first time we were there a man said, 'It is a totally different place,'" in reference to the changes that had taken place from the time Alfred left in 1955.

The changes never stopped.

When they returned in 2022 Linda found that "You could really feel it. Now you felt obligated to speak Spanish. It used to be just Low German."

During their visit in 2022, Alfred and Linda's immediate family all stayed at the Hotel Boquerón in Neuland. It is located across the street from the Mennonite co-operative and a franchise grocery store called Supermercado. On a quiet Sunday, Alfred noticed an official-looking man standing around in the parking lot waiting for something so he went over and asked, "What's going on?"

"Workers for the Mennonite cattle ranches are coming in," the man replied.

And sure enough at that moment the first bus drove up.

"The guy knew exactly for whom they were working. He was the ombudsman, the guy that looks after regulations. He didn't have a gun, but close to it," Alfred said.

He said to the ombudsman, "There are a lot them!"

"Yes, and it's hard to keep track" the ombudsman replied.

"They come Sunday and leave Friday. Three buses full came into the Neuland parking lot," Alfred recalled with a rodeo-announcer excitement like he was there corralling profits with his voice. The whole thing stirred memories of the time when Alfred and his siblings worked in the cotton fields, picking cotton by hand and trying to avoid the needles of the flowers that sometimes jabbed painfully under the nails if they were not careful. It was to say nothing of the overbearing heat that suffocated even the hardiest workers.

The education system had changed as well. When Alfred was a boy in the Chaco in the late 1940s and early 1950s, his education was solely in German. Today, half the subjects are taught in Spanish and half in German.

Even though most of the local ranch owners are German-speaking Mennonites the day-to-day operations require knowing Spanish.

"The cattle are getting injected. All instructions are in Spanish (so they) have to know Spanish," Alfred explained. "The younger ones, because they had education in Spanish and also TV comes from Asunción in Spanish, all the signs are now in Spanish. I would think that for the Mennonites, give them another fifty years and their native language will be Spanish."

Every facet of society is seeing the demise of the Mennonite's Low German language and the infiltration of Spanish.

"Neuland has its own hospital and the last time I was there, of the four doctors, only one was a Mennonite. The others were imports from Asunción. There was a little advertisement saying, 'If you want to speak German to a doctor his name is J. Wiens. His hours are blah blah blah, otherwise, you'll have to speak Spanish,'" Alfred mentioned.

Labour demands forced the isolated Mennonites to open up to the world—or at the very least, to the rest of the country. As they did, they began to lose some of their insularity with some economic benefits accruing, but one wonders if they have not also lost some strands of their culture that made them successful in the first place?

Alfred mentioned that it "doesn't mean they will totally intermarry with Spanish people because it is mainly Indigenous people that work for them."

The original Mennonite colonies started with around 2,500 people who'd come from Russia and Canada. In the early days they had a tough time. Many packed up and left for greener pastures. Some went to Germany but most went to Canada. The population dropped to 800 and levelled out, only because the rest couldn't leave.

"Some didn't have anyone in Canada that could sponsor them. Some didn't have German citizenship. So, they basically had to stay there. Quite a few also moved to the capital of Asunción," Alfred explained.

The population hemorrhage stopped and a solid and vibrant economy slowly built up over time. The population rose. Now there are roughly 2,500 people in Neuland. Fernheim is up to 5,000 and the original Menno Colony has around 12,000 people. In total, around 25,000 Mennonites live in the Chaco as of 2024.

The numbers are deceiving though. Since Paraguayans have been moving in and intermarrying with the Mennonites for many decades, the cultural line between the two groups is not as clearcut as it used to be. The same cannot be said of the Indigenous people. The Mennonites and the Indigenous live worlds apart, right next to one another.

An estimate by a local anthropologist suggested the Indigenous population in and around the Menno colonies was 30,000—about 25% higher than the Mennonite population.

In comparison, "the population of Paraguayans who are Spanish or mixed background of Guarani and Spanish is 6,000–7,000 in the colonies. They are the doctors, nurses, computer techs, etc. So, they're the ones intermarrying with the Mennonites," Alfred explained.

Paraguay has two official languages—Spanish and Guarani. It's the only country in the New World that has an official Indigenous language and while "Guarani is not written, the conversation between lawyers and clients, etcetera can take place officially in the Guarani language. In all of East Paraguay, the common language is Guarani," said Alfred.

With more marriages between Mennonites and Spanish-Paraguayans—the latter being a unique culture that blends Spanish, Guarani and other historic influences and loosely labelled as "Spanish"—resulted in a situation where "many Mennos adopted Spanish names," Alfred reported and then added, "Marriage with the technocrats!"

"The interesting part is Neuland, as the city centre, has maybe 1,600 people and there is an Indigenous community in the northeast that has maybe 3,000. Paraguayans are adjacent to the Indigenous but also adjacent to the Mennonites."

The social division between Mennos, Paraguayans and Indigenous is real but it is much more pronounced with the Indigenous in almost every way.

"A couple of years ago there was only one marriage between an Indigenous man and a Mennonite woman."

The woman happened to be on the board of Alfred's charity, which helps support education for Indigenous students—Verena Regehr—affectionately known as the *Indiana Mumsche* (Indian Mother).

"After her first husband died, they had a very good friend, a chief of the Nivaclé. We call them Chulupi. The chief came frequently to Walter and Verena and visited them. At this stage in her life she had been widowed four or five years. After Walter died Verena married this chief. Anyway, they were not married long before he died."

The Nivaclé man had been married previously to a Nivaclé woman and fathered a passel of children and had many grandchildren. When he died, his offspring buried him in a Nivaclé cemetery.

"Different than the Mennonite cemetery," Alfred added. "The interesting thing was Verena married him in an Indigenous ceremony. And then went to a Mennonite church and married as Mennonites. But church and state are different. If you want to marry (officially) you have to sign a document and send it to the government. She never did. It meant that her inheritance goes to her two daughters, not to his kids."

Verena was a permanent resident in Paraguay but had originally come from Switzerland. Her first husband was a Russian Mennonite.

The odd tripartite mix of Mennonites, Spanish and Indigenous had a noticeable influence, not just on the social fabric, but also on the urban environment.

The Mennonite culture of cleanliness and order where all members of the society are expected to fit in is in strong contrast to the Latin American cultural attitude of 'Don't worry about what others think, do your own thing.'

Where Mennonite villages and homes were meticulously tidy, orderly and clean, Spanish places resemble a more chaotic nature. It is similar in appearance to that found ubiquitously in Latin American cities. Broken sidewalks, disorganized garbage collection, the feel of place run by self-serving government officials and drug cartels greased with corruption that manifests in a physical urban environment lacking coherence and beauty. Yet, at the same time the sounds of tango, jazz and the ever-present tangle of timbales, trumpets and cowbells resonate in clubs, alleys and open doors every evening to create a culture united in social coherence, if not a physical one.

The social element stands out vividly in Spanish streets with women dressed to the nines while cat-walking to the grocery store or the smoke of barbecuing meat for tacos and asado that permeates the clothing of passersby. Shiny zippers, sunglasses and opulent jewellery offer the feminine flavour of sauciness that catches the eyes of men who wait, never too far from a soccer pitch built on some street corner with no formal address, who play fast and hard when the sun goes down. A cadence of strut and confidence radiates on every street corner in a sexually festive mode that rises and falls but never disappears.

The Mennonite areas by contrast offer the calming effects of order and unity but demand a brake be dragged heavily on human temperament and desire. The message is that carnal pleasures are a sin not to be indulged in, or at the very least, hidden behind closed doors.

In spite of the contrast between the two cultures, a blending has occurred in the Chaco and the differences between the Spanish and the Mennonites are perhaps not so extreme after all, at least not in comparison with the third group—the Indigenous peoples.

Alfred explained, "The Spanish section looks like the Mennonite section. The houses are maybe not quite so big. Some of the Mennonite houses are still having Russian styles, but not the Spaniards. They built slightly different structures. The Indigenous were still in grass huts."

The Indigenous area is also the most dangerous side of town.

"And they don't have police in Neuland. They have an Achtungsman. Someone keeping things in order. In Filadelfia there is a six-man military detachment. They have guns but most things don't get to the police (although) there was an incident of a Menno who was helping run a little store for the Indigenous. They broke in and when he came out from his house across the road they shot him. That was the only fatality I know of in the last thirty years. They did find the two guys. I don't know what happened to them."

In reality, changes in the Chaco since the Mennonites first arrived in 1926 have never really stopped. Distance had a lot to do with the changes.

As an economic geography professor and researcher Alfred had predicted what was going to happen long before it did. He even wrote about it and his predictions came true.

"When I started at Laurier there was pressure on profs to have three areas of research. It meant you could supervise more students. In my case it was Urban Economics, Regional Development of Paraguay and the Chaco, and Geographic Analysis from a non-aggregate approach."

"During my academic career I went a number of times (to Paraguay) because that was my research area. I originally envisioned that I would do a survey of the ranchers in the Chaco to see if they would use the Trans-Chaco Highway, which was a dirt-packed road at that time."

To do this research Alfred received a primary grant from Laurier as well as a Social Sciences and Humanities Research Council (SSHRC) grant from the Canadian government.

"At the beginning, the only exports we had from the Chaco was chicken, eggs, some cattle. We would produce butter but to get it to the market they had to fly it in with small planes. It just did not pay to fly butter five hundred kilometres."

It was a common theme I heard again and again. Mennonites were constantly experimenting with new business ideas.

Alfred had gone to visit a business that was trying to make full use of raw cowhides instead of shipping them offshore for others to turn into value-added products. When the business owner started, unfinished leather was being sent to Italy without further processing. The Italian and German leather industry really liked Paraguayan rawhide because there were very few fences in Paraguay and thus, very few scratches and rips in the rawhide. The Italians and Germans paid a premium for it. The rawhide would be sliced thin into an inside piece and an outside piece. "The outside is used for the backseats of BMWs and for the leather around steering wheels, and nice leather shoes," Alfred said with a beaming smile.

The Mennonite businessman saw an opportunity to use the leather locally and add value. "I talked to the guy that was operating it," Alfred said. "He started off by making leather wallets and now had two hundred employees." It was mostly a success.

Meanwhile, other businesses had pushed into new markets as well. All three colonies for example now have various products shipped in trucks to Asunción. "Fernheim, Menno, and Neuland produce butter and yogurt; 80% of yogurt production in Paraguay and also some in Bolivia and Chile. Each colony has its own brand and slightly different products. You can buy them in most stores in Asunción in little corner stores. People like that on a hot day. Instead of drinking yerba maté you can buy a yogurt. It's not that expensive."

Aside from the local producers selling yogurt or making high-end leather products, there's one thing that surpasses all else in the export market and it brings the Mennonites a lot of money—cattle.

"Beef is 80–85% of exports. Soybeans is the rest," Alfred said, being well acquainted with the statistics.

Yet when Alfred was young the top important crops were cotton and peanuts, not cattle. The economic shift to cattle was something he predicted would happen. It had everything to do with a new road and a long-dead German geographer named Johann Heinrich Von Thünen.

Von Thünen first described the relationship between land rent and land use. The economic spatial patterns of agricultural land use were described in his first book *The Isolated State*, published in 1826 in German. He argued that land use was a function of transportation costs, land rent and product perishability and that farmers will always choose to grow or use their land in the most economically rational way possible.

He proposed the idea that agricultural landscapes have four rings of agricultural activity. In the centre is an urban area where goods and services are bought and sold. The first ring closest to the urban market centre would be used for intensive farming and dairy—lettuce, grapes, milk, butter, etc. The second ring is forestland for heating fuel. Extensive grain crops such as wheat and rye form the third ring. The outermost ring is used for cattle ranching and beyond that land is considered useless.

"I used that theory when the Ruta Trans-Chaco Highway was going to be built in Paraguay," Alfred said.

Before the Ruta Trans-Chaco was constructed, the road was a glorified dirt highway "controlled by the military. Rain would produce massive potholes and you always had to have enough food because sometimes you had to wait a week until the road would dry out."

It was a terrible way to ship products that were heavy and even worse for those that had a time limit on them such as butter or meat before refrigerated trucks existed.

At one point the Paraguayan government wanted to know if it was worth it to build a fully paved road over 500 kilometres out to the isolated Mennonite colonies. It would be extremely expensive for the small country to undertake. The economic returns through an expanded tax base had to be viable, so the government hired a consulting firm from Canada to do a feasibility study.

The consulting firm concluded that with a better road the Mennonites would produce more of the same. "Three times as much cotton, four times as many eggs, seven times X and so on," Alfred said with disbelief at the stupidity of their conclusions.

"I wrote a short article against them, saying it was all wrong. According to (Von Thünen's) theory, once you open up the periphery (for example, by building a road that gives greater access and faster transportation), you're going to use a lot of land, instead of intensive labour, and that meant cattle ranches."

He published the article in *Menno*—the oldest continuous newspaper in Paraguay going back to 1930—which basically said, "If the road is completed then the Mennonites will have to change from cotton and peanut production to raising beef."

"It didn't take the Mennonites long to understand that. That is exactly what happened."

But the Mennonite leadership feared the social impacts the road would bring. They tried to soften the social influence of the outside world by maintaining some isolation through distance.

Before paving it took about twenty-four hours to get to the big city of Asunción, assuming all went smoothly. The distance prevented younger Mennonites from easily going to Asunción. Distance prevented temptation.

After paving it would take eight hours and the conservative Mennonite leadership worried it would allow young people too much access to the sins of the world.

A surveyor had taken three of the top Mennonite preachers up in his plane to scan the area prior to road construction. The intention was to get the pastors' opinions and suggestions on where the road should be built. The government had originally intended for the road to directly connect with each of the three colonies before continuing on to the Bolivian border.

Alfred talked to the pilot who took the preachers up that day and recalled that they had flown toward the Mennonite colonies and the pilot pointed out the cockpit window at each colony as they flew by. "There's the Menno Colony. There's Filadelfia. There's Neuland."

Alfred remembered the pilot surveyor saying, "he was asked by the three preachers, very conservative (they would censor books and only use the Bible) to put the road in between. They were afraid it would be a bad influence on young people because they would go to Asunción for nightlife."

The preachers said to the pilot, "You have to run the road through the middle so that none of the colonies will be directly connected." This way each colony would have to build a spur road which added extra distance and they hoped, maintain some isolation.

The Paraguayan government complied with the preachers' wishes.

Alfred laughed a little. "It was ridiculous because each of the colonies had to attach to the road and pay for it themselves." The distance of Fernheim to the highway is approximately fifteen kilometres. The Menno connection is ten kilometres and Neuland is also fifteen.

The extra ten to fifteen was hardly going to dissuade anyone from going to the big city. Although Linda commented that realistically, even with the new modern highway, "it was still quite a way. The young people couldn't go to Asunción and come back the same day."

Alfred, aware of how distance wasn't always a deterrent, quietly remarked that, "My brother Rudy ran away from home. He took the truck from Neuland colony to go to Asunción." Alfred was unsure why.

The comment piqued my interest. I later asked Rudy why he ran away and was met with a wall of silence. He became unapproachable in a way I had never seen before. Whatever happened back there in Paraguay, it would remain a mystery.

While distance did not deter Rudy, or others, truth be told, from leaving the Mennonite colonies, distance *did* explain the economic changes that arrived with the new road.

With a decrease in the time-distance factor through road improvements the economic changes were obvious to Alfred, except one thing that wasn't. He had miscalculated human nature.

When Von Thünen first proposed his agricultural land use theory, he hypothesized that cattle need a lot of land for grazing. With extensive land requirements, the land had to be cheap. Cheap grazing land would be farthest away from urban areas. Even today, this is obvious at a large scale. The regions of the world that have extensive cattle ranching such as North America's prairies, the South American Pampas or even the Mongolian Highlands, all occupy large areas well away from populated regions.

Thus, a difficulty arises when ranchers must get their product (a cow) to market. In Von Thünen's time, cattle were walked to the market and then butchered there, close to the point of sale in order to prevent spoilage. Since a cow loses weight with distance and cows are sold based mostly on weight, there's a trade-off between distance and value. If the distance is too far, the cow loses too much weight and literally become skin, bones and of little value. The tipping point in that calculation between distance, weight and value is the geographic line at which it no longer makes sense to raise cattle.

The Mennonite colonies, five hundred kilometres distant from the market city of Asunción, were simply too far away before the new road was built. Alfred recognized that if a paved road was constructed out to the Menno colonies the ability to move cattle easily over long distances would make ranching viable. With land being extremely cheap and mostly unused in the Chaco it would make economic sense to use it for grazing.

The one impediment was that shrubland and virgin forests needed to be converted to rangeland. Once cleared and planted in grass, cattle ranching would thrive, and that's exactly what happened almost everywhere, with one exception.

Years later, Alfred went to see the changes for himself. He noticed the Mennonite colonies had completely shifted to cattle ranching as predicted but there was also a strange anomaly he had not expected to find. There had always been some cattle ranchers that existed more to the east, near the Paraguay River, long before the road was built. After the road was built, oddly, they weren't using it.

"There were about two hundred (original ranchers). Most had their place on the Paraguay River" who'd long ago built cattle stations at the water's edge. From the river, cows would roam westward for hundreds of kilometres inland. When it came time to take the cattle to market the ranchers would have to go out and herd them all the way back to the Paraguay River before putting them on barges and sending them downriver to the abattoirs in Asunción. When the Ruta Trans-Chaco was built it ran right through the middle of their rangeland.

"I thought the road would have quite an impact on the (existing) native cattle ranchers," Alfred said.

From the river stations into the bush of the Chaco, "the cattle would be grazing natural savannah grasses for three hundred kilometres inland, so I thought these ranchers would take advantage of the road by trucking the cattle" directly from the ranges instead of herding them all the way back to the river. "I figured if you take a good cow and (herd) it three hundred kilometres she's gonna lose thirty pounds," so it made sense to use a truck and drive it to Asunción instead. "I asked the rancher T. Eaton, who was one of the biggest," if this calculation made sense.

The rancher did in fact agree with Professor Hecht's economic rationale. It made complete economic sense.

"So, can you not use the road to truck them?" he asked Eaton with some incredulity.

Eaton explained that the situation had nothing to do with economics. "I think you're right but first of all, many of these cattle ranchers don't live here. They either live in Argentina, Buenos Aires or Paris." The real issue was that many of the ranch owners were absentee landlords that had managers running their operations and the simple fact was, "The managers don't care."

Alfred was right about the economics but he and Von Thünen were wrong about human nature. People are not always economically rational.

In the end, the road did change almost everything in the Chaco, completely in line with Von Thünen's economic theory. Land was cleared and planted in grass for ranching. Native forests were uprooted and now they are mostly gone.

"There is basically no land left in the Chaco," Alfred confirmed. The price of land has increased significantly even though "until relatively recently land prices were less than the fencing cost to enclose it."

In some ways, it was a mirror image of what happened in the Ukraine. Cheap land was put into agricultural production. The population increased. More land was turned to agricultural production. Population increased again. Then they ran out of land. The gap between rich and poor increased. Tensions simmered and eventually violence broke out.

Alfred explained that the situation "sometimes looks like development in Russia between Mennonites and Russians. Wes Hiebert compared Mennonite villages and economic standing to adjacent Russian villages. In terms of wealth it was 20:1. In Paraguay, I would say that same ratio would be true. The question I sometimes have is, 'Can it get to the point where the natives outnumber the Mennonites by quite a bit; would it cause an uprising?' All you need is a Che Guevara or a Castro guy to get involved."

For the moment, the situation was calm and in 2022 Alfred was able to bring his entire family to the land he enjoyed as a young boy. In comparison to 1948, instead of living in poverty, he was able to enjoy a nice hotel, a comfortable bed and a good cigar by the pool with his children and grandchildren.

"The handmade cigars were pretty light in flavour. It wasn't the roughest tobacco around, that's for sure," Alfred smiled.

It was all a far cry from the one-room mud-brick house with a thatched roof and the beans and lard he had grown up with.

As Alfred liked to say of his own success, "He had arrived."

40. SPEAKING of ETHNICITIES

In 1981, Hecht, Pletsch and fellow scholars received a $200,000 grant, an incredible sum of money in those days, to study how different ethnic groups fared in Canada.

"We found that European immigrants integrate very quickly," Alfred summarized. It was hardly surprising but there were exceptions. Mennonites...for example.

In the early half of the 20th century the Manitoba provincial government decided that all teachers had to teach in English. That included the Mennonites who were told they could no longer teach in Low German. Lessons had to be in English, no exceptions.

The government was intent on assimilation. The Manitoba School Question, as it became known, was counter-productive. Instead of assimilating the Mennonites, it drove many of them out of the country. They went to Mexico and Paraguay where they could maintain their way of life including their language. They went to countries where they were tolerated, if not always fully accepted.

It was a great irony. After fleeing Russia and going to Canada where the government had given them special permission to practice their religious faith, sometimes in contradiction to general laws and norms of Canadian society, they were turning around and leaving when the government sought to rescind those special privileges.

"Canada might learn something from what happened in Paraguay," Alfred said.

While equal laws for everyone sounds fair, reasonable and even optimal, it was not historically common, and for good reasons.

"It was pretty normal to give groups of people special privileges as a way for some nobility getting farmers to come to their lands. A kind of servitude, I guess. Nobility wanted people, so they gave them privileges. You see this across Europe," and other places across the globe as well.

It's not that privileges cannot change as society changes but sometimes, it's best when the changes come not from government but from the people themselves.

For example, in Paraguay, "as Mennonites we had special exemption from the Paraguayan government to not go into the army."

Paraguay had a mandatory eighteen-month military service for each male over the age of eighteen.

"Not that Paraguay has been in a war since 1935 but as a small country with five countries surrounding it, they keep themselves armed and ready just in case," Alfred added. "But Mennonites had special exemptions as conscientious objectors. Because of our faith. But over time some individuals weren't really like that. They didn't mind going into the army."

Meanwhile, every other young Paraguayan man had to serve whether they wanted to or not.

"We thought it wasn't right, you know, that some of our guys didn't have to go in the army but we had regular Paraguayan workers who had to serve in the army."

Instead of thinking only of themselves, the Mennonites gave an intriguing proposal to the government. They said, "We will give up our special exemption if you allow any and all Paraguayans the opportunity to decline military service as well, if the individual is a conscientious objector."

Paraguay's parliament accepted the proposal.

In 1992 a new national constitution with Articles 37 and 129 outlined the parameters for exemptions from military service. Article 129 stated that *"conscientious objection for ethical and religious reason is recognized."*

De facto implementation, however, has not always worked out as the Mennonite community foresaw, but that's a different issue.

It was instead, as Alfred suggested, an interesting case study for Canada to consider with regard to the granting of special privileges. In a sense, it was a granting of privileges based on moral and ethical principles applicable to all. It was certainly different than the historical granting of privileges based largely on economic needs of a government or big business. It was also a vastly different approach than the current trend of the

Canadian government to kowtow to any number of ever-expanding identities that whine about never-ending grievances.

The question of special privileges has, in fact, long dogged debates in Canada and within the pre-existing Dominion. The Royal Proclamation of 1763 gave legal recognition to Aboriginal land title, rights and freedoms, unlike in the United States where the principle that *might-is-right* ruled. In 1774, the Quebec Act gave the Province of Quebec the right to favour Catholicism instead of Protestantism. It also granted the use of Civil Law instead of British Common Law and the seigneurial land system was allowed to continue, where the British government would have otherwise implemented a township system if not for the granting of these exceptions to French Canadiens. Special privileges and battles to retain them have continued to this day.

In the past, privileges were mostly based on ethnicity (culture) while today, strangely enough, more recent iterations of the granting of special privileges and funding are directed at groups based on race (physiology) such as Blacks and Visible Minorities.

The debates have simmered somewhat but never subsided over the issue of whether or not the granting of special privileges is right, wrong or fair. The question has created an uneasy, although not untenable, situation in Canada. Bouts of intense debate are common and occasionally even spasms of outright violence do occur. The mood of the Canadian nation shifts back and forth between tolerance and intolerance of minorities, never quite comfortable with either.

In times when assimilationist rhetoric rises and formal action by government takes place, those deeply attached to their ethnic identity over Canadian national identity have resisted. Some even leave Canada altogether to find freedom to be themselves, elsewhere. That has historically included the Mennonites, Amish, Japanese and even some First Nations such as the Sinixt.

Pletsch and Hecht's 1983 published study, *Ethnicity and Well-Being in Ontario and Toronto*, looked at the assimilation of immigrants. Although a long time ago now, more recent studies with a similar investigative question tend to reveal the same thing today. Some people integrate quickly such as the average German and Korean immigrant while others such as Old Order Mennonites, Sikhs, and fundamentalist Muslims integrate very slowly, if at all.

Alfred Hecht's proposal to consider Paraguay as a case study seemed like a good idea assuming those in power were willing to work for the common good of the country and not cling to their own special privileges.

41. RETURN to LAURIER

Country music played on the car radio as it often did whenever Alfred drove around town. A disquieting female voice was recalling a love lost and with the conventional four-on-the-floor beat at low volume came an emotional soothing as we made our way toward a confession.

Without the Steppe, Chaco, Pampas or Prairies, gauchos or cowboys anywhere in sight, southern Ontario's suburban four-laned roads and grassy medians had to suffice as a substitute for the necessary feeling of wide-open spaces required to subliminally match the music. Life, landscape and tradition of course don't always align.

"The Freedom Office asked me to give a little speech because he was in our faculty," Alfred said as we neared the Geography Department at Wilfred Laurier University—a place that Alfred had not seen in a long time. He retired from Laurier in 2006 and from his other teaching appointments, in 2011. He had gone back to Laurier a few times but as time passed, the visits were fewer and farther between. It was now 2024. The man he was talking about was a former colleague.

"He didn't have any relatives around. So I got there and here's this guy from Political Science standing in a uniform saluting him" at the farewell.

Alfred had asked him why he was standing in uniform saluting the man they had both come to pay their respects to.

The man explained that "We were both in the same Boy Scouts unit in Latvia. The tradition was, when one dies, the others give him the farewell. You know, salute."

Alfred added that "In the old days it was a gunshot salute but," he said wryly, "you can't do that at Laurier."

"That's been banned, too, eh?" I replied sarcastically.

We both let out a laugh of the kind that's indignant of absurdity, knowing attempt to correct it would be futile.

"Yeah, all the good and exciting things are banned," Alfred said.

"Yeah, no peanuts, no perfume, no guns."

The country music carried on, as did we. Alfred concentrated on the road, sticking close to the posted speed limit. The last comment had drawn him into a memory. He glanced sideways. "I have a very sensitive nose and the church has banned perfume, also!"

His sister Elsa also had the same sensitivity to perfume.

"Funny part is Hein, her husband, can't smell a thing," Alfred said while speeding up. "One day there was a skunk in Elsa's garden. She had a perfect garden. Well, a skunk was eating her carrots. She asked Hein to get rid of that skunk."

Hein and Elsa are a picture-perfect couple who dote on each other like innocent teenagers in love. They're well into their nineties now but Hein would do anything for Elsa and Elsa would do anything for him.

"Hein took an old blanket, went right up to the skunk and put the blanket over it. The skunk sprayed but Hein couldn't smell a thing. He drowned the skunk in a barrel of water. They burnt the blanket (and maybe) burnt his clothes too," Alfred recalled.

We turned onto the campus of Wilfred Laurier University and soon found a handicap spot in front of the Laurier Giving office.

Cec Joyal, Development Officer of Individual & Legacy Giving at WLU, had been in charge of all endowments for as long as Alfred was there. She, Alfred and some other colleagues worked together to set up a scholarship fund for students wanting to go abroad. The fund was significant enough on its own. It could be considered a lasting legacy in its own right but of course that would only be going halfway. Why stop at the creation of a travel fund for Laurier students? The fund was only one goal, on a lofty list.

We went in, spoke to Cec briefly and then ventured over to the Geography Department. I wanted to see the place where it all happened and it seemed Alfred did too, although there was a hint of reticence in his voice. I wondered why.

42. INSIDE LAURIER

Wilfred Laurier University and Professor Hecht got along famously. They were well suited for one another during their time together but times change. Professor Emeritus Alfred Hecht retired from WLU in 2006 with auspiciously good timing.

He and I walked over to the Department of Geography and Environmental Sciences where Alfred had spent so much of his life and career. At the entrance to the building we stepped into a beautifully constructed glass elevator attached to the outside.

"We decided we wanted a new elevator here and the Vice-President financed it. Put it adjacent to the building," Alfred said, intuitively answering my silent question.

Artfully integrated, the elevator looked as though the designers, engineers and architects worked seamlessly together with skill, pride and attention to detail. It's strange to say but it felt good. As we rode up, we left behind the small and unassuming geology department on the ground floor before landing on the second.

"There was an agreement between universities. Waterloo had a big Geology Department, so we did not expand geology," Alfred said, again answering a question on the tip of my tongue.

The elevator door opened and we stepped into a hallway with a vastly different mood. The walls were painted in glum grey. The hallway itself was empty and the ceiling lights were turned off.

Perhaps turning off the lights was done in some noble effort to save the planet? Whatever the reason, it gave the impression that human life was unwelcome here.

As we sauntered down the hallway through a ghostly ambience a Chinese proverb came to mind, "The first generation creates wealth. The second generation maintains it. The third generation destroys it."

Across the Western world there were significant pressures on university budgets and have been for a long time. The problems were not yet apparent when Alfred left Laurier in 2006. Truth be told, the problems were not restricted to money. By almost all metrics—enrollment numbers, grade inflation, declining entry requirements, number of registered patents, social legitimacy—post-secondary education had been flashing red for some time and the situation was only getting worse with every passing year. Some say it began around 2015.

Arising social forces at this moment were suddenly promoting the antithesis of what higher education was originally intended to be. Instead of a place of open, independent inquiry and serious debate about the nature of reality, these new social forces were snuffing out free speech. Tribal group think was coalescing and the sanctity of tenure also came under threat. That year was a pivot point when the internal rot of political correctness and cancel culture rose to the surface and fully exposed itself.

The Manichean shift hit students first.

In Canada, it happened in a publicly explosive way right here at Wilfred Laurier University when the Lindsay Shepherd affair broke.

Lindsay Shepherd was a Master's student who was financially supporting her studies by working as a teaching assistant. Late in the fall semester of 2017, she played an innocuous video for one of the communications classes she had been teaching. The video was used as a prop around which class discussion could ensue. Apparently, the class went well and the students were eagerly engaged in debate.

The video was a short clip of an interview between Steve Paikin, TV show host of The Agenda and renowned clinical psychologist and University of Toronto professor Dr. Jordan Peterson. The interview had originally aired on one of the province's largest public broadcasters. Steve Paikin and The Agenda could hardly be called controversial.

Shepherd played the clip and conducted herself precisely as any good teacher should.

However, Shepherd's thesis advisor named Nathan Rambukkana, a large, burly man with a lisp, whine and the facial demeanour of resentment, claimed that a student in Shepherd's class was offended and had lodged a complaint. Rambukkana requested that Shepherd meet with him, insinuating she was about to be scolded for doing something inappropriate.

Shepherd felt uneasy. Something was askew. Worried, she called her mother on the other side of the country prior to the meeting. Her mother, with prescient advice, told Lindsay to record everything.

At the meeting were Rambukkana, the program coordinator Herbert Pimlott and Adria Joel, a Diversity and Equity Officer.

It turned out that Shepherd was right to be worried. The three accused her of "creating a toxic climate for some of the students."

They wouldn't say who complained nor could they adequately explain what they meant by *toxic*. The meeting was classic Sovietesque secret tribunal stuff. It was unprofessional, egregiously manipulative and the interrogation of twenty-two-year-old Lindsay Shepherd really had no other purpose than for Rambukkana to flex power and control.

Shepherd secretly recorded the whole conversation and sent it off to various news outlets shortly afterwards. *The National Post*, a major Canadian newspaper, picked it up. One of their top reporters, Katie Blatchford, wrote a scathing piece against Rambukkana specifically and Laurier generally.

The audio recording also went public.

Shepherd could be heard defending herself quite well, pointing out that she was doing exactly what any university instructor was supposed to do—facilitate debate. Rambukkana and Pimlott on the other hand could be heard making ridiculous accusations of insensitivity. But as Shepherd hit back the interrogators seemed to realize she was outgunning them intellectually and morally. Rambukkana came across as a bully, Pimlott as morally weak and Adria Joel as a useful idiot.

Not prepared for Shepherd's intelligence and common sense, the three continued with their manipulative badgering. It was almost comical until Shepherd broke down and began to cry. Yet, even with tears in her eyes and a gulp in her throat she never once backed down from her interrogators. It was stellar stuff and it left most of those who listened to it feeling furious with righteous anger toward the interrogators.

Laurier's President Deborah MacLatchy apologized on behalf of the university for the deplorable actions of Rambukkana, Pimlott and Joel but she did it with a feckless ambiguity that only enraged people even further.

"Giving life to these principles (free expression) while respecting fundamentally important human rights and our institutional values of diversity and inclusion, is not a simple matter," MacLatchy wrote.

Rambukkana also penned a public apology that came across as a convoluted excuse rather than a genuine apology.

Sensing the lack of repentance and stubborn refusal by the bullies to take personal responsibility for their egregious behaviour, and standing up for the important principle of free speech, Shepherd launched a lawsuit in May of 2018 against the university, Rambukkana, Pimlott, Joel and an unnamed student.

The whole affair shocked the public into realizing that their publicly funded educational institutions might just, in fact, be run by conniving and manipulative sycophants.

Of course, Wilfred Laurier University, like other universities, had faced moments of public notoriety in the past. There was the rubber-chicken hacking incident of the 1970s and the panty-raid incident of 1989 but this was something far different. This wasn't about bad behaviour among the students. This was about bad behaviour among the faculty.

Laurier's administration was unprepared for the backlash, not because the event with Shepherd was unique but because similar events were becoming common in universities and colleges everywhere and Laurier's administration was responding in kind, like others had, with the usual appeasement to the authoritarian Left and political correctness instead of standing up for what was right and honourable.

The Lindsay Shepherd Affair became a poster child in Canada for what happens when the insidious destruction of political correctness infects an educational institution.

But Laurier was not alone. In a disturbing trend across the entire West, it appeared that universities were becoming ideologically undermined in a not too dissimilar fashion to that experienced in the East under Stalin, Hitler and Mao.

To the average observer it all seemed to rush in out of the blue. As Ernest Hemingway's character in the novel *The Sun Also Rises*, Mike Campbell says of bankruptcy, it happened "gradually, then all at once."

The National Association of Scholars (NAS), an American non-profit organization whose mission "fosters intellectual freedom," had been keeping track and seemed to concur. It had compiled of list of professors, administrators and students that had been "cancelled"—the new form of mob rule.

The first one was Edward O. Wilson, a well-known ecologist, in 1975. Few noticed. A new victim of cancel culture was then added no more than about once every four years after Wilson. Again, few took notice. Then things changed all at once. The list exploded. Seven people were added in a single year, 2015.

Dr. Jordan Peterson was put on the list the following year, along with another seven people. Lindsay Shepherd was added in 2017. The peak came in 2021 with sixty-two academics making the list. In 2022, things were not much better but cancel culture now faced pushback, which began to dampen its ugly ferocity.

Many of the older faculty who worked so hard to raise higher education to new heights in the latter half of the 20th century by expanding its reach and bringing the best of open inquiry to the masses were left watching with dismay as it seemed to crumble away. Alfred said in a tone of requisite sadness, "That was after my time."

We turned and walked down the hall toward the Geography and Environmental Sciences Department. Suddenly, he stopped as his eye caught a letter-sized piece of paper attached to a corkboard on the wall. He bent down a little to take a closer look.

It was advertising a course. The recruitment poster had the course name, professor, course description and a few other details.

Classes that have low enrollment are often advertised like this. If successful, the professor, or the part-time instructor, can increase enrollment and avoid having their course and their paycheque put on the chopping block.

If it's a new course without credentials, no history, and no reputation among students, it's a tough sell unless the professor is already known, liked and respected. Of course, if the latter were true there should be no need to advertise.

It was more likely that the course had been around for a while but the professor was awful. Word travels fast among students.

Alfred, with his experience as the chair, knew the routine. He casually said, "Most students self-select profs." They never choose the bad ones.

We carried on, then stopped a few feet shy of the entrance to the department where double doors were swung open but no one was visible to be seen inside.

Alfred turned to the other side of the hall and looked up at a display board on the red brick wall. Behind the display glass were the portraits of the department's former and existing faculty.

"(Mary-Louise Byrne) is the chair now," Alfred said, pointing at her portrait up top. "We had a big debate when we hired her from Windsor. Her references weren't that strong," he said, inhaling with the hissing sound of disapproval. "But at that time, we were under some pressure to hire women, you know."

He scanned down. "Gordy, he was good. A lot of grants came in." His eyes and memory dropped a little further down. "Don't know that guy."

Distant voices carried in the air but Alfred didn't hear them. He was still looking at the faces.

"Eric Creighton, I know. He came in one or two years before (me). He was a physical geographer when they started climatology. The government would provide money to nearly everybody that had a good record (in climatology)."

We turned and within a few short steps sauntered into the foyer of the department office. A friendly voice called out, "Alfred!"

"No kidding. You're still here," Alfred replied, instantly recognizing the tall, slim man that appeared.

"Yeah, still here. What happened?"

"I'm trying to get a job," Alfred replied sarcastically.

Grant Simpson had a narrow face and the youthful look of a man that jogged every day. At the age of twenty-three he had been hired as the Geospatial Technical Support Specialist for the department. In other words, he was the indispensable guy that keeps the labs running faithfully and consistently every year. He was now sixty years old. "I'm looking at retirement. It's a hard reality," he admitted.

Alfred and Grant ran through the current roster of names and places—Ken Hewitt was in the Himalayas, Phil Marsh in Inuvik and Brendan Walker up north as well.

Alfred looked over at a door not twenty feet away. "In the Dean's office there was a special desk," he insinuated with a wide grin.

"That desk is probably still in there," Grant confirmed before mentioning there had been lots of changes over the last ten years, which was precisely the last time Alfred had come to visit, with Linda in tow.

Alfred raised his eyebrows with a piqued interest.

"Attrition of faculty," Grant explained. "A lot of empty offices. We said we need replacements. We got a couple of Indigenous hires."

Alfred nodded, knowing the power of politics all too well. "Universities make up rules. Want to hire ten Indigenous, ten Black faculty, and so on."

"Yeah, EDI or whatever they're calling it," Grant said with frustration. "There is money for that but then when you ask for replacement needs there is a significant lag. It's quite distressing when you look at the number of faculty that have left and how many positions haven't been filled."

The faint smell of cannabis suddenly drifted in from the hallway.

"When I started here, biology was over there (with) bad smells," Alfred said, acknowledging the change in the air. "A physical geographer from Lithuania, Gunars Subins, always smoked a pipe (and) there was a geologist from Western (who) smoked cigars. He did open his window, but it was a little too much."

Grant smiled as memories were jogged.

"Nowadays, I try to go for a three-kilometre walk," Alfred said. "I take a cigar with me." He held up his hand and wiggled his fingers. "If you got nothing in your hand you feel kind of dumb, you know."

Others had entered the room and joined the conversation. Josling suggestions were made about smoking and health but were quickly deflected by Alfred. "Hey, you remember Ken Hewitt? Boy, could he play ping pong."

"I think Ken took a fourth-year group to the Inca Trail and he could probably outlast all of them," Grant mused.

"Yeah, one of the major fourth-year trips."

"They haven't done a big fourth-year trip for a couple of years. Never go international again. It's too expensive," Grant said with some resignation.

Disappointment, well-hidden as it was on Alfred's face, was still apparent nonetheless. The shortest of silences was evidence enough that the statement hit him hard. Learning in a flash that the international field schools had gone by the wayside would be hard to take for anyone who was proud of what they had created. To see it fall apart now, would be tough.

Alfred drifted into nostalgia, perhaps as a counterweight to grief. "I remember one time we took a group to Germany…"

The trip had included Pletsch, a bus, students and a lot of drinking. Alfred shifted from Germany back to Canada again, not that the two countries weren't deeply intertwined in his mind's eye.

"I used to work with the Viessmann Research Centre on Modern Europe (at WLU) and Pierre Cyclos was Director when I retired. I noticed he was still on faculty. He must be near eighty!"

"Some faculty just drop off and we never see them again," said Grant.

"Mike Flaymore?" Alfred questioned before adding a few more names.

The response from Grant Simpson was the same with each one. "Gone."

Just then two middle-aged men walked in without hurry.

Alfred took in a deep breath and exclaimed, "No kidding. I think I know this guy!"

One of them was a man named Alex MacLean. "The last time I saw you was with Russell Muncaster," he said with a boyish glow.

Russell Muncaster had been a man of great significance in WLU's history but time waits for no one. "Russell is in bad shape," Alfred said softly. "He was the chair before I was and then he became Dean and then Vice-President. He had a stroke three years ago. Paralyzed his left side."

Most of Professor Hecht's students and colleagues just called him Al. The informality and openness with everyone left an endearing impression on others and so it was with Alex MacLean.

MacLean had been hired as a lab technician at Laurier after graduating as a student. "I had you for economic geography in second year," he said to Al with a look of some adoration.

The reminiscing continued among an increasing crowd and like a fly on the wall, what stood out to me was how much Laurier was both unique and ordinary.

It is always the people that make a place succeed or fail. A truism of change among every institution and business is that new people who replace the original cadre will either use the existing foundation to springboard to even greater heights or they will ignore the foundational structure built by those that came before. Some of the new faculty, administrators and Laurier's President Deborah MacLatchy had taken the latter approach. They had vastly different ideas about what Laurier was going to be rather than having gratitude for what it was.

"The first generation creates. The second generation maintains. The third generation destroys."

How fast could something go from great to terrible? How quickly could it all fall apart? From inside the foyer of the Department of Geography and Environmental Sciences at Wilfred Laurier University, I was getting the impression the answer might be, *surprisingly quickly*.

When Alfred Hecht was chair of the department, he created a strong graduate program, a successful International Study Abroad program with a healthy endowment fund for students and he founded the Hans

Viessmann Research Centre on Modern Europe. Creation of all these had of course required collaboration. Hecht hadn't done it alone. Likeminded people with a shared vision were necessary for all of it to come together. That cohesive, productive, collegial group existed when Alfred was at Laurier. It led to great success with Alfred leading much of it.

In the era after Alfred retired, collegiality dissolved. But Laurier was no outlier. Post-secondary institutions everywhere today show the telltale signs of descending into the proverbial destruction phase. Universities are suffocating under a lack of merit in hiring, antagonistic faculty, and an ideological woke cancer not unlike communist ideology that threatens to kill the university system entirely. Each university has its own unique circumstances, of course. Some are in more trouble than others.

In some ways Laurier had become a locally unique symbol of the dysfunction. The current Department of Geography and Environmental Sciences had mostly avoided the worst of the societal issues but sometimes, like all work places, a single person can be the cause of great angst.

The present chair of the Department of Geography and Environmental Studies, Mary-Louise Byrne, arrived just as Professor Hecht was about to retire.

"We had to put her in," Alfred said again as he retold his stories to those now listening. "Although it wasn't a first pick. They wanted more women, you know. Anyway, she went in."

After Byrne took over as chair of the department, Alfred retired.

"And apparently, everything went to Hell after that," he said with indignation.

While the Lindsay Shepherd affair happened long after Alfred retired it was interesting to consider that Nathan Rambukkana, as a highly manipulative man, had perhaps become the norm and not the exception. Seven years after the event, in 2024 Rambukkana was still teaching at Laurier although he had changed his appearance. He now sported a full beard and flared his chest in biography portraits. Herbert Pimlott also changed his appearance. He became She. *Hillary* Pimlott was also now claiming a special area of research expertise in "Anti-Trans Language."

University faculties across the West today, if they hire men at all, seemed to be hiring men of Rambukkana and Pimlott's ilk—conniving, manipulative, questionable self-esteem and certainly not as intellectually astute as their forebears. Academia was increasingly hiring the worst among men but for the most part, it was only hiring women.

During this same period woke totalitarianism arrived on scene. Recognizable through jingoistic slogans such as *You Belong Here* and mantras dedicated to *Safe Spaces* it had become the norm in academic institutions. Some argued that academia's entire decline arrived on the heels of women.

It was a touchy subject but some have claimed that a phenomenon referred to as "male flight" was at the root of the problems.[17]

The *theory of male flight* proposes that when a profession switches from predominately male to predominantly female, somewhere around a 40/60 tipping point, the profession experiences a rapid exodus of the remaining 40% of men. Once this happens the profession loses social status in the eyes of society and financial support plunges.

It happened to high school teachers and interior designers. Those two professions used to be dominated by men and they carried strong social status and prestige along with generous salaries. Now they are both heavily dominated by women and have lost their status.

High school teachers, because they are supported by government, have to a certain degree avoided the theory's expected decline in wages. Interior designers have not been so lucky. As a profession directly accountable to their perceived value in the marketplace, they are not looked upon so favourably any longer. An average plumber in Canada now makes more per year at $70,093 than does an interior designer at $64,674 according to the employment website Indeed.

The issue revolves around social status and there's no way of getting around it. It's evolutionary. The theory of male flight argues that at a deep evolutionary level men compete with other men, not women, for intraspecies dominance. That's a good thing. When men dominate a profession, their inherent competition with one another elevates and pushes innovation and excellence forward. Society in return, rewards them for that.

Women don't have the same intraspecies competitive need for excellence, especially when challenging ideas. When women dominate a formerly male-dominated profession, innovation tends to vanish. So too vanishes the creation of new insights, technologies, ideas and the expansion of universal theories and laws.

Society always notices and eventually withdraws support.

Academia, for example, was supposed to be society's central laboratory for the testing of ideas. Now that academia is dominated by women it seems to be following the anticipated trajectory of male flight to a tee. Ideas are squelched. Innovation has gone down. Men are leaving in droves. Public support is in decline.

Ironically, as I was writing this, the very next day on October 22, 2024, the *National Post* newspaper ran an opinion piece by staff writer Carson Jerema titled, *Defund the Professors. Every Last One.* Thirty years ago when men dominated academia the headline would have caused bewilderment. It wouldn't make sense to say such a thing. Today, it does.

The public is tired of the internal nonsense within academia and it's probably too late to recover.

When universities reach that tipping point where 60% of faculty and students are female, men do seem to leave in droves. And they don't show any signs of going back. But who can blame them?

Men favour truth over harmony. Women favour harmony over truth.

When the female preference for harmony dominates the classroom, it becomes the antithesis of what makes a strong, healthy place of serious inquiry. The female preference for harmony dooms universities to failure.

The issue is actually more about men than women. A demographic shift to female dominance means the university can no longer be a place where men can be at their competitive best—challenging ideas in brutal fits of wit, intelligence and the occasional fist fight in order to win mastery over all others in the arena of truth.

Harmony, enforced by women, made universities stifling and boring. So, the men left.

Universities have become *safe spaces*. Controversial ideas, at least anything deemed controversial by those in power, are suppressed through the excuse of causing harm to some imaginary group's collective feelings.

It's not that individual women can't be great leaders. History is replete with examples of individually powerful and highly capable women in positions of leadership including Catherine the Great, Joan of Arc, Margaret Thatcher and Tulsi Gabbard.

It's also true that some professions skew toward harmony instead of truth. Nursing, for example. Not a single patient would want nurses to be testing new ideas and probing the boundaries of truth or trying to innovate while being cared for. Patients want what is already known and conventionally agreed upon. Nursing is thus a realm where harmony and conformity are of utmost importance. It is a profession that remains the domain of women.

For an arena that battles between harmony and truth we need look no further than politics. A politician that only tells the truth never gets elected but a politician that always tells lies is despised and punted. It's an arena where skilled men and women can both do well but once again, it's best that a government be composed of far more men than women if effective, competent and truthful leadership is desired.

It's not that individual women don't seek truth. Some of the world's best researchers have been women.

The issue, according to the theory of male flight, is that in professions which seek truth, demand innovation, or require physical strength, problems will arise when there is a *dominance* of women.

The feminine preference for harmony is the root of the problem.

Since women have taken over academic institutions by sheer numbers alone, men are leaving and the only men still hired as faculty appear to be the emasculated ones such as Rambukkanna and Mister, or is it *Miss* Pimlott? Without a majority of men on faculty and as students, the universities are predictably devolving into nothing worth saving.

The theory of male flight is ironically one of the very ideas that needs to be questioned, challenged and investigated further. The university would have been the place to do it. The Social Sciences would have been the perfect branch where researchers could construct a viable *male flight hypothesis*, gather evidence and attempt to nullify the hypothesis. But if the theory of male flight has some validity, I can only imagine that instead of testing it we will find the idea being suppressed in the halls of academia. The usual excuse (*"It's harmful"*) will surface and then be followed by frenzied, hysterical, mobbish attacks. The detrimental effects from the dominance of women in academia will never be allowed to be questioned, at least not in academia itself.

One of Alfred's own creations, The Viessmann Research Centre on Modern Europe, seemed to have suffered the effects of this detrimental dominance of the feminine.

Inaugurated in 2000 and funded by Herr Dr. Dr. Hans Viessmann, it was displaying all the classic signs of ideological rot in 2024. When Hecht retired from the Centre in 2006, it took less than a decade before a new board shifted the focus of the research centre to the latest fad at the time called "sustainability." The research centre's name was changed to the Viessmann Centre for Engagement and Research in Sustainability (VERIS). The research centre later fixated on 'diversity, equity and inclusion' with the usual garble of ambiguous terms plastered throughout their marketing materials and mission statements, a vocabulary signalling allegiance to harmony and conformity. Clarity of purpose, competition and truth were eliminated.

The research centre's board of directors and staff are of course, more than 60% female. The research centre's rudder had rotted away and fallen off after Alfred disembarked from the proverbial helm.

"The first generation creates. The second generation maintains. The third generation destroys."

It still wasn't clear the proverb was accurate. Maybe the decline in academia had nothing to do with generations, or the dominance of women, or any other cause currently on offer. And it certainly wasn't true that the past was all roses either.

"There was a guy at Laurier. He was a real jerk. He would dictate who could get tenure. Two guys from England in the History Department went around and in no time, they had 60% support for a labour union," Alfred remembered.

"If there is a union in place, everyone has to pay union dues. Even if you didn't want to sign up."

Barry Boots had been angry about the whole thing, "Why should I have to join a union?" he had asked.

Alfred had been more cordially resigned to the wave of changes although as a fiscally conservative gentleman, he didn't sign it but enough people did for it to become official. "Then part-time staff got their own union," Alfred said. "Luckily the years I was at Laurier the faculty were never on strike. But the part-time went on strike. The staff went on strike."

He shook his head a little. "If you look at what they were getting paid while on strike for three weeks, (well) you're gonna get less money than (the administration) were originally willing to give."

Although these things happened after Alfred had retired from Laurier, and also did not directly involve his department, it hurt him to see his university go through negative publicity.

We turned and walked casually down the hallway, rode the elevator to the ground floor, exited and walked away from Laurier.

We would meet former colleagues from that point onward, characters in their own right who left indelible marks on Laurier and the world, at coffeeshops instead. There at least, the lights would still be turned on.

43. SHARPE

When he walked into the coffeeshop, he began peppering *us* with questions. Perhaps that personable curiosity toward others facilitated Bob Sharpe's rise up the academic ranks to Assistant Dean at Wilfred Laurier University.

He held that position under a man named David Doherty who moved on to become President of Mount Royal University at the same time I was teaching geography there. It didn't take long for Bob and I to realize we shared some mutual acquaintances.

We had made our way to the back of Covenant Cafe on Erb Street West and made ourselves comfortable in plush velvet chairs. Up front, young conservative Mennonite women in black dresses with pincushion coverings on their heads worked the busy counter.

Bob has a smile that gave off an aura of a pleasant man. His hair was combed forward and a sharp nose above a reddish beard going grey accented his narrow face. He was older than first impression would suggest although upon closer inspection, the jaundiced whites of his eyes gave indications this was a man with an overloaded liver. And where livers go, hearts go too.

Bob and Alfred had bonded as student and mentor.

Alfred hired Bob as an Associate Professor in the Department of Geography and Environmental Studies at WLU and it didn't take long for Bob, who was teaching urban geography, to become known as *the walking professor*.

Bob is retired now but the friendship between him and Alfred had been highly beneficial to both, outside of academia.

Alfred got a good deal when Bob sold his family cottage at Maple Lake in Haliburton County to him. Like most of the original places in the Muskokas and Haliburton, it was an outback fishing cottage that old men or young families with low expectations and rustic desires would go in the summer months and leave the big city behind. As Toronto and its surroundings grew, cottage country became increasingly popular with everyone including the wealthy.

But Alfred bought the place from Bob before that and he loved that. The cottage—a term often disputed by Linda who preferred the word *cabin*. It was not much more than a sturdy roof, wall boards with windy cracks between, a potbelly stove to warm the inside and an outhouse not much farther out than the limits of illumination on a strong flashlight.

It was a place of refuge for Alfred. The quality of the fishing had gone down in the later years but nonetheless, the *cabin* was Alfred's rugged mistress first introduced to him by Bob.

But long before the cottage transfer and even before Alfred hired Bob at WLU, Bob had been doing an urban planning degree at the University of Waterloo, at a time when "downtown Kitchener was kind of a wasteland. A de-industrialized hollowed-out core."

Bob explained that "Kitchener used to be Berlin. It was the only non-Francophone and non-Anglophone city in Canada, which is quite a claim. Because of that it has a really unique culture. Germanic influence. Very entrepreneurial in its origins. Quite removed from Toronto. Autonomous in its development but all of that crashed."

During his studies at Waterloo he was shocked by *how* they taught, or more accurately, *didn't* teach.

"They never once took us to Kitchener," he exclaimed.

"Really?" I asked somewhat astounded. As a former urban planning student myself and then a teacher of urban geography at Mount Royal University, I had always included field trips that explored the city. I knew the importance of getting out in the real world. Some things simply can't be taught in the classroom.

It was truly shocking what Bob was saying especially since university curricula from the 1980s onward focused heavily on two major topics—managing growth and reconstructing deindustrialized cities.

In the era of globalization, North America's manufacturing went offshore and the industrial cities fell into decline and decay. America's Northeast, the *Rust Belt*, felt the greatest burden but the urban carnage also extended into the Canadian industrial core in southern Ontario. Kitchener was one of the cities especially hard hit.

Kitchener would have been a perfect case study to examine the deindustrializing effects of a globalizing economy at the time. Planning students at the University of Waterloo could have quite literally walked to Kitchener's downtown core to examine the consequences of globalization. It seemed a shocking oversight on the part of the University of Waterloo urban planning faculty to miss out on such an opportunity.

"Not once!" Bob reiterated. "A lot of things were happening in Kitchener that were very interesting. To this day I don't understand why there wasn't a stronger field component in our education. So I decided to change all that."

He built a whole program dedicated to walking the streets. A field school of sorts. "I became known as the walking professor," he beamed. "We walked everywhere. That was essentially the course and then I even built it into my grad course. I taught PhD and Master's students and we took them walking. Showed them what was happening in Kitchener."

We both glanced over at Alfred who was savouring his coffee in slow sips.

"I'm sure Al has driven you around the downtown. Maybe not? He's more a Waterloo bias."

"Kitchener has too many red lights," Alfred retorted.

Bob looked directly at Alfred now and said, "He was my Master's degree supervisor. He was great."

Alfred let a subtle smile slip out.

From a bubbly exterior, Bob Sharpe carried on with talk about his 2006 Honda Fit and fuel efficiency. It seemed to be an intellectual focus on saving the planet through electric vehicles, mass transit and so-called efficiencies. It's common to see men and women with a deep grief turn their focus toward the intellect of the mind in order to suppress emotions of the heart. And then suddenly it came out. Bob mentioned that his wife died in 2019 from cancer.

"Didn't expect her to die so soon. The doctors said, 'You have one year to live.' And they were bang on," Bob remembered.

Bob and Shelly made the best of a bad situation.

"The last year was really good. She was only ill the last month. We went all over. Vienna three times, Vancouver, best cities. The last year was wonderful."

Bob diverted his sorrow again, suggesting his son was having a hard time with the death of his mother but it seemed obvious who was really holding the mountain of grief. He then mentioned he had heart disease and was going for surgery in less than two weeks. Where the liver goes, the heart goes too.

"I have to go for heart surgery," said Bob.

Alfred sat up in his chair and attempted to soften Sharpe's worry by describing his own surgery many years earlier, while adding a touch of humour to break the tension.

"I went into the surgery and there were two Chinese doctors. One man, one woman. I said, 'Hey, I heard you go through the leg and up' and he said, 'No it's too far and I can't because I'm left-handed.' Anyway, he put a stent in here (pointing to his heart). He said, 'You might have a little heart attack on the table but I'll do my best.' As soon as he started, he said to the nurse, 'Give me a bigger reamer!'"

"Just like plumbing!" I added.

"Yeah, just like plumbing! You know, that was twenty years ago and I am still here, no problem," Alfred said directing his attention at Bob.

"Mine is more severe than that. My dad died when he was fifty-eight. My brother had the same thing, open heart surgery. Mine is March 26, 2024."

Alfred seemed comfortable with his age and accomplishments and his place in the world. I wondered quietly if Alfred's faith had something to do with that sense of contentment—the knowledge that when God says your time is up, that's it, and that's fine. Although admittedly, Alfred had never lost his wife.

Bob and Alfred turned to rattling off the names of people they knew and checked notes on who was still alive and who still attended social events at the university.

"I don't go to those events anymore. I feel kind of old and depressed. Covid really set me back," Bob admitted.

Alfred returned to a previous topic. "So, you were with David Doherty?"

"Yup. He went straight to MRU."

The small colleges in Canada, especially those with a long history, often began as religious colleges. They tended to have a pattern of collegiality among faculty and students. Those students usually left with a purpose, community connections and leadership. Laurier was one such example in Ontario. Mount Royal in Alberta, and perhaps others such as Thompson Rivers and Langara in British Columbia or Mount Alison in Nova Scotia, would claim similar histories if one were to ask.

"Laurier was such a small community when I started there. People knew each other, Arts and Science were together. They're not anymore," said Bob.

Alfred pointed out that in Canada a "college is typically run by a president that has control over almost all governance decisions. A good president makes a good college. The university model is bicameral; faculty and administration share governance. It sounds more democratic but it typically becomes more political and top heavy in bureaucracy. More than a few colleges that ran well for a hundred years thought they were progressing when they became a university only to find the best attributes of collegiality and tight-knit relationships with students disappeared quite quickly after the transition."

It was true. Administratively top-heavy problems were reeking a noticeable toll.

"When I first started at Laurier there was a President, Vice-President, Dean and Department chair and then faculty. Then all of a sudden...there was a Vice-President for Advancement. Then we had an Associate Vice-President for Human Relations. Then a Vice-Pres. for Faculty. Then the Deans got Associate Deans for Student Affairs, then Dean for Faculty Affairs and Associate Dean for Staff Affairs, etc.," Alfred said.

To me it hit home.

"I saw that at Mount Royal," I added. "When I started in 2008 it was a very collegial place. Then it switched to a university and the collegiality disappeared. New research staff came in with no interest in teaching and administrative positions exploded. Some of us used to joke there were so many people in administration after it became a university that no one was left to teach."

"Yeah," Bob agreed. "Similar to Laurier. Laurier is really old, 1911."

"Same as Mount Royal, 1910," I replied.

"Was it a religious college?"

"Originally, yes."

"A similar trajectory."

Alfred then brought up the topic of our visit to Wilfred Laurier University a couple of days earlier.

"Were there a lot of people around?" Bob asked. "Because I've been in a couple of times and there's nobody there."

"Two guys and the Executive Assistant only. Mary-Louise Byrne is the chair now (but) she wasn't there."

"That's kind of shocking," Bob replied.

"They all work from home. This guy Grant who's been there a long time said Geography has been losing faculty positions left, right and centre."

"Yeah, even though it moved to Science, it didn't really help."

"It hinders," Alfred said firmly. "It really has gone down," he said with more than a tinge of disappointment. "Byrne thinks of herself as a big scientist."

Bob shook his head a little while Alfred described how a number of years earlier he found out the department was moving to the Sciences. "My judgement in the long run, was that it was very bad because Laurier is not known for its sciences. If you want to take a BSc go to Waterloo."

"Yeah, most of the students are Arts students," Bob confirmed.

"Or business, so when Grant told us (they're) losing faculty, I thought, 'It's because of that.' Now it's called the Department of Geography and Environmental Studies but moving it into the science area they are with the smaller departments of chemistry, physics and biology.

Well, those departments are peanuts in comparison to the ones at the University of Waterloo."

Alfred took another sip of coffee before hitting hard.

"They are joining the small dogs instead of the big dogs."

Bob nodded.

"And they cancelled the joint grad programs years ago," Alfred said.

Bob Sharpe had stayed on longer at WLU, retiring after Alfred. "That was happening when I was there," he confirmed. "I could tell it was happening because there was no collegiality anymore, so many retirements. PhD students could have independent committees. They didn't need each other anymore."

"I don't think they are going to be able to keep the program. You need critical mass. Originally we had a Master's program with four graduate students, (then during) that first year (of expansion) we had fourteen students."

"That's pretty good," Bob said. "I think a part of the reason for the change was the faculty that was hired, when still in Arts, became research chairs. They think they don't really need the undergrad program. Research chairs are mostly research chairs."

"Yeah, well I'm beyond that," Alfred huffed a little.

Bob nodded in agreement.

Alfred turned back to the more soothing subjects of camaraderie among men—competition, guns, cars and cottages.

"For the cottage at Maple Lake...Linda never accepted the word cottage because it never had indoor plumbing."

"Worse than that, the fireplace didn't work properly," Bob said as a new smile came over him, "And no insulation! It was great. I grew up there."

"Alfred Pletsch and I built that outhouse, good for 100 years, five feet deep."

"And it had a window to the sea," Bob added with fondness.

While the quaint and rustic cabin did not always appeal to the rest of the Hecht family, for Alfred and Bob it was a refuge and Alfred had always been grateful to Bob Sharpe for selling it to him.

"The reason why *we* sold it was that four-hour drive," Alfred said.

Bob half laughed. "That's why I said, 'Yeah, take it.'"

"We had it twenty years!" Alfred exclaimed.

They both beamed with the smiles of a fond nostalgia.

Suddenly the coffeeshop baristas were sweeping and upturning chairs as a cue to make it known they wanted to close.

We obliged and scurried away from the expiring benevolence of the Mennonite baristas with brooms.

44. SALLOUM

An interior design of simple lines, institutional cleanliness and subdued Victorian mouldings greeted us as we walked into the modern retirement home. In an open meeting area on the ground floor Alfred and I helped ourselves to free coffee at a kitchen countertop that was recessed into an alcove, before going over and sitting down at one of a few tables where a man named Jerry Salloum was sitting.

A mild-mannered man with the look of deep thoughts bubbling behind the soft face. Straight grey hair was parted on the left in a not too dissimilar fashion to Alfred's hairstyle, although Jerry was a few pounds lighter. Jerry was an Anglican priest and apparently a good one at that.

"I have Alfred to thank because I was a nobody," Jerry said after introductions.

It struck me as an odd thing to say but deprecating humour can have its place. Jerry explained that he had lacklustre academic credentials—only a Bachelor's degree—when Alfred first hired him to teach in the Geography Department at Laurier. Salloum and Hecht became friends after Alfred hired him to teach physical geography courses at the Brantford branch campus.

The conversation between two old friends turned quickly to philosophical discussions about religious doctrines. Jerry came from the Anglican faith and Alfred from a Mennonite background. In the world of theologians, faith and competitive friends, the two are polar opposites.

Jerry explained their religious philosophical differences as a matter of, "Grace versus Works."

Anglicans place faith in *Grace*.

Mennonites see good works as a way to secure their place in Heaven.

Smiles came over both as they recalled a moment together.

"I'd come into Alfred's office," Jerry said, "and asked him for a book of…favours," intimating the notion that God has recorded everyone in a book who is destined to go to Heaven.

Alfred had pulled out a notebook from his office desk in response, flipped through it before looking up and replying in a dry tone, "Jerry, your name is here but it's written in pencil."

They both laughed.

The Wilfred Laurier University campus in Brantford was an experimental offshoot. It wanted to attract students from the immediate surrounding regions of Brantford and Hamilton who might choose to go there instead of driving all the way up to the main campus in Kitchener-Waterloo. It needed good teachers if was going to succeed. Since Jerry had taught high school geography, Alfred hired him and sent him down to Brantford to teach undergraduate geography courses. It worked.

Jerry was a great teacher. He got good evaluations and brought in new students.

As a Mennonite who rewards good work, Alfred hired Jerry to do even more courses for Laurier. Since Jerry only had a Bachelor's degree it would be hard to justify having him on faculty at that moment so Alfred helped him get into a Master's degree program.

Alfred became Jerry's supervisor.

"This way," Alfred explained, "I could say that he had a Master's degree *in progress*." It was good enough to allow Jerry to teach with only a Bachelor's degree. It's a common practice now in universities. When they have someone with potential but not enough credentials, they sign them up for a higher-level program so they can get them teaching right away.

"I don't know why he hired me," Jerry said again. This time it struck me as not just self-deprecating for comedic effect but a genuine belief in not being good enough.

I leaned in a little, locked eyes and asked, "Do you see yourself as unworthy?"

Jerry looked momentarily shocked at the question but then responded, "Yes."

It all seemed to come together. The man had spent his entire life feeling a sense of unworthiness, which apparently came from his mother's demands more than his father, he suggested.

It also struck me that we were suddenly delving into questions of faith and allegiance. Could it be that the Anglican faith attracts those who feel unworthy? Could it be that the Anglican faith, so devoted to the idea of grace, automatically attracts those who wonder if they are worthy of unconditional love and acceptance and thus, respond externally with self-deprecation?

By contrast, does the Mennonite faith, which puts an emphasis on working hard and making something of yourself, come with a stern drive of achievement but maybe also a heavy dose of judgement?

Just then, Alfred began to explain through metaphor that questioning one's worth is probably a universal phenomenon. "Paraguay is such a different setting. It does not necessarily transfer here to North America. But some of the values certainly did. You know, I didn't have a father growing up so in my case, I don't ever remember my mother hugging me. There were seven of us kids."

"There is another explanation for your mother never hugging you," Jerry said with a wicked grin.

"What's that?"

"She didn't like you."

Alfred displayed no surface reaction whatsoever. He simply carried on, remembering his mother telling another person that her kids, including Alfred, didn't know the difference between a horse and a cow. So, living in Paraguay as farmers had no future.

"So, what is the difference between a horse and cow?" Jerry asked facetiously.

Alfred smiled now and replied with his own wicked grin, "You pat a cow on the back and she won't kick. You pat a horse on the back, she kicks and that is the end of you."

They chuckled a little before Alfred added, "I think to some degree she was right. When we got to Canada, I went to high school. Rudy finished high school in extension. My younger sister, who has died now, finished high school and went to university. We all went to university. I went on, the others went to teacher's college, the only one that didn't was Helene. One year younger, she sometimes reminds me that she had to learn a practical nursing course for six months and then work and help Mom out with money so the rest could go to university. School was private and expensive. We got good marks."

The conversation turned back to Jerry. He had colon cancer. There was a history of it in his family and I wondered how much the emotional effects of one's belief in their own self-worth affect health. Here was a man who was a very good teacher and priest, highly valued by those around him, yet in his own eyes he seemed unable to see the good man he was.

Jerry was eighty-five. He was having trouble recalling things, although heaping praise upon Alfred came in abundance.

Unfortunately, the signs of dementia and the effects of the cancer were noticeable. There was slippage in memory, repetitive statements and an obsessive worry over the control of money. We spent thirty minutes with a good man who seemed unable to see what others saw in him before he politely terminated the conversation.

"You'll have to excuse me. I have to find my wallet," said Jerry.

Jerome Edward Salloum passed away four months later on July 23, 2024.

45. SIDE HUSTLE

A professor's salary is not going to make anyone rich. Alfred had successfully climbed the career ladder, successfully mentored countless students, raised a family and made a name for himself. When he fully retired from teaching in 2011, the last teaching position held was at Fachhochschule in Germany, he still wanted to do one more thing—make some real money.

The opportunity had actually begun with an unexpected phone call from a former student just prior to retirement.

"Al, what do you think about a shopping centre at the intersection at 401 and Hwy. 4?" the former grad student named John McCash asked over the phone. McCash had started his own real estate firm in Cambridge, Ontario after graduating from Laurier.

Alfred replied, "It has great accessibility. So, why are you calling me?"

"Are you interested in doing the feasibility study?"

"Yes, but only if I can use my fourth-year students."

"That would be great; to say we're hiring students!" McCash shot back.

Alfred took on the project. He needed data on consumer purchases in the region. He hired graduate students to make phone calls asking people about their shopping habits.

"I started with three men and four women," Alfred laughed a little. "Only one of the men had a voice on the phone that didn't irritate people!"

Two men, apparently sounding too pushy or questionable or something, felt the sting of rejection as people regularly hung up on them. The friendly women and the reassuring voice from one man eventually allowed the team to get enough data.

"We interviewed 910 (people). I had to document it all. I also did a gravity model from each township. I knew income. I knew also, from other data, what proportion they would spend on department store-type merchandize. Theoretically the shopping centre would have $808,000 potential income. The company said, 'Great!'"

But there was a little shopping centre down the road a kilometre and a half away that objected.

"I had to prove the new (shopping centre) would not affect the old one negatively. According to my calculation the old one would lose…in the first year but after a couple of years, the pass-by traffic, they could catch some of that extra traffic," and actually generate a positive return for both the new and old stores. "According to my analysis, theoretical and survey, it would generate good money."

In the province of Ontario, the proposed shopping centre needed approval from the government and since the little shopping centre down the road objected, a hearing had to be held to prove the big new shopping centre wouldn't unduly impact the existing one. The case went to Ontario Municipal Board hearings.

"The OMB had two older guys, one had been a planner, the other, a retail business owner of some sort. This was an early retirement job for them."

Alfred represented the development company—Cadillac-Fairview Corporation.

"It was like a law case. They got me on the stand and peppered me with questions."

He presented the research findings from the nine hundred surveys.

"They were grilling me with questions, then shut down for the day. They said you cannot talk to anybody."

The company booked a hotel room nearby and Alfred, John McCash and a company lawyer discussed strategy all night. When they returned the next day the opposition said, "We noticed that you have slightly different measurements."

Alfred explained. "I had sub-contracted that work out to our cartographer and to our physical geographer. The cartographer had a wheel that moved to the very centre of the proposed site. The other guy had just put the measurement right up to it. I tried to explain (the minor discrepancy) but the judge said 'There is a problem so throw it out.'"

Suddenly, all they had left were the survey results and the opposition wasn't even sure those actually existed. The time between the work and the hearings was extensive. In that time a few of Alfred's graduate students had used the work they had done on the survey for their graduate and PhD theses. In other words the full dataset was available at the WLU library for anyone to check.

The company sent someone to see and sure enough, all the data was there. Alfred's team made their case and won.

"But by that time shopping centres were no longer in anymore. (Cadillac-Fairview) asked if they could put in 500,000 square feet of big box instead of a shopping centre. So, they did. Highway 4 and Highway 401."

Alfred added with a smile, "They have a nice restaurant there. Texas Lone Star Grill."

Cadillac-Fairview paid him well for his consulting services, "and with that I got into the housing business."

The first property didn't go well. He invested in one unit of a six-unit townhouse project in London, Ontario. The project was only half built and ran into construction problems. Alfred had to get out shortly after getting in.

"Experience is a good teacher but it's the most expensive. I lost about $50,000. It doesn't sound like much but it was my first (and last) investment where I didn't have control." Alfred added, "Money is too precious to get into something that is not yours."

He turned instead to using his skills as an economic analyst. He generated a wealth of data on housing prices and market variables far beyond what an average real estate assessor would ever do. He ran regression analyses on his data set and knew exactly what each house should cost in order to generate the highest cash flow. With that knowledge in hand, he would wait until the right one came on the market and then pounce.

The first opportunity actually came with the sale of his daughter and son-in-law's house. It was in good condition. It fit his criteria and they were willing to sell to Dad at a good price. He snapped it up for $205,000, he rented it out and it produced cashflow very quickly and worked out well. Alfred bought numerous rental houses after that, which generated healthy cashflow as well but not without a couple of hiccups.

Sometimes renters need to leave early or a landlord wants them to leave for various reasons. Under amicable landlord-tenant relationships, the landlord will often offer a hand, like renting a truck to help the tenant move. Normally, that's not needed because it's a common tradition for people in Canada to help their friends move. A couple of guys and a truck and it's done in a day. No big deal. But one of Alfred's tenants was such a problem, obviously a manipulative individual, that he concocted a story claiming he needed $10,000 from Alfred in order to move out.

Alfred's religious faith would not allow him to sue.

"We help people out," Alfred explained. He gave the tenant $10,000.

His son Marv still reels whenever the topic comes up. He believed his father should have "kicked the guy to the curb" so to speak and definitely not handed over $10,000.

It wasn't the only tenant who tested Alfred's patience, and chequebook.

"Usually I did a check on where the (applicant) previously rented. One of the references for this (potential tenant) had given her dad. When I called, her dad said, 'I would never rent to her.' I couldn't believe it!" Alfred said with the look of shock.

He wrote a rejection letter to the potential tenant who then turned around and "accused me of racial bias because her husband was Black."

Alfred couldn't believe this woman would try to use the race-card against him, which of course, only solidified his decision not to rent to her.

Aside from a couple of bad actors, the real estate business went well. At the high point in his post-retirement side hustle, he had six rental units. They generated far more income than a retired professor's pension ever could. While he gained fame as a professor he became wealthy as a real estate investor.

He gradually sold off his holdings at various peaks, timing the market and getting top dollar. By 2024, on the cusp of a Canada-wide real estate melt, he had only one left.

46. FISHING STORIES at JACK'S

Alfred's brother-in-law, Wayne Toews, loved to spend time fishing at remote lakes that shimmer like pockmarked puddles in the scoured bedrock of the Canadian Shield; a geological formation that defines the character of northern Manitoba and Ontario. Covered in thin-soiled forests and isolation, the word 'remote' is a terribly weak adjective to describe the wilderness landscape. Wayne loved to escape the world by flying out there to fish. He built himself a plane.

"But a friend took it up and crashed it," Alfred reported as he, Linda and I sat down for dinner at Jack's restaurant. Located at the St. Jacobs Farmer's Market complex where hustle and bustle occur every day but especially on the weekends as tourists from Toronto and surroundings arrive looking for schnitzel and handicrafts, Jack's offers a place to rest.

Leatherette booths, burgers and some sort of pasta dish are always on the menu at Jack's. So was trout today. Alfred and I both ordered it.

Alfred mentioned that he often joined Wayne on fishing trips. There was a third fellow, too.

The only one in the trio who didn't own a plane was Alfred. The other fellow had his float plane parked on the river at Selkirk, Manitoba halfway between Lake Winnipeg and the city of Winnipeg. Lake Winnipeg is a little larger than the state of Israel which is to say, it's too big for really good fishing. The best fishing was to be had in the small lakes at least two hundred kilometres away with clear water, no pollution and few humans. Only accessible by foot or air was best.

The trio had their favourite spot. As Alfred described the round lake an image of a meteor strike hole filled with water came to mind.

"That is the best fishing lake there is, you know!" Alfred said, not giving away the actual name or location. "We stored an aluminum boat in the bush" at the edge of a sandy beach. "That was kinda neat (and) usually if we flew at 10 a.m., by 2 o'clock we had our limit."

Many of the fish they caught were too small or outside the regulations and therefore they'd put them back in the water. While Alfred loved fishing Wayne Toews was a level above. Wayne knew everything about fishing, awards and special moments cast and caught on the end of a reel.

"On one occasion...I got this fish and I said, 'It is not that big. Maybe I should throw it back,'" Alfred remembered.

Wayne took a quick look and replied, "No, we're gonna keep this one." He put the fish into a cooler of ice-water and when the three returned to Winnipeg, Wayne took Alfred's fish home with him. Later he showed up at Alfred's place with the fish, stuffed and mounted on a trophy plaque.

"He presented me with this...stuffed fish I had caught!" Alfred said beaming.

The fish sits like the prize that it is on the wall in the Hecht's family room above the fireplace.

Linda jumped in to add, "It's a prized perch!"

"Master Angler Award for Manitoba," Alfred added coyly for a second time.

The waitress came by just then with our meals. As we ate, Alfred told of how they would also drive from Winnipeg to just north of Kenora, a good hour and a half away, where there were also a couple of good lakes. "Usually before noon we had the limit and then drove back, sometimes arriving before 6 o'clock."

"Yeah," Linda said as she put her utensils down to speak. "The first time they came in with all these fish, they said, 'Okay, it's the women's turn. They can do all the cleaning.' I had never done that before and haven't since."

"I think it was good enough grounds to get a divorce. But we didn't proceed," Alfred said jokingly, which was followed by a small round of laughter from Alfred and myself. Linda was not nearly as amused.

Not always off with the men in the far reaches of northern Canada, one of Alfred's fondest memories was going to the cottage they'd bought off Bob Sharpe. The cottage was a place Linda liked and Alfred cherished.

For Alfred, especially rewarding was time spent with his grandchildren out there; a time especially fond, emotive and revealing.

His granddaughter Rebecca, now a teenage girl with a raspy voice suited for jazz and leadership, with straight black hair and slim build carried a commanding presence larger than her age would suggest.

Without saying much of anything, it was clear Alfred is deeply fond of his granddaughter. The shared trait of strong wills, I suspect, has something to do with it but that only scratches the surface.

"I used to take Rebecca and Joseph when young (up to) Maple Lake."

The fishing was decent enough and "when we got back to shore, you gotta clean. Either you fillet it or you scrape off the outside of the fish. Before you do that, you had to cut off the head. Ha!" Alfred said, laughing to himself as he remembered what would happen next.

Rebecca would say, "Grandpa, just hold it down and cut it off!" He chuckled again at the thought of his young granddaughter having zero signs of squeamishness. "She had no repulsion or restriction on seeing the blood."

Rebecca would say with authority and glee, "Chop it off Grandpa! Just chop it off!"

"But that cabin was a four-hour drive, you know. It wasn't the best fishing lake." Alfred looked down at the trout and fries on his plate and added, "British (people) always put vinegar on their fries. Argh, even Barry Boots. Well, each to his own."

47. REGRETS

The list of regrets was short but distinct. There were only two.

"When I was growing up, I thought maybe I should be in business. Canada, being a cold country, I would have liked to have a shop to sell nice heavy-duty woollen sweaters or pullovers. Well, that never came to be. In part, all cars now have heaters, houses have heaters. So, you don't see sweater-wearing much now."

There was also a deeper, grittier, more primordial influence that turned him off the sweater-selling business and it had nothing to do with modern indoor heating.

"One of my colleagues always wore a sweater from September 'til March and he never washed it. You could smell him from three yards away!"

In typical Canadian fashion, nobody said a thing.

"I think he got so used to it, that he did not know. All faculty members...stayed away from him. He had a little historical house on the Grand River" without heating or shower, only an outhouse. "If he had to stay overnight there, the next morning he had obviously not showered. It turned me off the idea of having a nice store selling big thick sweaters!"

The other thing Alfred had mild regrets about was the unfulfilled desire to own or manage a fly-in fishing lodge somewhere up north.

"On one occasion these guys came into the bar (we were at and) they had the old fishing stories. I said to myself, 'That's an ideal life: catch the fish, fry the fish and tell stories of how the big one got away.'"

But on one fishing expedition with friend Merle Hunsberger, they flew in to a fishing lodge on a native reserve west of Timmins, Ontario. The cheap rental accommodations enticed them to go.

"When we got there, there was this little hut, double bunk beds, very small kitchen and an outhouse (with) a sign that says *Watch Out for*

Bears. The guy who flew us in said, 'The black bears are out in force already.' That soured me a little on having a fly-in lodge."

Aside from the bears and smelly sweaters, "my mom never allowed me to (consider any other path). She would remind me that my dad had been a teacher, my uncle had been a teacher, my Aunt Emma had been a teacher..."

48. LEGACY

Inside every person is an evolutionary drive to leave a legacy. Women leave children and relationships. Men must leave behind something they either build or create. Whether that's a stone wall, a business or an endowment fund, the legacy looms large in every man's conscience and Alfred Hecht was no exception.

Education had always been a driving force in his life from the time his father sent a letter to his brother Rudy saying, "Everything you have you can lose but what you have in your head no one can take away from you."

For Alfred, the benefits of an education were enormous, and obvious. Education brought him out of poverty, propelled him to a fabulous career, allowed him to raise a family and gave him opportunity to be a mentor to others. It was only natural that he would leave a legacy dedicated to education. And it was only natural that his support would go to those who helped him in the past and were most in need now. He turned his attention to Indigenous students in the Chaco region of Paraguay.

The first thing he needed to do was register a charity with the federal tax department. In 2014, he submitted an application.

The government found it suspicious. Behind closed doors, they were asking themselves if this was some sort of money laundering scheme to get money out of an obscure South American country.

"When I applied to the CRA (Canada Revenue Agency) to set up a charity they said, *'Paraguay?'* I argued that (the Indigenous people) helped us Mennonites a lot because they knew the environment pretty good and they would help us clear the bush but they couldn't read and write."

Nowadays machines have mostly replaced labour. Demand for labour has gone down and Alfred, even more, could see they needed to have an education in order to find alternate work.

The Canadian government accepted his application.

However, in order to satisfy the bureaucratic paperwork requirements Alfred made an unassuming error. He filled in the title box as a descriptor of the charity's purpose. He wrote, "Scholarship/Bursary for Indigenous Students in the Neuland Settlement Region of the Chaco of Paraguay."

Alfred explained that, "It was a working name. Then all of a sudden the (CRA agent) said, 'Well, you've got it!'"

The temporary working name became the official name.

"Ha!" Alfred exclaimed. "So, on the actual tax receipt I have to have the full name—Scholarship/Bursary for Indigenous Students in the Neuland Settlement Region of the Chaco of Paraguay."

The purpose of the charity was to help Indigenous students in Paraguay receive an education.

"We support them getting a high school education. There is an NGO that's pretty big that organizes elementary education. They look after some twenty elementary schools in that region. There is one high school run by the same organization but it's very expensive." The government of Paraguay does not contribute to the funding of high schools and since the school had to pay the teachers, the cost per student was around $500 per year. Most of the students simply couldn't afford that. "That's when our charity jumped in," Alfred explained.

The first year, 2015, there were only a few donors. By 2023, they were supporting fifty-seven students.

The board of directors in Canada includes Alfred Hecht as chair. Jerry Salloum's wife Nancy is on the board in addition to Roma Carlson and Yvonne Douglas. A committee in Paraguay administers the applications and selects the students to be funded. Verena Regehr is the chair of the committee in Paraguay.

Of course, where money is involved, emotions and an overabundance of compassion can be a problem.

Verena Regehr, the Indian Mother, originally moved to Paraguay from Switzerland with her husband. She's the kind of person who wants to help every soul in need and Alfred has had to be the one to sometimes say, *No.*

The students mostly come from the Nivaclé and Ayoreo Indigenous tribes who live in the region. In some cases, the Ayoreo villages are over two hundred kilometres away. They can't just go back home each day to eat. "So who's gonna feed them?" Alfred asked rhetorically.

Verena Regehr wanted to use some of the charity money to help feed students. Alfred had to insist, "Sorry, our money is only for education, not for food."

Managing the money and adhering to the purpose is one of the tasks Alfred does well, even if it's not a role he wanted. There was also a request at one time for insulin and once again, he had to remind Verena that the fund is for education, not medical supplies.

Instead, "Linda and I threw in $5,000 of our personal money to buy insulin," he said.

But as the old Chinese proverb states, "No good deed goes unpunished" and nowhere was that more true than here.

"Because we have supported the students for quite some time the message is spreading throughout the Chaco, 'Hey, go talk to Verena Regehr, they have some support from abroad' and for them *abroad money* must be like water, it just keeps on flowing."

The last time there was a request to use funds for other purposes, "I threatened, I said, 'We were thinking to stop the charity.' She came back saying, 'Not yet, not yet.'"

While the Indian Mother has been trying to expand the charity's purpose she has also, without a doubt, been a needed guardian in her own way as well. For example, the last time Alfred and Linda were in Paraguay they went to the school, sat on the benches with around one hundred students in attendance, and listened to a sales pitch by the new school president and some of his admin staff. The fancy PowerPoint presentation was essentially proposing that the school take the money and designate where it would go.

Alfred remembered, "I was sitting there and Verena was on the other side. I could clearly see her looking at me (to say), 'Don't fall for this!'"

There will of course come a time when Alfred no longer runs the charity. He could shut it all down, or ask someone else to continue it.

At this point I teased Alfred a little. "You'll have to be careful. You might be accused of promoting cultural genocide."

On May 29, 2021 the Canadian Broadcasting Corporation (CBC) reported that 215 mass graves of Indigenous children had been discovered at a former Indian residential school site in Kamloops, British Columbia. The narrative that followed claimed that Canada was a genocidal nation that had murdered Indigenous children and allowed priests and nuns to secretly bury the bodies in mass graves.

Yet evidence to support the wild accusations of mass murder, genocide or any other such atrocities, was seriously lacking. Three years later and millions of dollars spent, not a single body was ever exhumed. No forensic evidence of mass murder was ever found to substantiate the wild claims. The book, *Grave Error: How the Media Misled Us,* published in 2023, clearly refuted the entire genocide narrative.

Yet, most Canadians seemed to have internalized a mental position of self-loathing in response to the stories. According to polling data, three years after the event, 85% of Canadians still believed the false government narrative that had been perpetrated mostly by the country's government-funded public broadcaster, the CBC.

As Winston Churchill once said, "A lie gets halfway around the world before the truth has a chance to get its pants on."

The truth had not even managed to rouse itself awake in Canada. To this day most Canadians still believe the lie. *Oh well.*

I warned Alfred again jokingly that his charity, which supported Indigenous people in Paraguay who wanted to go to school, much in the same way government and religious organizations in Canada had supported Indigenous people by giving them an opportunity to access employment in modern society via education through the residential school system, could be construed as "destroying Indigenous culture." The taunt was light-hearted but not unserious. One could not simply wave off the self-loathing that seemed to overcome Canadian society. But so far, Alfred had not had to deal with such accusations, although negative sentiment of so-called colonial oppression, certainly simmered among some Indigenous people in Paraguay just as it did among some in Canada.

Nonetheless, the charity was Alfred Hecht's legacy and gift that brought the opportunity of education to those lacking the financial means to obtain it on their own. And there were others gladly willing to be a part of it, especially as repayment to the Indigenous people who helped them out many years prior.

Franz Friesen, his wife Anna and their whole family contribute every year. Why? Because as Anna Friesen, who lived in Paraguay at the same time as Alfred and her future husband Franz, said emphatically, "The Indigenous people helped us tremendously in the Chaco and if we can help them now, we will!"

Sadly, Canadian donations to charities have been declining every year since the 1970s. Alfred's charity, however, was bucking the trend. In spite of this, the need still outweighs demand. There are still far more students who could be supported. With the insatiable need, his charity is an honourable venture. It was exactly as was to be expected of Alfred Hecht.

His, was a fine legacy.

REFERENCES

[1] Steinfeld is the prior German name. The village is now called Kam'yane Pole. It is located in the Dnipropetrovsk Oblast of Ukraine.

[2] Driedger, MaryLou. "What in the World Was the Judenplan?" May 7, 2021, www.maryloudriedger2.wordpress.com

[3] Weidemann, Erika Lee. "A Malleable Identity: The Immigration of Ethnic Germans to North America, 1947–1957." Dissertation, Graduate and Professional Studies, Texas A&M University. March 17, 2020.

[4] Friesen, Karl. "Audio recording of an interview with Franz Friesen by his son Karl Friesen." Winnipeg, Manitoba, 2023.

[5] Schloneger, Florence. *Sara's Trek*. Newton, Kansas: Faith and Life Press, 1981.

[6] Popowycz, Jennifer. "The Last Million: Eastern European Displaced Persons in Postwar Germany." The National WWII Museum, New Orleans. April 4, 2022. www.nationalww2museum.org

[7] Chapter XVI, "Germany in Defeat, The Carpet." Center for Military History. www.history.army.mil

[8] Chapter XVII, "Germany in Defeat, Zone and Sector Access to Berlin." Center for Military History. www.history.army.mil, 289.

[9] Warkentin, J.W. "Carving a Home out of the Primeval Forest." Anabaptistwiki.org, 1950.

[10,11,12,13,14] Remus, Harold. *I Remember Laurier: Reflections by Retirees on Life at Laurier*, Waterloo, Ontario: Wilfred Laurier University Press, 2011, pg. 71, 72, 41, 45, 45.

[15] "Battle of Hué." www.wikipedia.org. Retrieved August 8, 2024.

[16] This chapter is an adaptation of Alfred Hecht's contribution in Harold Remus' book, *I Remember Laurier: Reflections by Retirees on Life at Laurier*, Waterloo, Ontario: Wilfred Laurier University Press, 2011. pp. 128–132.

[17] "Why aren't we talking about the real reason male college enrollment is dropping?" by Celeste Davis, Matriarchal Blessing, Oct. 6, 2024. celestemdavis.substack.com.

[*] Alexandrovka (a farming estate) Rayon (Rayon is part of an "Oblast"), Izyum Izyumskiy Rayon, Kharkivs'ka Region, Kharkov (a.k.a. Kharkivs'ka) USSR. Location: 49.1666667 N. 37.4166667 E

APPENDIX
CURRICULUM VITAE

ALFRED HECHT, B.Sc., M.A., Ph.D. (University Professor)
Born: 26 Feb. 1942 – Steinfeld, Ukraine
Son of Leonidas and Susanna (Krause)
Husband to Linda A., daughter of John and Tina Huebert
Married June 26, 1965
Children: Marvin A., Melinda M.
Waterloo, Ontario, Canada

APPOINTMENTS IN CANADA

2007	University of Waterloo, taught graduate course 'Industrial Location Models'
2006-present	Professor Emeritus, Wilfred Laurier University
1982-2006	Full Professor, Wilfred Laurier University
1988, 1991	University of Guelph, taught graduate course, 'Regional Economics'
1989, 1990	University of Waterloo, taught graduate course, 'Industrial Location Models'
1976-1982	Associate Professor, Wilfred Laurier University
1970	Summer School Instructor, University of Manitoba
1967-1968	Counsellor, Department of Manpower and Immigration, Manitoba
1968-1969	High school teacher in Portage La Prairie, Manitoba
1964-1963	High school teacher in Portage La Prairie, Manitoba (Phys, Math, Chemistry & Geography)

APPOINTMENTS ABROAD

Oct-Feb/2009-10	Visiting Professor, Fachhochschule, Hof, Germany
April-July/09	Canadian Studies, Visiting Professor, University of Kiel, Germany
May-June/03	Canadian Studies, Visiting Professor, Marburg, Germany
Oct-March/98	Visiting Professor, Fachhochschule, Hof, Germany
May-July/97	Visiting Professor, Philipps University, Marburg, Germany
June 1990	Visiting Professor, Philipps University, Marburg, Germany
April-July/87	Visiting Professor, Justus-Liebeg University, Giessen, West Germany
April-July/87	Visiting Professor, Philipps University, Marburg, West Germany
Oct-March/79	Visiting Professor, Philipps University, Marburg, West Germany
April-Sept/79	Visiting Professor, John F. Kennedy Institute of North American Studies, Freie University Berlin
April-Aug/76	Visiting Professor, John F. Kennedy Institute of North American Studies, Freie University Berlin

ADMINISTRATION

- Associate Director, Viessmann Research Centre on Modern Europe, 2005-2011
- Director, Viessmann Research Centre of Modern Europe, 2001-2005
- Director, Laurier International and International Liaison Officer, 1999-2005
- Wilfred Laurier University Senate Academic Planning Committee, 2001-2005
- Director, Waterloo-Laurier Graduate program in Geography, 1998-2000
- Wilfred Laurier University Senate Academic Planning Committee, 1998-2000
- Chair, Department of Geography and Environmental Studies, 1976-1979 / 1989-1997
- Department Graduate Officer, 1973-1976, 1983-1986, 1988-1990
- Urban Studies Option Coordinator, 1974-1998
- Member, Executive of the joint Waterloo-Laurier Graduate Program in Geography, 1992-98 (Main force in establishing this joint Graduate program. (It has more than 120 Grad students in Masters Arts, Master of Environmental Studies and PhDs)
- Member, Senate Honorary Degree Committee, 1992-1998
- Dean's Advisory Committee, 1989-1997
- Member, Wilfred Laurier Board of Governor's Development and Community Relations Committee, 1996-1998.
- Member, WLU's Board of Governors, 1992-1996
- Member, WLU's Board of Governors, Executive, 1993-1996
- Member, WLU's Board Property Committee, 1992-1995
- Member, WLU's Board Audit Committee, 1993-1993
- Member, WLU's Board Investment Committee, 1992-1993
- Member, WLU's Senate Executive, 1992-1996
- Geography Department Graduate Officer for 7 years, 1973-1976, 1982-1986)
- Secretary, Council of Deans of Arts and Science of Ontario for 2 years, 1977-79
- Executive Member, Canadian Association of Geographers 1992-1994
- WLU/Philipps University Exchange Program Coordinator, 1984-1996
- WLU/Baden-Württemburg Exchange Coordinator, 1989-1996

FORMAL EDUCATION

- PhD, Clark University, Worcester, Massachusetts, 1972 (Major in Geography, Minor in Economics)
- M.A., University of Manitoba, 1968, (Major in Geography, Minor in Statistics)
- B.Sc., United College/University of Manitoba, 1964 (Physics, Calculus, Chemistry)
- High School education, 1961, Winnipeg, Manitoba, Canada
- Elementary education, 1954, Gnadental, Chaco, Paraguay

HONOURS

- Alexander von Humbolt Fellow (26 months) – Germany, 1980, 1983, 1986, 2002
- Honorary Degree, Dr. rar, nat. h.c., Freie University of Berlin, February 18, 2000
- Visiting Fellow, Australian Defense Forces Academy, University of New South Wales, Australia, February—May, 1993
- Conrad Grebel College Fellow, Waterloo University, 1985-present
- Canada Council Doctoral Fellow, 1971-1972
- Clark University Fellow, 1969-1972 (graduate)

TEACHING AREAS

<u>Undergraduate</u>
Economic Geography – Industrial location – Research Methods – Urban Studies: Latin American Cities – Internal Structure of Cities - Models of Geographic Systems – Advanced Canadian Urban Geography

<u>Graduate</u>
Canada's Regional Space Economy, Seminar in Economic Location Models, Advanced. Urban Analysis Seminar, Regional Disparities and Regional Development, Regional Economics

<u>Abroad</u>
Canada's Regional Economy, Regional Development Theories and Models, Special English. Colloquium Expressions and Sayings, Geography of Canada, Canadian Urbanism (taught in. German), Economic Geography of Canada (taught in German), Socio-Economic Dimensions of Canadian Urbanism, Regional Geography of North America (taught in German), Economic Geography of North America (taught in German), Problems of North American Cities (taught in German), Quantitative Methods in Economic Geography (taught in German).

PUBLICATIONS

Thesis and Dissertation

Hecht, Alfred. "An Analysis of Urban Residential-Work Structures and the Impact of Industrial Decentralization: A Non-aggregated Areal Approach", Ph.D. Thesis, School of Geography, Clark University, 1972, 264 pp.

Hecht, Alfred, "An Investigation of Central Place Aspects of Portage La Prairie with Special Emphasis on the Establishment of Hierarchy and the Delimitation of the Complementary Region", M.A. Thesis, Department of Geography, University of Manitoba, 1968, 258 pp.

Books/Monographs

Hecht, Alfred and Regina Salvador (eds), The Evolution of Integration in Europe, 20 years after the fall of the Berlin Wall, Special Issue—2010, GeolNova. 230 pp. ISSN:0874-6440

Lugovoy, O., Dashkeyev, V., Mazayev, I., Fonchenko, D., Polyakov, E., Hecht, A., Analysis of economic growth in regions: geographic and institutional aspects. Consortium for Economic Policy and Research Advice – Moscow, Gaider Institute for Economic Policy, 2007, 222 pp. ISBN 978-5-93255-240-7

Prikhodko, S., Volovik, N., Hecht, A., Sharpe, B., Mandres, M., Special Economic Zones. Consortium for Economic Policy Research and Advice – Moscow, Gaidar Institute for Economic Policy, 2007, 247 pp. ISBN 978-5-93255-207-0

Hecht, Alfred and Alfred Pletsch (eds) Canadian Urban and Regional Socio-Economic Perspectives: Conditions at the beginning of the 21st Century. Schriften der Universität Marburg. 120, Marburg-Kanada Studien 2, Marburg, Germany, 2004, 308 pp. ISBN: 3-8185-0398-2.

Zhdanov, V., O. Kuznetsova, V. Mau, V. Plyukhin, S. Prikhodko, M.J. Wojciechowski and A. Hecht, Problems Related to Development of the Kaliningrad Region as an Exclave Territory of the Russian Federation. Consortium for Economic Policy Research and Advice – Moscow. Gaidar Institute for Economic Policy, WCER and ANE, Moscow, 2002, 249 pp. ISBN 5-93255-078-3.

Boots, B., S. Drobyshevsky, O. Kochetkova, G. Matginov, V. Petrov, G. Federov, A. Hecht, A. Shekhovtov, A. Yudin, Typology. of Russian Regions, Consortium for Economic Policy Research and Advice, CIDA, AUCC, Gaider Institute for Economic Policy, WCER and ANE, Moscow, 2022, 412 pp. ISBN 5-83255-071-6.

Hecht, Alfred and Alfred Pletsch (eds), Geographies of Germany and Canada: Paradigms, Concepts, Stereotypes, Images. Braunchweig, Germany: Georg-Eckert-Institute, 1997, 352 pp.

Hecht, Alfred, Bob Sharpe and Amy. Wong. Ethnicity and Well-being in Ontario and Toronto, Heft 92, Marburger Geographische Schriften, Marburg: Geographishes Institute der Universität Marburg, 1983, 192 pp.

Hecht, Alfred (ed.), Regional Developments in the Peripheries of Canada and Europe. Winnipeg: Manitoba Geographical Series, Vol. 18, 1983, 255 pp.

Articles and Chapters in Books

Hecht, Alfred, 'The Changing Canadian Economy: From Resources to Knowledge", in Tremblay, Rémy & Chicoine, Hugues 9 dirs.) The Geographies. of Canada. Bruxelles: P.I.E. Peter Lang, 242 pages, 2013.

Hecht, Alfred, "Laurier Looks Abroad: Marburg, and Laurier International", in Harold Remus, general editor, Rose Blackmore and Boyd McDonald, editors, I Remember Laurier, Reflections by Retirees on Life at WLU, Wilfred Laurier University Press, 2011, pp 128-133. ISBN 978-1-55458-383-6.

Marinel, Mandres (WLU, Canada) and Alfred Hecht (WLU-VERS, Canada), "Intra-European Migration: Magnitudes and Intensities of Contemporary Flows", Special Issue GeolNova, 2010, pp 169-186.

Hecht, Alfred, "The 'Baltic Main. Street' highway proposal", Baltic Rim Economies, Issue No. 3, June 17, 2008, pp. 30-31.

Hecht, Alfred, "The Kaliningrad Oblast of the Russian Federation: Its Development Prospects on the Conceptual Baltic Main Street', GeolNova, Numero 12, 2006, pp 297-323.

Hecht, Alfred, "Ethnicity and Home Language Retention in Canada", In a book edited by Peter Kirsch and Waldemar Zacharasiewicz, entitled The Protection of Cultural and Linguistic Diversity in Canada and Europe: Chances and Obstacles of Multiculturalism, University of Wien: Centre of Canadian Studies, University of Wien, 2003.

Hecht, Alfred, (with Bob Sharpe and Alfred Pletsch), "Virtual Geography Texts on Canada and Germany" in The Monograph, Vol. 52, No. 3, 2001, pp 29-31.

Hecht, Alfred (with Alfred Pletsch), "Virtual Geography Texts on Canada and Germany: Final report and Assessment", in Ahornblätter, Schriften der Universitätsbibliothek Marburg, Nr. 14, 2001, 62-81.

Hecht, Alfred (with Alfred Pletsch), "Allemange et le Canada par internet", Historiens & Geographies, no. 372, 2000, pp 55-56.

Hecht, Alfred, 'Selective Canadian Geography Texts. on the Internet – A. Learning device for students and teachers anywhere in the World", in International Textbook Research, Vol. 22, Nr.2, 2000, pp 201-217.

Hecht, Alfred (with Alfred Pletsch);Virtual Geography Texts (VGTs) on Canada and Germany – Background of a Pilot Project", in International Textbook Research Vol. 22, Nr. 2, 2000, pp 173-181

Hecht, Alfred (with Ulrike Gerhard, Alfred Pletsch), "Viruelle geographische texte uber Deutschland und Kanada, das Internet als Medium im bi-trilingual Unterricht". Geographie Praxis, Nr. 1642: 12-15.

Hecht, Alfred, Ahornblätter, Schriften der Universitätsbibliothek Marburg, Nr. 13, 2000, pp 133-234.

Hecht, Alfred (with A. Pletsch), "The Virtual Geography Textbook on Canada and Germany", In, Ahornblätter, Schriften der Universitätsbibliothek Marburg, Nr. 12, 1999, pp 81-100.

Hecht, Alfred (with. Alfred Pletsch), "Virtuelle Geographiebucher – Utopic oder neue Wege im UNterricht", In, Der Schulgeograph, Zeitschrift des Hessischen Schulgeographen-verbandes. no. 2, 1998, pp 3-6.

Hecht, Alfred, (with Steve Meyer), "University growth poles in Canada: An Empirical Assessment", Canadian Journal of Regional Science, Vol. XIX, NO.3, 1996, pp.263-282.

Hecht, Alfred, "Mennoniten, Juden and Ukrainer. – Aspekte ihrer gesellschaftlichen und wirtschaftlichen Integration in Kanada", in 1997 Jahrbuch der Marburger Gesellschaft, Fachbereich Geographic, Marburg, Germany, 1998, pp 60-67.

Hecht, Alfred, "A Socioeconomic Comparison of Jews, Mennonites and Ukrainians in Canada, The Prairies and Winnipeg", in Ahornblätter, Schriften der Universitätsbibliothek Marburg, Nr.11, 1998, pp. 45-73.

Hecht, Alfred (with Alfred Pletsch), "Introduction/Einleitung" in Hecht, A.&A. Pletsch 9eds.), Geographies of Germany and Canada: Paradigms, Concepts, Stereotypes, Images. Braunschweig: Georg-Eckert Institut, 1997, pp 15-34.

Hecht, Alfred (with Warren Stauch), "An Overview of Ontario's Geography Curriculum Policies and its European/German Content", Hecht, A.&A. Pletsch (eds.) Geographies of Germany and Canada: Paradigms, Concepts, Stereotypes, Images. Braunschweig: Georg-Eckert Institut, 1997, pp 135-148.

Hecht, Alfred (with Marinel Mandres Harald Blauder & Alfred Pletsch), Geographies of Germany and Canada: Paradigms, Concepts, Stereotypes, Images. Braunschweig: Georg-Eckert Institut, 1997, pp 201-350.

Hecht, Alfred (with Alfred Pletsch), "Ein Bericht uber die Deutsch-Kanadische Schulbuchcommission in Geographie", Internationale Schulbuchforschung/International Textbook Research, Jahrgang 79, Nr. 1, 1997, pp. 100-106.

Hecht, Alfred (with Trudy E. Bunting), "Birth Pains of a new Regional Shopping Centre, Cambridge Mall: Theories, Tools and Speculations of the Geographer in the Retail Planning Forum", in The Dynamics of Dispersed City: Geographic and Planning Perspectives on Waterloo Region by P. Fillion, T. E. Bunting and K. Curits (eds), University of Waterloo, Geography Department Monograph Series, 1996, pp. 273-302.

Hecht, Alfred (with Ekhart Ehlers), "Die Polargrenze des Anbaus: Struturwandel in der Alten und Neuen Welt", Geographische Rundschau. Heft 46, No. 2, 1994, pp. 104-110.

Hecht, Alfred, "Mennonites and the Canadian Society: A Financial Well-Being Comparison", in C Redekop, V. Krahn and S. Steiner (eds.) Anabaptist/Mennonite Faith and Economics. New York: University Press of America, 1994, pp. 237-253.

Hecht, Alfred, "Income variation and religious association in Canada; with special emphasis on Mennonites", Die Erde, Heft 124, 1993, pp. 195-208.

Hecht, Alfred (with Eckart Ehlers), " A Model of the Canadian Northern Agricultural Frontier", Ontario Geography. No. 39, 1992, pp. 35-45.

Hecht, Alfred, Review Essay: "Regional Development and Regional Policies"; based on Regional Policy in a Changing World, by N. Hansen, B. Higgins and J. Savoie, New York: Plenum Press, 1990, 311 pp., Canadian Journal of Regional Science. Vol. XIV, No. 3, 1991, pp.447-453.

Hecht, Alfred (with Alfred Pletsch), "Regionale Geographie und Ihre Prezeption in Kanada – Eine Betrachtung aus Anlass des Todes von Carl Schott", Geographische Zeitschrift, Vol. 79, No. 3, 1991, pp. 131-137.

Hecht, Alfred, (with Brian Cey), "The Spatial Inventive Surface of Canada Through Time", Ontario Geography. No. 35, 1991, pp. 14-25.

Hecht, Alfred (with Alfred Pletsch), "Ontario-Geographischer Wandel in einer Pionerprovinz Kanadas", Jahrbuch der Marburger Gesellschaft, 1990, pp. 35-38.

Hecht, Alfred, 'Geography", The Mennonite Encyclopedia. Scottdale, Pen.: Herald Press, Vol. V, 1989, pp. 332-333.

Hecht, Alfred (with Alfred Pletsch), "The Presentation of Germany in Canadian High School Text and Reference Books and Atlases", Ahornblätter 3, Schriften der Universitätsbibliothek Marburg 48, 1990, pp. 133-156.

Hecht, Alfred (with Alfred Pletsch), " The Geography of Germany as seen in the Canadian Geography High School Texts", Internationale Schulbuchforschung. 12 Jahrgang, 1990, pp. 405-522.

Hecht, Alfred (with Harald Bathelt), "Key Technology Industries in the Waterloo Region: Canada's technology Triangle (CTT)", The Canadian Geographer, Vol. 34, No. 3, 1990, pp. 225-234.

Hecht, Alfred (with Jim W. Davidson and Herb A. Witney), "The Pilgrimage to Graceland", in G. Rinschede and S.M. Bhardwaj (eds.) Pilgrimage in the United States, Vol. 5, Geographie Religionum, Berline: Dietrich Reimer, 1990, pp. 229-252.

Hecht, Alfred (with Barry N. Boots), "Spatial perspectives on Canadian Provincialism and Regionalism", Canadian Journal of Regional Science, Vol. 12, No. 2, 1989, pp. 187-204.

Hecht, Alfred (with Alfred Pletsch), "Kanada und die BRD im Spiegel ihrer Erdkundebucher", Zeitschrift der Gesellschaft fur Kanada-Studien, Vol. 15, 1989, pp. 97-107.

Hecht, Alfred, "Die. Wirtschatliceh Entwicklung der Mennoniten-Kolonien im Chaco: - Ein Theoretisches Perspecktive", Mennoblatt, 58 Jahrgang, No. 17, 1. September 1989, pp. 8-10.

Hecht, Alfred (with Alfred Pletsch), "The Canadian North: A Socio-Economic Invasion of the Native Milieu", Ahornblätter 2, Schriften der Universitätsbibliothek Marburg, 42, 1989, pp. 7-36.

Hecht, Alfred, "The Socio-Economic Core-Periphery Structures in Canada: A Present Analysis", Zeitschrift der Gesellschaft für Kanada-Studien, Vol. 13, 1988, pp. 23-51.

Hecht, Alfred, "Pioniere im Chaco Südamerikas: Indianer Mennoniten – Paraguayer", Jahrbuchen der Marburger Geographischen Gesellschaft, 1988, pp. 21-24.

Hecht, Alfred (with G Braun), "The Canadian Migration Scene: An Explanatory Geographical Analysis", in Manuskript zur Emperische, Theoretische und Angewandte Ergionaleforschung, Department of Geography, Freie University of Berlin, Vol. 15b, 1988, 44 pp.

Hecht, Alfred, "Probleme der Kulterelen und Religiösischen Gruppen Kanadas: am Biespiel der Mennoniten", in Band 1, Jahrbuch der Marburger Geographischen Gesellschaft, 1987, pp. 23-27.

Hecht, Alfred (with Barry N. Boots and John F. Peters), "Residential Relocation and the Urban Spatial Activity Structure", in H. Schröder-Lanz (ed.) Stadtgestalt-Forschung. Trierer Geographische Studien, 4/5, 1982/86, pp. 543-557.

Hecht, Alfred (with Wolfgang Andres), "Zustanddekommen der Partnerscahft zwischen der Philipps Universität Marburg und der Wilfred Laurier Universität, Waterloo, Ontario", Kanada in Marburg, Beiträge der Philipps Universität, zur Kanada-Forschung, Universitätsbibliothek Marburg, Germany, 1986, pp. 9-16.

Hecht, Alfred, "Variation in the Socio-Cultural Boundaries of Ontario's French Ethnic Population: A Geographic Interpretation", Revue Interdisciplinaire Des Etudes Canadiennes en France, Tomes 2, Vol. 21, 1986, pp. 115-127.

Hecht, Alfred, "Income Differences Between Ontario's Ethnic Groups", in Proceedings, Canadian Association of Geographers, Trois Rivieres, Quebec, 1985, pp. 263-291.

Hecht (with Ludgar Muller-Wille and Alfred Pletsch), "Ethnic Aspects of Central Canada – An Introduction", in A. Pletsch 9ed.) Ethnicity in Canada: International Examples and Perspectives. Marburger Geographische Schriften, Marburg: Geographisches Institute der Universität Marburg, Heft 96, 1985, p. 1-33.

Hecht, Alfred, "Ethnic Groups as Charter Groups in Ontario, Canada", in A. Pletsch (ed.) Ethnicity in Canada – International Examples and Perspectives. Marburger Geographische Schriften, Marburg: Geographisches Institute der Universität Marburg, Heft 96, 1985, pp. 134-153.

Hecht, Alfred (with Cathy Wesol and Bob Scharpe), "Peripheral Location of Indian People in Ontario", in A. Hecht (ed.), Regional Development in the Peripheries of Canada and Europe. Winnipeg: Manitoba Geographical Studies, Vol. 9, 1983, 52-80.

Hecht, Alfred (with Ernst Giese), "Regional Variation of Development in the Soviet Union", in Regional Development in the Peripheries of Canada and Europe. Winnipeg: Manitoba Geographical Studies, Vol. 8, 1983, pp. 205-244.

Hecht, Alfred (with Winfied J. Fretz), "Food Production Under Conditions of Increased Uncertainty: The Chaco Example", in K. Hewitt (ed.) Interpretations of Calamity. England: Allan and Unwin, 1983, pp. 162-180.

Hecht, Alfred, "The Germans in the Anglo-Saxon Milieu in Central Canada", in M.S. batts, W. Riedel and R. Symington (eds.) German-Canadian Studies in the 1980s. Vancouver: German-Canadian Studies Symposium, 4 Publication, 1983, pp. 110-142.

Hecht, Alfred, "The Regional Economy of the Maritimes" Funk and Wagnalls Encyclopedia. 1983, new Brunswick, Vol. 18, 416-420, Newfoundland, Vol. 18, 431-435, Nova Scotia, Vol. 233-237 and Prince Edward Island, Vol. 21, 279-284.

Hecht, Alfred (with Karl Lenz), "Die Entwichlung einer neuen wirtschaftlichen Kernregion in Kanada", Die Erde, Heft 113, 1982, pp. 273-279.

Hecht, Alfred, "Regional Well-being in Canada and the European Economic Community", in H. Becker (ed.) Kulturgeographische Prozessforschung in Kanada. Bamburger Geographische Schriften, No. 4, 1982, pp. 45-64.

Hecht, Alfred, 'Relationships and Tensions between the Mennonites and the Indians in the Paraguay Chaco", in H. Loewen (ed.) Mennonite Images. Winnipeg: Hyperian Press, 1980, pp. 165-176.

Hecht, Alfred (with Brandon J. Lander and Brian Lorch), "Regional Development in Northern Ontario", in C. Schott and A. Pletsch (eds.) Kanada naturraum und Entwicklungspotential. Marburger Geographisches Schriften, Marburg: Geographisches Institute der Universität Marburg, Heft 79, 1979, pp. 207-226.

Hecht, Alfred, "The Geographic Dimensions of Changing World Economic Order: With Specific Reference to Paraguay", Die Erde, Vol. 109, 1978, pp. 397-416.

Hecht, Alfred, "Die anglo-und frankokanadiesche Stadt. Ein Sozio-ökonomischer Vergleich am Beispiel von Hamilton and Quebec", in H.J. Niederche and H. Schroeder-Lanz (eds.) Beitrage zur Landeskundlich - Linguistischen Kenntnis von Quebec. Trier, West Germany: Trier University, 1977, pp. 87-112.

Hecht, Alfred, "Exploring the Urban Industrial Relocation Process", Journal of Geography, Vol. 76, 1977, pp. 15-18.

Hecht, Alfred (with Richard A. Brown), "Residential Relocation within the Physical and Socio-Economic Space of an Urban Area", Monograph, No. 3, 1976, pp. 23-30.

Hecht, Alfred, "The Agricultural Economy of the Mennonite Settlers in Paraguay: Impact of a Road," Ekistics, Vol. 42, No. 248, 1976, pp. 42-47.

Hecht, Alfred (with Brian Lorch), " Regional Growth Rate Relationships in Manufacturing Employment in Ontario", Regional Geography. Vol. 8, XXIII, International Geographic Congress, Moscow, 1976, pp. 125-130.

Hecht, Alfred, "Industrial Decentralization and the Changing Residential Locations of Employees", East Lakes Geographer, Vol. 6, No. 4, 1975, pp. 69-90.

Hecht, Alfred, "The Agricultural Economy of the Mennonite Settlers in the Chaco Region of Paraguay", Growth and Change, Vol. 6, No. 4, 1975, pp. 14-20.

Hecht, Alfred, "The Journey to Work Distance in Relation to the Socio-Economic Characteristic of Workers, Canadian Geographer. Vol. XVIII, No. 4, 1974, pp. 367-370.

Hecht, Alfred, "Residential Locations Under Stress of Urban Industrial Decentralization", Proceedings of the Association of American Geographers. Vol. 5, 1973, pp. 103-111.

Hecht, Alfred, "Spatial Dynamics in Classical Location Theory", The Monadnock, Vol. XLV, 1971, pp. 52-56.

Hecht, Alfred (with Peggy Lentz), "Forrester's Urban System Model: Evaluation and Experiments", Occasional Papers in Regional Science, No. 1, Graduate School of Geography, Clark University, 1971.

Hecht, Alfred, "A Commentary on the New Manitoba Grade XII Geography Course", The Manitoba Geography Teacher, Vol. 2, No. 1, 1969 (note).

COMMUNITY ACTIVITIES

Member, Board of Rockway Mennonite Collegiate (1995-97)
Chair, Grace MB Church pastoral search committee (2009)
Chair, Grace MB Church Finance Committee (2003-06)
Chair, Grace MB Church Board (2003-06)
Moderator, Waterloo Grace MB Church (2006-07)
Member, Finance Board of the Ontario Mennonite Brethren Conference (1996-97)
President, Canadian Association of Geographers—Ontario Division (1992-94)
Member, Glencairn MB Church Council (1989-96)
Former Member, Ontario MB Board of Education
Moderator, Waterloo MB Church (1983-86)
Former Member, Editorial Board of Mennogespräch
Former Member, Ontario Mennonite Historical Society

THESIS SUPERVISED STUDENTS

PhDs at Laurier

Edmund N. Okoree (2000), Co-supervised with Russell Muncaster
Sue Lucas (1999), Co-supervised with Bob Sharpe
Kimberly Naqvi (1999)
Marinel Mandres (1998)

Master Theses

C. Charman (2001)	K.B. Naqvi (1986)
N. Bauer (2000)	A. Weiss (1986)
C. Stefan (1999)	R. Campbell (1985)
K. Chapman (1998)	M. Beetham (1983)
A. Gosztonyi (1997)	R. Sharpe (1983)
T. Hammers (1996)	A. Wong (1982)
R. Furtado (1995)	PJ DeBoer (1980)
M. Lavers (1995)	M.M. Laine (1979)
L. Kucsma (1993)	J.B. Lander (1979)
C.J. Wright (1991)	V. Konkle (1977)
Y. Wu (1991)	J. McCash (1976)
J. Torretto (1990)	B.J. Lorch (1975)
B. Ceh (1989)	G.W. Brown (1974)
S. Meyers (1989)	R.J. Worral (1974)
J. Ghosh (1986)	

Honours Theses Supervised

K. Geddes (2000)
J. Henderson (2000)
K. Chapman (1995)
K.L. Bishop (1995)
C. Adams (1994)
A. Boothroyd (1994)
T. Hammers (1994)
S. Schneider (1994)
B. Dufault (1992)
R. Lee (1992)
N. Messenger (1992)
M. Van Veen (1992)
D. Wells (1992)
G. Chalk (1990)
A. Darby (1990)
S. Dungey (1990)
S. Large (1990)
S. Vargas (1990)
B.J. Foran (1989)
P. Morgan (1988)
C. Picton (1986)
T. Schwindt (1986)
R.J. Simpson (1986)
H.S. Oeji (1985)
J. Taylor (1985)
L. Warburton (1985)
J. Kerr (1985)
M. Kramarich (1983)
P.E. Hanson (1983)
C.F. Fleming (1983)

R.W. Dufort (1983)
L.B. Currie (1983)
A.C. Weiss (1982)
D.P. Neil (1982)
B. MacLeod (1982)
L. Cadman (1982)
J.E.W. Beach (1982)
C.M. Wesol (1981)
M.W. Beetham (1981)
D.P. Friesen (1981)
S.A. Gellner (1981)
M.F. Dutka (1979)
D. Piggot (1979)
R. Andrey (1978)
C. Drimmie (1978)
G. Finkbeiner (1978)
J. Chamberlain (1977)
J.M. Foran (1976)
J.E. Zemek (1976)
R. Dickson (1975)
A. Hendelman (1975)
W. Howard (1975)
V. Konkle (1975)
J.D. Radke (1975)
R.C. Steiner (1975)
G.J. Duncan (1974)
B.J. Lorch (1974)
P.E. Moores (1974)
B. Sheardown (1973)
D. Shewfelt (1973)

AUTHOR BIO

Mark Hecht is a Canadian teacher and writer.

He taught geography at Mount Royal University for eleven years and was given the 2014 *MRU Award for Excellence in Teaching*.

His writings have been published in *Areo magazine, Merion West, The Canadian Journal* and *The Vancouver Sun* among others.

His academic contributions include textbook chapters, debate articles and editing for Mount Royal University, ABC-CLIO, John Wiley & Sons, and other major publishers.

Mark Hecht is the nephew of Alfred Hecht. Together they share a passion for geography, history and story-telling.

Being tasked with writing *Uncle Alfred's* biography was an honour beyond words for Mark.

Mark Hecht grew up in the Okanagan Valley of British Columbia. He currently resides on Vancouver Island where you will find him writing his next book.

INDEX

Alexander von Humbolt University, 94, 11, 139

Amish, 56, 57, 80, 134, 135, 137, 167, 190

Asunción, 4, 49, 59, 94, 127, 172, 173, 177, 179–182

Buenos Aires, 47, 48, 182

Chortitza, 10, 14, 15, 22

Czechoslovakia, 26, 27, 30, 33

Einsatzgruppen, 18

Elsa Hecht, 15, 24, 27, 38, 42, 48, 53, 90, 120, 189

Fernheim, 47, 60–62, 164, 175, 179, 182

Franz Friesen, 15, 24, 26–28, 30–38, 52, 54, 120, 154, 231

Freie University, Berlin, 86, 93, 107, 108, 132, 143, 149

Grönau, 42–44, 46

Gruenfeld, 1, 13, 15, 22

Heintzelman (ship), 48

Helene Toews (nee Hecht), 15, 16, 27, 38, 42, 216

Helene Hecht (nee Krause), 15

Hitler Youth, 74, 119–121

Inflation, 4–6, 59, 60, 171

Johanna Toews (nee Hecht), 16, 26, 34–35, 37, 38, 42

Judenplan, 14, 15

Kaliningrad, 146, 147

Leonidas Hecht, 12, 13, 15, 19, 23, 117

Manitoba, University of, 76, 86, 87, 89, 90, 93, 97, 102

Marvin Hecht, 73, 75, 80–83, 100, 131, 162–168, 220

Melinda Hecht-Enns, 75, 83, 84, 134, 135, 136

Molotschna, 10, 22

Neuland, 13, 49, 59, 60, 172–177, 180

Oberdorf, 26, 27, 29, 31, 40

Pacifism, 9, 47, 52, 53, 56, 80, 134

Philipps University, Marburg, 93, 96, 118, 125, 126, 128, 130, 132, 142, 149

Rudolf Hecht, 4, 15, 23, 24, 27, 35, 38, 42, 50, 55, 96, 120, 180, 181, 216, 226

Ruta Trans-Chaco, 178, 182

Stalin, Joseph, 1, 9, 15, 22, 29, 30, 41, 112–114, 193

Stalingrad, 22, 29

Susanna Hecht (nee Krause), 12, 13, 26–28, 30–38, 41–43, 94, 100

Susanne Dueck (nee Friesen), 15, 25–28, 30, 33, 38, 42, 44

Steinfeld, 1, 8, 15, 23, 25

Viessmann Research Centre, 132, 150, 197, 198

Volendam (ship), 48

Volendam Colony, 48

Von Thünen, 178–183

Wilfred Laurier University, 67, 68, 93, 103–108, 122–126, 130–132, 142, 150, 163, 165, 178, 179, 188–193, 198, 203, 210, 214

Alfred Hecht

www.ingramcontent.com/pod-product-compliance
Lightning Source LLC
Chambersburg PA
CBHW050338010526
44119CB00049B/598